IMPACT OF RESERVATION POLICIES: INDIA'S QUOTA POLITICS DURING THE POST-INDEPENDENCE PERIOD, 1950-2011

By
Sai Ma

A dissertation submitted to Johns Hopkins University in conformity with the requirements for the degree of Doctor of Philosophy

Baltimore, Maryland
November, 2011

ProQuest LLC
789 East Eisenhower Parkway
P.O. Box 1346
Ann Arbor, MI 48106-1346

Abstract

India has witnessed a "second democratic upsurge", which involved the broad and intensive political participation among the disadvantaged social groups, since the late 1980s. This dissertation focuses on the politics of historically disadvantaged caste groups, especially Other Backward Classes (OBCs). It assumes that Reservation Policies (RPs) played a constructive role. Through examining the case studies of Tamil Nadu, Uttar Pradesh and West Bengal, I explain three findings and three aspects of policy methodology.

The first finding is that the new social categories, such as the OBCs, are shaped or strengthened by the state. Through reviewing the Constitutional debates, Indian Census, and procedure of Caste Certificate issuance, I argue that the identity of OBC groups is a construction originating in or strengthened by RPs. The formation of such identity is an irreversible process. Based on this finding, I find that rigidity of state continuously using the same/incorrect standards of caste recognition unintentionally created new identity politics. This is illustrated by the "Creamy Layer" phenomenon. Thirdly, with its caste-based identification, limited reservation benefits and elites' interpretation of RPs, the state has strengthened casteism in the political landscape. I especially analyze resource effect and interpretive effect of RPs, arguing that insufficient allocation of resources and manipulation of interpreting RPs by the political elite caused a politics of contention on quotas.

On the methodological front, this dissertation provides a good case for policy research. It supports three hypotheses of policy approach: 1) Scope of programs: compared with the targeted programs in Uttar Pradesh, universal programs in Tamil Nadu shape a broader political coalition among welfare supporters. 2) Program spending: the policy beneficiaries in Tamil Nadu tend to participate in a more collective matter than Uttar Pradesh because more generously, more evenly and longer welfare benefits are provided. 3) Interpretation of programs: beneficiaries' political attitudes and behaviors tend to be manipulated by elite groups' interpretation of policies. Finally, I emphasize the importance of research into the relationship between welfare regimes and political participation.

Advisor: Walter K. Andersen

Readers: Sunil Khilnani, Pravin Krishna, Cinnamon Dornsife, and Pranab Bardhan

Table of Contents

List of Figures

Preface

The dissertation is about the Indian politics of the lower castes, especially the Other Backward Classes (OBCs), with an emphasis on Reservation Policies' constructive role in it. My study addresses the question why Reservation Policies, aiming to diminish inequality and caste eventually, has strengthened them. It is important to understand this policy process because 1) Reservation Policies, unintentionally but in its direct effect, shaped or strengthened the social and political formation of these lower caste groups. 2) India has undergone wide-ranging political transformations and political conflicts caused by Reservation Policies. I hope this research will help the decision-makers reconsider their choices of distributing quotas among the disadvantaged social groups in India.

I could not have completed this study without the active cooperation and help of a large number of people. My fist debt is to five great scholars – Walter Andersen, Sunil Khilnani, Pravin Krishna, Cinnamon Dornsife, and Pranab Bardhan. I am especially thankful for my advisor Dr. Walter Andersen, who was a source of encouragement and advice. As my mentor, he is one of the most supportive members for my dissertation. He not only made many useful suggestions for the improvement of the text, but he also helped solve a lot of difficult questions during my fieldwork in India, such as the issuance of a research visa and helping set up appointments with high-level officials.

I would also like to thank Professor Sunil Khilnani and Professor Pranab Bardhan, whose great understanding of Indian Studies has enlightened my research. Professor Pranab Bardhan went through the entire draft more than once and contributed a great deal to its improvement. I also extend my thanks to Ms. Cinnamon Dornsife and Professor Pravin Krishna, who gave me useful suggestions as we discussed my research.

I went to India twice in 2006 and 2008 for field studies. During my stay, the National Institute of Public Finance and Policy (NIPFP) and the Center of Policy Research (CPR) hosted me for research. Here, I would like to express my thanks to the scholars at the NIPFP including Tapas Kumar Sen, Anit Nath Mukherjee etc. Their willing of cooperation and hospitality made my field work a pleasurable experience. My greatest thanks go to Dr. Govinda Rao, Director of NIPFP, who provided not only all the useful sources available at NIPFP, but also analyzed with great care the feasibility of my field studies in the Indian states. I would like to thank Professor Suhas Palshikar for his suggestions on parts of the study. My research was also enlightened by Dr. Madhav Godbole, who shared important views of Finance Secretary at Indian Administrative Service with me.

Furthermore, I am grateful to the officials and administrators, at the Ministry of Social Justice and Empowerment, Ministry of Finance, Ministry of Human Resource Development, Planning Commission, and Finance Commission. Due to confidentiality issues, I cannot reveal their names. I would like to thank the state government officials at Backward Classes Welfare Department in West Bengal, Backward Class Department in Maharashtra and Backward Classes and Most Backward Classes Welfare Department in Tamil Nadu. Thanks are also due to the librarians at the NIPFP library, the library of Finance Department, and the library of Planning Commission, who helped in locating useful material for the study.

Finally, and most importantly, I dedicate this volume to my parents Lili Liu and Tai Ma and my grandmother Yongyi Liu, who love and support me with unconditionallly. I would like to dedicate my work especially to my brave and strong mother, who is currently struggling with cancer.

Chapter 1

Introducing Framework: Welfare Regimes in India

"New Policies create a new politics"
E. E. Schattschneider, "Politics, Pressures and the Tariff", 1935: 288

"Too often social scientists...forget that policies, once enacted, restructure subsequent political processes. Analysts typically look only for synchronic determinants of policies—for example, in current social interests or in existing political alliances. In addition, however, we must examine patterns unfolding over time...We must make social policies the starting points as well as the end points of analysis"

Theda Skocpol, "Protecting Soldiers and Mothers", 1992:58

1.1 Research Objectives

This dissertation is a study of India's redistributive policies in the post-Independence period. The impact of regime types and the impact of policys on patterns of political attitudes and behavior of certain social groups has not received the scholarly attention it deserves. An earlier generation of scholars interested in the welfare state investigated the welfare system in isolation from its political and social context. For example, the study of policy impacts on social groups would have rarely been considered a legitimate area of enquiry in a modernization theory. In contrast, the more recent neo-Marxist scholarship tends to reduce political analysis to economic forces. Scholars with the dependency perspective would not analyze the state's redistributive role within capitalist development.[1] Important exceptions to these dominant analytical tendencies have emerged recently. These include the studies of Andrea Louise Campbell and Paul Pierson.[2]

[1] Dependency theory is predicated on the notion that resources flow from a "periphery" of underdeveloped states to a "core" of wealthy states, thus enriching the latter at the expense of the former.
[2] Campbell, Andrea Louise. How Policies Make Citizens: Senior Citizen Activism and the American Welfare State. Princeton University Press, 2003. Pierson, Paul. "When Effect Becomes Cause, Policy Feedback and Political Change." World Politics, 1993: 595-628.

Systematic analysis of the role of policy in social and political development, however, has not been explored sufficiently.

According to Campbell, public policies can confer resources, motivate interest in government affairs by tying well-being to government action, define groups for mobilization, and even shape the content and meaning of democratic citizenship.[3] To avoid the analytical pitfalls of both the modernization and neo-Marxist perspectives, I have adopted an alternative perspective: *the impact of policy,* explaining both choices and constraints under certain social and political context. At the heart of my dissertation is the exploration of post-independence India's lower caste participation in politics dependent on policy impact of welfare states. The analytical issue this dissertation raises about India goes beyond the often-discussed question of suitable development strategy, or the fundamental issues such as land redistribution. The dissertation discusses the issue of Reservation Policies (RPs) and its effects on the lower caste communities.[4]

1.2 Research Questions and Propositions

India has always witnessed a wide gap between the rich and the poor. This disparity has only increased over the years in spite of three decades of economic liberalization and development. The Gini coefficients that indicates rich-poor gap increased from 0.29 in 1973-74 to 0.34 (Uniform Reference Period) or 0.30 (Mixed Reference Period) in 2004-05. (Table 1.1) It is important to note that India's welfare situation has been considered a significant political issue within India. Mohandas K. Gandhi and Jawaharlal Nehru were ideologically committed to the cause of the bottom layer. Indira Gandhi made *garibi hatao* (eradicate poverty) a central slogan in her mobilization strategy. India's Planning Commission has tended to treat poverty as a basic problem. A focus of redistributive policy is made still more meaningful by the fact that the

---

[3] Ibid.

[4] Reservation Policies(RPs) is one type of redistributive policies which gives a percentage of quotas to the lower castes in the governments, educational institutions and legislatures.

country's policymakers have utilized different strategies affecting the living conditions of the subaltern. For instance, land reforms have been continuously set upon India's political agenda to improve employment and wage conditions for the landless agricultural laborers. Another important effort by Indian policy makers is targeting the lower castes for equal opportunities. Just as with land and poverty issues, caste issues, such as reservations for the Other Backward Classes (OBCs), have been put on the table to alleviate inequality in India's society.

Table 1.1: Gini Coefficient for India (1973-2005)

1973-74		1977-78		1983-84		1993-94		1999-2000		2004-05 (URP*)	
Rural	Urban	Rural	Urban	Rural	Urban	Rural	Urban	Rural	Urban	Rural	Urban
0.28	0.30	0.34	0.34	0.30	0.33	0.28	0.34	0.26	0.34	0.30	0.37

Note: * URP - Uniform Reference Period
** MRP - Mixed Reference Period
Source: Unofficial estimates of Planning Commission; 61st Round 2004-05 MRP

This dissertation attempts to answer the following questions: whether and how did policies (Reservation Policies in this case) facilitate the source distribution among the targeted people? How and why did the states differ in compensating for the inequality? Who are the truly needy? In what form have the states participated in the politics? In what way and to what extent did different levels of interest groups bargain for welfare expansion? To address these questions, this dissertation adopts a comparative analytical framework complemented by small-N case studies of three states in India—*Uttar Pradesh, Tamil Nadu and West Bengal.* For each of these selected cases, I employ a historical institutionalist approach and argue that policy regime matters. Welfare policy regimes, characterized by specific sets of programs, laws/regulations, and decision-making processes, create institutional niches to help pro-welfare state interests overcome collective action problems. Overall, this research sets out to investigate the evolution and character of Reservation Policies (RPs) in India to ascertain whether or to what extent it constitutes a distinct model of welfare provision.

The research of the participation-policy nexus in India is significant in two aspects. First, it attempts to provide a subnational perspective for analyzing conditions and patterns of welfare policy formation. This study will counter the simply positive/negative nexus between participation and policy by disaggregating the state involvement mechanism. Second, the study employs a historical institutionalism approach, emphasizing traditional policy impacts on current political process which have rarely been explored in the literature.

This study selects the post-Independence period in India for two reasons. First, RPs was created and developed within this period of time when the Indian polity experienced democratizing process. This constitutes a preconditioned environment to examine the participation-policy nexus. Second, this period has witnessed intensifying and varying degree of democratization at the subnational level. This approach helps study the incentive structures and institutional capacity of individual states. Third, it does not deny the rapidly growing non-government contributions (especially in terms of education and health), although it assumes that Indian governments are still the major redistributive mechanisms.

Again, this is a study of RPs that influences the political, economic and social status of the lower-caste groups. It is designed not only as an investigation of political performance, but also as an explication of the redistributive role of varying welfare regimes at state level in India. I show that the ability of the politically active to mobilize is in part a legacy of existing public policies: policy influences the amount and nature of a group's political activity, often exacerbating rather than ameliorating existing participatory inequalities.

The failure to mitigate the lower-castes inferior status is a consequence of institutionalized patterns of domination within India. Over the past few decades, India has been ruled by an alliance of nationalist political elites who have wielded power through a dominant party in control of a democratic system. This system has had poor political and organizational capacity to implement redistributive goals. The ruling alliance between political authorities and the more dynamic, propertied classes has generated 6% economic growth on average from 1981 to 2010 (Table 1.2), though the growth has generated an uneven impact. Pranab Bardhan indicated the failure of "trickle down" theory in rural India as early as 1986.[5] According to Bardhan, economic and political benefits have accrued to a small minority (upper-middle classes and professional) in the industrial and agricultural sectors. Lower-caste social groups have been left out of this arrangement had few outlets if they can not pose a significant political threat toward dominant alliance.

Table 1.2: Gross Domestic Product in India (1981-2010)

Percentage (%)

Year	Gross Domestic Product	Year	Gross Domestic Product	Year	Gross Domestic Product
1981	6.176	1991	2.136	2001	3.885
1982	4.072	1992	4.385	2002	4.558
1983	6.365	1993	4.939	2003	6.852
1984	4.647	1994	6.199	2004	8.106
1985	4.891	1995	7.351	2005	9.167
1986	4.88	1996	7.56	2006	9 658
1987	4.153	1997	10.328	2007	9.886
1988	8.258	1998	5.288	2008	6.396
1989	6.81	1999	3.273	2009	5.678
1990	5.63	2000	4.44	2010	9.668

Source International Monetary Fund - 2010 World Economic Outlook

[5] Bardhan, Pranab "Poverty and Trickle-down in Rural India—A Quantitative Analysis " In *Agricultural Change and Rural Poverty*, by J W Mellor and G M Desai, 76-94 New Delhi Oxford University Press, 1986

Surely the guidelines and constraints from the central government for redistributive programs cannot be ignored. However, the states have shown specific characteristics of welfare provisions towards the lower caste groups. While the ideology, organization, and patterns of class alliance in a communist state such as West Bengal can suggest one kind of welfare provision, so can state capacities to facilitate redistributive gains along caste lines in some other state such as Tamil Nadu and Uttar Pradesh. The range of redistributive choices available is delineated here through a comparative analysis of regional contexts within India. The former communist government in the State of West Bengal, for instance, had undertaken some successful reforms aimed at altering socio-economic conditions of the rural poor, including the poor *Brahmins* as well as those from the poor lower caste. By comparisons, the government led by the Dravida Munnetra Kazhagam (DMK) Party in Tamil Nadu was able to bring about some changes of certain selected subaltern groups, such as the Dalit groups, the women and the old because these groups had been politicized. The government of Uttar Pradesh, however, stands in a marked contrast to both of the above cases. It probably represents the general tendency of redistributing in the Hindi belt in favor of the Hindu peasant castes (Other Backward Classes) and Dalit (Scheduled Castes) groups in the past few decades.[6] If sustained, these policy efforts promise to have more impact on rural-urban issues in West Bengal, on anti-Brahmin issues in Tamil Nadu and on poverty issues in Uttar Pradesh.[7] These three Indian states, then, highlight a small but significant range of redistributive options possible for the lower castes within certain social-structural constraints. The core task of this study is to explain the conditions that potentiate these small but significant redistributive possibilities.

[6] Mayawati, the Chief Minister of Uttar Pradesh, began to woo the upper castes for electoral support in the 2000s

[7] Dalit movements feature Uttar Pradesh politics under the leadership of the Dalit Chief Minister K Mayawati and her Dalit party BSP This dissertation, however, emphasizes the politics of Backward Castes who were closely interacted with the *Kisan* issues in Uttar Pradesh context

1.3 Analytical Framework: Conceptualization of India's Welfare Regimes

According to Esping-Andersen (1990), welfare states have been analyzed in both narrow and broad terms. Those who take the narrow view focus on specific social welfare policies, including income transfers, social insurance for pensions and health care, public housing and personal social services and assistance, etc. In the broader view, these issues are considered integral components in the welfare-state complex. The state's larger role in managing and organizing the economic and social development has been crucial. Esping-Andersen (1990) put the western contemporary welfare states into three categories: social democratic, conservative corporatist, and liberal. In the "liberal" welfare state, modest social-insurance plans predominate, mainly catering to low-income state dependents. In turn, the state encourages the market by subsidizing private welfare schemes. The consequence is stratification between state-welfare recipients with relatively equal poverty and the mainstream population with market-differentiated welfare. Archetypical examples of this model are the United States, Canada and Australia. In the "conservative and strongly corporatist" welfare states, such as Austria, France, Germany and Italy, corporatism displaces the market as a provider of welfare. This model emphasizes class and status in access to welfare benefits and is influenced by family and church traditions. The third category consists of the small Nordic countries where the principles of universalism of social rights predominate. That is, target populations have been extensively or fully covered with egalitarian benefits and widely accessible social services, guaranteeing that workers come to enjoy rights identical to those of the better-off.[8] Estimated data in Table 1.3 shows that the percentage of GDP devoted to social spending exceeds 25 percent of GDP in the Scandinavian countries (Sweden, Denmark etc.) and Germany and lower than 20 percent in the US, Australia, Canada, and Japan amongst others. (Table 1.3)

---

[8] Esping-Andersen, Gosta *The Three Worlds of Welfare Capitalism* Cambridge Princeton University Press, 1990

Table 1.3 From Gross Public toTotal Net Social Spending as a Share of GDP, Social Expenditure in Percentage of GDP at Market Prices, 2007

Denmark	26.1
Sweden	27.3
Germany	25.2
United States	16.2
Australia	16.0
Canada	16.9
Japan	18.7

Source: Social Expenditure Database; www.oecd.org/els/social/expenditure

The above-mentioned welfare state models and relevant arguments are only for countries within the Organization for Economic Cooperation and Development (OECD). The existing literature does not sufficiently explain the changing trend of welfare spending in the Less Developed Countries (LDCs), such as India. This dissertation is worth exploring because there has been a good deal of discussion about an Indian model of economic development, yet analysis of its welfare components is in its infancy. Existing studies for welfare polices in India are significant for introducing preliminary research, but they are still descriptive and thus there is a need to build a theoretical base.

In Indian studies, two broad categories of explanations have been employed to explain variation in macroeconomic policy. One category of explanations takes a bottom-up approach, indicating that redistributive policies are promoted along social cleavages, such as caste, religion, languages and so forth. Grassroots politics, or non-party formation, driven by social movements and social institutions are an important part of this model (Weiner, 1962; Rudolphs, 1987; Varshney, 1999). In the case of welfare policy making, this group of scholars employ social institutions, such as caste associations, in explaining the possible welfare policies for the subaltern people. Lloyd Rudolph and Susanne Rudolph (1987) refer to this as "involuted pluralism", arguing that fragmentation and multiplicity certainly complicate negotiations between the political elites and demand groups. The other category of explanations is based on a top-down model, emphasizing the role of the state apparatus—the polity's systems of collective group and electoral interest representation, as well as its structure of decision-making authority. They argue that the performance of governments is related either to the strong-soft state distinction (Mygdal, 1988; Rudolph and Rudolph, 1987), or the extent of deinstitutionalization of the Indian state (Kohli, 1991), or specific party organizations (Kohli, 1987) and party systems (Chibber, 2001; *Yadav*, 2003). The recent literature (Jenkins, 2004; Sinha, 2004) finds that semi-autonomous lower levels of government have an independent or even intervening impact on policy making and implementation. However, these arguments are mainly focused on economic growth and investment flows in the reform years, leaving important welfare aspects untouched.

My analysis goes beyond existing studies by providing an alternative model of the determinants of welfare politics in India. Rather than the above-mentioned literatures treating policy as the result of political forces, I take policy as the cause of those forces, which often dramatically reshapes social, economic and political conditions. The analysis of policy feedback constitutes a major research frontier within the framework of "historical institutionalism". Historical institutionalist analysis is based on a few key claims: that the understanding of political processes emphasizes path dependence and unintended consequences; that structural constraints on individual actions, especially those emanating from governments, are important sources of political behavior; and that the detailed investigation of carefully chosen, comparatively informed case studies is a powerful tool for uncovering the source of political change (Pierson 1993).[9] Regarding past major policies as starting points, I argue that long-term adoption of specific public policies provides incentives and resources for particular groups and such policy responses lead to unintended consequences.

According to Skocpol (1992), the two major types of policy impact are: 1) the transformation of state capacities; and 2) changes in social groups and their political goals and capabilities. The former type of policy impact changes the incentives and resources of

[9] Pierson, Paul. "When Effect Becomes Cause, Policy Feedback and Political Change." *World Politics*, 1993: 595-628.

government elites who in turn create administrative possibilities to affect future prospects for new policies. The latter type of policy impact provides motivation and resources for beneficiaries to mobilize in favor of programmatic maintenance or expansion. Over time, policy regimes will come into being with specific mechanisms. This dissertation mainly focuses on the latter policy impact. Employing historical institutionalism approach, I argue that the different policy regimes across Indian states determine the divergent trends of political participation among the lower caste social groups. Overall, I will explore whether such a creature as an "Indian welfare model" actually exists, and, if so, what it is and how it developed.

Welfare regime type is considered in the light of the linkages between economic growth and human development. Within this system, welfare provisions should be provided by the government alone. Welfare regime type, it is argued – at least in the case of India—closely reflects the nature of the regional redistributive policies. The ideology, organization and class alliance underlying a party-dominated regime affect the redistributive performance of that regime. This study will examine these questions by comparing Indian policy at the state level, a regime capable of introducing elements of redistribution into the development tends to display the following characteristics: a coherent leadership, an ideological and organizational commitment to exclude propertied interests from direct participation in the process of governance, a practical attitude toward facilitating a non-threatening as well as a predictable political atmosphere for the majority.

Below the federal government in India, the state (or provincial) governments in India play a more important role in designing and implementing welfare policies. For instance, it is the state governments rather than the central government that incur the bulk of expenditure on social sectors. Table 1.4 compares the shares of the states and of the central government in the early 1990s, early 2000s and late 2000s, where we can see, despite a downward trend, the contribution of the subnational governments to social-sector expenditure is substantial and much larger than that of the centre. Despite an overall downward trend of the Social Sector Expenditure (SSE) on average (Table 1.5 and Figure 1. 1), the fiscal priority for the social sectors has shown a divergent trend across the states in the reform years (Table 1.6, 1990-2011). Some states such as Maharashtra show a rare increase in the SSE-Total Expenditure (TE) ratio, while other traditional "welfare states" such as West Bengal face a clear decline in similar areas.

Table 1.4: Share of States in the Total Social Sector Expenditure of Center and States (%), 1990-91, 1999-2000 and 2006-07

Major Heads	Share of States (%)		
	1990-91	1999-2000	2006-07
1. Medical, public health water supply and sanitation	89.0	87.9	84.5
2. Education, art and culture	87.8	87.5	87.5
3.,Family welfare	52.3	40.9	33.7
4. Housing	67.3	37.4	49.1
5. Urban development	79.1	94.3	96.3
6. Labor and employment	59.6	59.2	57.1
7. Social security and welfare	93.7	81.4	97.0
8. Others	96.6	84.7	41.9
9. Social Services (1 to 8)	80.1	79.0	76.4
10. Rural development	90.0	66.2	51.8
11 Total (9+10)	85.1	72.6	64.1

Note Others include scientific services and research, broadcasting, information and publicity, the information given in the table relates to actual expenditures
Source calculated from *Indian Public Finance Statistics*, Ministry of Finance, GOI, 2009

Table 1.5 and Figure1.1: Trends in Aggregate Social Sector Expenditure, 1990-2005

	1990-95 (Avg.)	**1996-00** (Avg.)	**2001-05** (Avg.)
TE/GDP	16.0	15.2	17.5
SSE/GDP	5.9	5.6	5.7
SSE/TE	36.8	36.9	32.5

Note Avg Average, SSE Social Sector Expenditure, TE Total Expenditure
Sources Budget Documents of State Governments and Census Reports, Reserve Bank of India

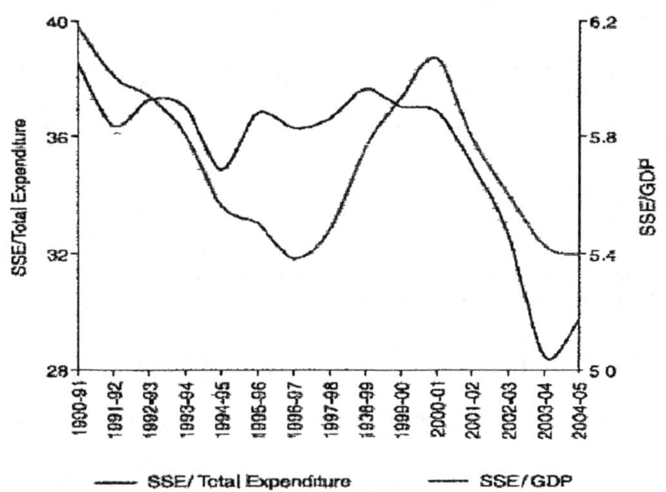

Table 1.6: Major Indicators of Expenditure in Major Indian States: 1990-91, 2001-02 and 2010-11

States	SSE/TE (%)		
	1990-91	2001-02	2010-11 (BE)
Andhra Pradesh	41.7	35.6	35.8
Bihar	38.3	43.7	42.8
Gujarat	36.4	35.6	38.6
Haryana	32.4	37.0	39.2
Karnataka	37.0	38.3	34.8
Kerala	43.7	39.9	39.5
Madhya Pradesh	41.3	42.3	44.3
Maharashtra	35.2	36.6	40.5
Orissa	36.5	36.8	25.8
Punjab	28.1	27.6	42.4
Rajasthan	39.5	41.3	39.3

Tamil Nadu	45.1	39.4	37.9
Uttar Pradesh	38.5	33.1	42.9
West Bengal	46.9	36.0	34.8

Notes: 1. TE: Total Expenditure; GSDP: Gross State Domestic Product;
SSE: Social Sector Expenditure; BE: Budget Estimate
2. Expenditure under different heads has been estimated as the sum of revenue expenditure and capital expenditure (including loans and advances net of repayments).
Source: Budget Documents from State Governments, Reserve Bank of India

A comparative political analysis of Indian states reveals different welfare regime types in alleviating inferior status of lower-caste groups. In this dissertation, I investigate the redistributive attempts of three different policy regimes within India: Tamil Nadu, Uttar Pradesh and West Bengal. These provide similarities and differences regarding regime ideology and organization on the one hand, and the effectiveness of the programs on the other. The conceptual framework governing our analysis is set out in the enclosed table. (Table 1.7)

Table 1.7: Welfare Regimes in India, the Case of OBCs

	Tamil Nadu	West Bengal	Uttar Pradesh
Targeted Beneficiaries	Non-*Brahmins* (including all castes lower than *Brahmins* in the hierarchical Hindu system)	Middle and small farmers, can be clubbed with the middle castes	The middle castes between the *Brahmins* and *Dalits*
Ideological Legacies	Dravidian; anti-Brahmin	Communist; reformist	Socialism; pro-peasants
Political Elite	Dravidians (lower castes)	Upper-caste Communists	Socialists
Institutional Supports	Two-party (pro-lower caste) system;	One-party domination* (upper-caste	Multi-party competition

		leadership)	
Welfare Regime Type	Dravidian-Democratic	Democratic-Developmental	*Kisan*-Socialist

Note: * One-party dominance was officially ended when Mamata Banerjee's Trinamool Congress, a non-communist party, won 2011 state election in West Bengal.

1.4 Research Methods; Account of Research and Fieldwork

As a methodological orientation, I assume that the consequences of the impacts of policy are more important than policies themselves. Policy impact, in this dissertation, refers to the following questions: who gets benefits, how generous they are, and how are they interpreted. The distributional consequences are profound. Policy begets participation begets policy in a cycle that does not lead to equal protection of interests, but in outcomes biased toward the politically active. It may be that the very quality of democratic government is shaped by the kinds of policies it pursues.

The empirical materials for this study were collected mainly during field trips to India in 2006 and 2008-9. It becomes clear that the case of Reservation Policies (RPs) has received greater research attention than the other areas when it comes to the topic of "Caste and Politics". Research efforts were more or less equally divided between West Bengal, Tamil Nadu and Uttar Pradesh. Aside from the use of such printed materials as government documents (published and unpublished) and newspapers (mainly in English), information was collected mainly through interviews with the relevant members of both the state and civil society. Those interviewed included political leaders, government bureaucrats, intellectuals, lower caste peasants and others, who are likely to affect and be affected by RPs.

This study also examines the growing significance of policy impacts. I have closely monitored the economic diversification among the lower caste communities that has occurred in these states of India. In reporting the results of that research, I draw attention to the significant impacts that RPs had for identity formation, resource distribution and interpretation among the caste communities. Subsequent investigations over the online reports and newspapers have shown that this trend has continued undiminished. Three states were chosen because they represent a continuum of maximum to minimum government efforts in mitigating the caste issues in face of lower-caste political activities. Tamil Nadu represents the maximum and long-time effort, and West Bengal represents the minimum and sporadic effort. Uttar Pradesh falls between these two on the continuum. Within these states, village-level studies were also chosen so as to capture the nature of variation. The intellectual aim of the investigation was to compare and isolate the conditions under which political intervention on behalf of the lower castes was likely to be successful.

During the fieldwork, I did not quite follow the research methods and the sequence suggested by textbooks: derive hypothesis, specify research methods, collect data, and present conclusions. As Atul Kohli states, this sequence may be useful for testing ideas, but constricting when answering "why" and "how" questions in a relatively unexplored terrain.[10] The situation I've explored is practical, constructive and somewhat unexpected. For example, the interviews I have done in Jaldhaka villages in northeastern West Bengal have shown a complicated picture: most of the Other Backward Classes (OBCs) are also tribal people, who claim to enjoy both the tribal and caste reservations.[11]

I am particularly interested in the consequences that economic and political changes had for the lower castes. I started by investigating how the local targeted lower castes tended to gain access to the welfare programs. This brought me into contact with various categories of OBCs

[10] Kohli, Atul. *The State and Development in the Third World.* Princeton University Press, 1986.

[11] Although Other Backward Classes is used as a similar term with Other Backward Classes, I will strictly follow the Other Backward Classes because it was created by the central government of India to identify economically and socially disadvantaged caste communities along with Scheduled Castes (SCs) and Scheduled Tribes (STs).

who continued to benefit from the welfare programs after they became better off. The result of this investigation confirmed the decreasing role that RPs have played in improving equality between low and high echelons within a single caste hierarchy. It, however, forms one important part of my research of the "Creamy Layer" phenomenon.[12]

In additional to my own data, I have utilized a large variety of secondary sources and official materials. These include numerous studies written by fellow researchers and other publications based on surveys and case studies. To a lesser degree, my study also uses official statistics and other documentation produced by state organs. However, the government agencies have limited insights into operation of RPs which have formed a major part of caste –related policies. The defective coverage of "Creamy Layer" among the Other Backward Classes (OBCs) has not been rectified by the decadal censuses, which update the existing stock of knowledge regarding population composition and dynamics. For example, the inclusion of *Vokkaliga* and *Lingayats* in Karnataka's OBC list has created controversies.[13] The strongly quantitative nature of such analyses formed a welcome supplement to my own more qualitative research. For instance, I assess the impact of governmental programs carried out in Uttar Pradesh and Tamil Nadu based on the data provided by K. Srinivasan and S. Kumar (1999).[14] Within the context of themes I shall refer repeatedly to these secondary sources as well as the official reports.

[12] "Creamy Layer" refers to relatively wealthier and better educated members of the Other Backward Classes (OBCs) who should be excluded from the quotas granted to the OBCs at the educational institutions, governments and parliaments if financial conditions are not qualified for reservation benefits.

[13] Devaraj Urs formed a Backward Classes Commission under L G Havanur, who in his report dropped Lingayats from the Backward Classes list. During the tenure of Ramakrishna Hegde, the T Venkataswamy commission came into being and recommended dropping Vokkaligas from the backward list, which was opposed. See Dandavati, Padmaraj. "The Saga of Quotas in Karnataka." *Deccan Herald.* September 13, 2005. http://www.deccanherald.com/deccanherald/sep132005/state1910142005912.asp.

[14] K. Srinivasan, Sanjay Kumar. "Economic and Caste Criteria in Definition of Backwardness." *Economic and Political Weekly*, 1999: 3052-3057.

1.5 Composition of the study

The structure of the study contains eight chapters, including chapters on policy approach and policy impacts, and an individual chapter on the phenomenon of "Creamy Layer". Chapter 2 details the conceptualization of welfare regime types and constructs the mechanism of policy impacts. In Chapter 3, I introduce Reservation Policies (RPs) and point out the uniqueness of these policies. In Chapter 4, the caste criterion adopted in RPs has helped shape new social categories, especially the ideological and attitudinal aspects among the lower castes in the political area. This chapter hints at the causal connections between the RPs and political participation among the lower caste communities, which are explored systematically in the following three chapters.

In Chapter 5, I discuss resource effect of RPs. Over time, the political elites avoided including non-Brahmin caste groups in the participatory arena, who have become disproportionately active in recent years. This chapter elaborates political contention among the lower caste regarding the reservation programs. Chapter 6 starts by figuring the major interpreters of the RPs. It mainly discusses the interpretation of the party elites that directly influences the participatory trend among the lower caste voters.

From Chapter 3 through Chapter 6, I discuss RPs and the process of the policy impacts comprehensively. How did the lower-caste participation increase over time and how did the reservation programs contribute to that increase? In short, how does policy influence participation? I attempt to create a linkage between participation and policy in three aspects: the group identity formation, the political and economic source distribution, as well as the interpretation of the distinctive message sent through welfare policies. Chapter 7 focuses on the special group created by RPs –"Creamy Layer". It also gives an account for the political implications of proposed changes in welfare program's design, such as the introduction of exclusion of "Creamy Layer". Such policy threatens to exclude the better-off lower castes from reservation benefits. It works to break the tie between their well-being and government action, yet strengthens the politics of "Creamy Layer".

The final chapter summarizes the study's findings about the relationship between policy and participation. Does redistribution of reservation benefits exacerbate political inequality, erasing India's democratizing effect? Indeed, cleavages could become exposed or deepened among this population around the welfare programs. Proposals to change the program's spending, coverage and interpretation tend to polarize or integrate among the differentiated interests. Yet, this has been hidden by Reservation Policies' universal, if somewhat redistributive principles.

1.6 Terminology

State: According to Mooij (1996), "state" refers to the state apparatus—a set of political, administrative and coercive institutions and organizations, more or less well coordinated by an executive authority: the government.[15] "State" implies the constituent units of the Indian federation. Gujarat is a western Indian State/province.

Backward Castes: those whose ritual rank and occupational status are above "untouchables" but who themselves remain socially and economically depressed. Also referred to as Other Backward Classes (OBCs).

Scheduled Castes: a list of socially deprived (formerly referred to as "untouchables") castes prepared by the British Government in 1935. The schedule of castes was intended to increase representation of scheduled-caste members in the legislature, in government employment, and in university placement.

[15] Mooij, J. E. "Food Policy and Politics. The Public Distribution System in Karnataka and Kerala, South India." 1996.

Scheduled Tribes: a list of indigenous tribal populations who are entitled to much of the same compensatory treatment as scheduled castes. They live largely in the mountainous areas.

"Untouchables": Administrative parlance now employs the term "Scheduled Castes" while rights activists and the population more generally employ the term "*Dalits.*"

Upper castes: technically those occupying the first three major caste categories (thereby excluding the backward castes) and can also be termed as "twice-born".

Lower Castes: those relatively lower in the caste system, including *Dalits*. The term of "Lower Castes" means the lower-order of the four major hereditary classes, namely Brahman, Kshatriya, Vaisya, and *Shudra* into which Hindu society was virtually divided.[16] Lower Castes mainly refer to Other Backward Classes (OBCs) in this dissertation. It is different from the "upper castes" Brahmans and "intermediate castes" "Kshatriya" which can be termed as "forward castes"; it should also be differentiated from the Scheduled Castes and Scheduled Tribes.

Reservation Policies (RPs): it is referred as a quota system whereby a percentage of posts are reserved in enrollment at educational institutions and employment in Government and in the public sector economic units, in order to mitigate backwardness of the socially and educationally backward communities.

Creamy Layer (CL): Creamy Layer is defined by the Sattanathan Commission in 1970 as economically privileged segments of any group receiving quota benefits.

---

[16] *Dalits* are a fifth category in the Hinduist system.

Chapter 2

A Policy Approach

Executive Summary: the dissertation employs a policy approach to study the effects of Reservation Policies on caste-based politics in India. This chapter looks at three aspects of policy analysis - 1) scope of programs, 2) program spending and 3) interpretation of programs. I develop three hypotheses of policy process towards participatory and ideological outcomes. -1) *compared to the liberal programs, universal programs shape a broad political coalition among social welfare supporters. 2) Policy beneficiaries tend to participate in a more collective matter if more generously, more evenly and the longer the welfare benefits are provided. 3) Beneficiaries' political attitudes and behaviors* tend to be manipulated by the *elite groups' interpretation of policies.*

2.1 Introduction

Political scientists have increasingly recognized that public policies are not merely the outcomes of the political process, but are endogenous to it. Beginning with Schattschneider in 1935, policy-as-explanative-variable has survived in various forms within Political Science. To test and develop the basic hypothesis of "policy makes politics", various studies have analyzed the feedback effects of policies, not only upon state and elite actors, but also upon mass publics.

The designs and effects of policies are catalogued in order to seek the relationships between specific programs/welfare regimes and political outcomes. "This is precisely what policy taxonomy might do for the study of politics. To break through the weak and designative vocabulary of public law is perhaps to bring public policy-government-into a proper, analyzable, relationship with those dimensions of political science that are already well developed. In hard and practical terms, a good taxonomy of policies might ennoble this underdeveloped part of the field by converting these important phenomena into 'variables,' which make them more esthetic to the scientists in political science."[17] Lowi (1964) argues that the various natures of policy (distributive, redistributive and regulatory) produce different kinds of politics. Titmuss (1974) and Esping-Andersen (1990) assort different welfare regimes that generate differences in political ideology and mobilization patterns. Skocpol (1992) advances the concept of gendered politics. She draws a contrast between the failed "paternalist" social programs, which aimed to benefit the American working man; and the successful "maternalist" programs, which targeted women and mothers. She argues that the differences between "paternalist" and "maternalist" policies show the changing structure of the American polity and condition the subsequent policies. Pierson (1993) differentiates resource effects and interpretive effects. The former effects provide policy beneficiaries with the access to the political stages. The latter inform the beneficiaries of their roles in the political system. These claims have been tested by a few empirical studies of the public policies in the western countries, with case studies of Mothers' Pensions (Skocpol 1992), Social Security (Campbell 2003) in the United States, Social Care Policies in Germany (Ostner 1998), as well as a variety of universal and targeted programs in Sweden and other Scandinavian countries (Katzenstein 1985 and Kumlin 2002).

Although a few programs were explored to test the claims, this nascent field has yet to progress far enough to generalize from the extant case studies. Thus far, the empirical cases have been drawn primarily from the western countries. The existing explanations range from external factors (such as industrialization and globalization), social group factors (such as worker groups or capitalists) and statist factors (statist institutions). When one turns to the developing countries and when new programs and the impact of policys are studied, a couple of new methodological questions emerge. What are the feedback effects that programs generate in developing countries? What program characteristics produce which kinds of effects? Through what channels do welfare policies affect the political behavior and attitudes of the beneficiaries and the broader public?

---

[17] Lowi, Theodore J. "Four Systems of Policy, Politics, and Choice." *Public Administration Review* 32, no. 4 (1972): 298-310. P. 299

This chapter attempts to lay a theoretical foundation for the study of public policy effects in developing countries such as India. It deals with three primary aspects of program design (scope [universal vs. selective], spending [size of benefits, duration of benefits and benefit distribution], and,interpretation. With promoting political information, political learning and political efficacy, these program designs can shape political interests and group identities, therefore influencing political attitudes and political participation. In this chapter, I first look at the extant typology of welfare regimes (liberal, conservative corporative and social democratic) and the relevant approaches (the external driving forces, social group studies and statist institutions) that explain whether and how these welfare regimes sustain. Then I suggest a policy approach, among other approaches, which provides new insights over the causal-effective relationship between policies and political outcomes. Subsequently I delineate the mechanisms that link those policy characteristics with political participation and political attitudes. Finally, I attempt to seek the appropriate level of analysis for the case of India.

2.2 Welfare State and Its Sustainability

A welfare state is a system in which the state is a major provider of social and economic security for the country's population by means of pensions, social security benefits, free health care, and so forth. Esping-Andersen classifies the welfare states in the western countries into three categories: liberal, corporatist and social democracy. The liberal regime, exemplified by the US and Australia is a residualist welfare regime. Capitalist and market economy is the main mechanism for promoting welfare in a liberal regime. Welfare benefits go to the "deserving poor" at the minimalist. Only the "the people most in need" are targeted and only the worst of their distresses are alleviated, for fear of creating disincentives against participating in the labor market The corporatist regime, such as that in Germany, France and other Continental European countries, is a conservative welfare regime. Society is seen as a cooperative venture, with various groups (labor and capital, men and women, etc.) each having their distinct role to participate. The task of corporatist public policy is to ensure social cohesion and social stability. Welfare resources are typically earnings-related and hence status-preserving. Sweden and other Scandinavia countries represent the social democratic regimes, which had been characterized by class politics and socialist economics, though the conservative parties have gained strength in all of them, partly in reaction to the very generous welfare policies. Social democratic regimes are highly egalitarian in terms of welfare distribution. Welfare benefits are typically of a universal kind, either through promoting high levels of employment and earnings or through redistributive taxes. (Table 2.1)

Table 2.1: Three Worlds of Western Welfare States

	Liberal (U.S., Canada, Australia)	Corporatist (Germany, France, Italy, Austria)	Social Democratic (Sweden and other small Nordic countries)
Welfare goals	Poor relief	Social cohesion and stability	Social equality
Spending	Modest	Generous	Generous
Driving force	Market economy	Social groups	Socialist Ideology
Policy beneficiaries	Most deserving poor	Workers, capitalists etc.	All the citizens

Source: Esping-Andersen. 1990. Gøsta. *The Three Worlds of Welfare Capitalism*

These three worlds share the common redistributive means, for its various goals, of providing welfare benefits for the disadvantaged. The underlying welfare goals are seen by liberals as a means of poor relief, by corporatists as a manner of promoting social cohesion, and by social democrats as an instrument of social equality.

A number of theories have been applied to explain whether and how the welfare states sustain themselves. Some researchers see the external factors (industrialization and globalization) as the driving force behind social policies. For instance, the states embrace neoliberal policies and retrench welfare programs in order to maintain international competitiveness in an industrializing and globalizing world. Moreover, there are a group of sociologists arguing for the crucial role played by the various social groups – such as the working class and the progressively minded businessmen. They politically press for the pro-worker or pro-capitalist welfare policies. A more recent explanation was advanced by the statist researchers such as Theda Skocpol. Skocpol proposes the crucial roles played by the state and party organization through which politicians and interest groups pursue policies. These political elites and political institutions have effects on the identities, goals and capacities of social groups involved in policy making. In this dissertation, I attempt to provide a policy approach, which is aimed at bridging the statist and sociologist approaches to analyze the politics of quotas in India. This approach not only emphasizes the policies designed by decision makers that influence social groups in certain ways, but also stresses policy effects that further affect the statist institutions and policy makers.

2.3 The Mechanism of Policy Approach

How do welfare states sustain themselves? Generally, welfare states (especially those with generous and universal programs) are sustained by generating their own political support. The basic mechanism is producing self-interested public preferences favoring state intervention. Policy recipients back up their preferences with political activity. More specifically, they exert political pressure to maintain or expand the programs from which they benefit, or retrench the programs from which they suffer. The politically relevant resource empowers the targeted beneficiaries to engage in political activities.

What characteristics of government programs produce the effects outlined above? The research of welfare policy includes three basic/core research questions. First, who gets benefits? Second, how generous are the benefits? Third, how are the benefits administered? Such designs shape procedures and norms, create institutional niches, and provide political resources to help/hinder those pro-welfare state interests to resist the welfare rollbacks. By identifying and analyzing these three aspects of policy impacts, I offer some tentative hypotheses that help illuminate how program characteristics drive the participatory capacities and attitudes of the beneficiaries. This section considers political relevance of three aspects of program design: 1) scope of programs; 2) mode of spending; 3) program administration.

2.3.1 Scope of Programs: Universal or Targeted?

Scope of programs – whether it is universal or targeted– is one of the most politically consequential aspects of program design (Rothstein 1998). Scope is often correlated with other important aspects of program design, such as mode of spending and interpretation.

Hypothesis: The liberal nature (cost containment, market-oriented, means-tested character) of targeted programs tends to divide constituents' collective support for welfare expansion; By contrast, universal programs that enhance common social citizen rights shape a broad political coalition among social welfare supporters.

What are the political implications of these two types of programs' distributional effects? The universal/target design can affect the following aspects: 1) the socio-economic status of the program recipients; 2) the level of dependence of the recipients on the programs; and 3) the political attitudes of the recipients towards the programs. (Table 2.2)

Table 2.2: Scope of Programs and its Effects

Scope of program	The socio-economic status	Level of dependence on the program	Political ideology and partisan effect
Targeted	Dividing group interests	Modest	Liberal
Universal	Shaping common interests	Large	Leftist

Variations in these aspects can result in differing political patterns. First of all, the social-economic status may be changing in response to the targeted/universal programs. For those under the universal programs, they gradually shape a similar group identity by sharing the common interests around the welfare programs. On the other hand, the beneficiaries of the targeted programs could hardly change their pre-existing status due to their modest dependence on the program. To a larger extent, the limited targeting is likely to divide the interests among the beneficiaries who are under the targeted program and those who are not. The mechanism of reshaping the group identities will be discussed in the following section.

The second factor is the level of dependence of the beneficiaries on the program. Universal programs are politically protected due to the high dependency of the beneficiaries. The famous case is the Social Security program in the U.S.. Social security is called the real third rail of American politics and has shown its strong political roots among the seniors. Often targeted programs' political weakness stems from its low "dependability" as they provide an exit of public program for more affluent beneficiaries who are consequently less dependent on the government program. For instance, Medicare in the US does not cover many routine aspects of health care and imposes significant premiums and deductibles rather than providing first dollar coverage. This encourages the development of a private supplementary insurance market for more affluent beneficiaries. The design of Medicare left an opening for private provision. This reduced the stake that high-income seniors have in the public program, thus reducing the political pressure to improve Medicare benefits.[18]

There is a third way in which scope of programs is relevant with politics: the ideological and partisan effects. Such political attitudes vary across program experiences. The democratizing effect of the universal programs places the recipients to the left on the ideological scale. These recipients, as a result, tend to provide more support for a state role than those under the targeted programs.[19] As regards the targeted programs with a liberal nature, the beneficiaries have no

[18] Oberlander, Jonathan. *The Political Life of Medicare* Chicago: University of Chicago, 2003.
[19] Kumlin, Staffan. "Institutions—experiences—preferences. How welfare state design affects political trust and ideology." In *Restructuring the welfare state Political institutions and policy change* , by B. Rothstein & S. Steinmo. New York: Palgrave Macmillan.

incentives to promote the state's role since the sporadic targeting can hardly have an equalizing effect among those beneficiaries. This may dampen the political preference to public provisions. Therefore, compared to the targeting design, the universal design secures support for programs by claiming political equality.

2.3.2 Program Spending: Size, Distribution and Duration

Program spending is a second characteristic of the impact of policy. It influences the likelihood of political participation by recipients and the broader public. The mode of spending includes: 1) the size of benefits; 2) benefit distribution within recipient population; 3) duration of benefits.

Hypothesis: *The more generous, more evenly and the longer the welfare benefits are provided, in a more collective matter beneficiaries tend to participate politically.. In contrast, programs which are scarcely funded, more unequally distributed, and more episodic in nature, lack the same incentive, which results in disincentives to political participation.*

The size of benefits matters. For some programs, the spending has to be intentionally kept low so that they do not provide a disincentive to work.[20] Skimpy welfare benefits leave most program recipients poor and thus have little effect on their participation. For other programs, the benefits have to be large enough to lift the beneficiaries out of poverty, which positively affects their participation in politics. For instance, the funding for Social Security has been kept large enough to lift most senior recipients out of poverty, positively affecting senior participation in politics.[21] A contrasting example relates to the social welfare assistance programs. With the modest funding, the programs serve to assist the weak sections of people (such as the unemployed

---

[20] Gilens, Martin. *Why Americans Hate Welfare Race, Media, and the Politics of Antipoverty Policy* University of Chicago Press, 1999.

[21] Campbell, Andrea Louise *How Policies Make Citizens Senior Citizen Activism and the American Welfare State* Princeton University Press, 2003.

workers). But the funding source is kept so low that few beneficiaries are interested in relevant political activities.

In addition to the size of the benefits, distribution within recipient populations also matters. Under the same program, some beneficiaries can receive higher benefits than the others. "Targeting within universalism" is an often overlooked political effect of spending design: redistributing more benefits toward some sections of citizens than the others. For example, Medicare-related participation is more common among low-income seniors because they are less healthy, use more Medicare benefits, and are more likely to be solely dependent on the program for health insurance.[22] It thus helps narrow the gap between the poor and rich in terms of health care. However, this redistributional aspect of the programs leads to unequal consequences in some other cases. Reservation Policies in India tend to benefit the richer section of the lower castes, thereby enhancing their political and economic status and further broadening the gap between the richer and poorer sections within the lower caste communities.

The third aspect of program spending is duration of benefits. The duration of benefits is a factor particularly relevant to programs' participatory effects. This aspect is strongly correlated with the scope design. For those recipients of the means-tested benefits, there is low incentive to participate politically for the programs since they may pass in and out of eligibility as their incomes and life situations change. Universal programs, where recipients may benefit for the rest of their lives, tend to produce political participation. For instance, the one-shot nature of some welfare programs, such as college loans, can hardly lead to mass participatory activities. By contrast, Social Security ensures the seniors' life and thus makes that program widely supported and untouchable politically.

To sum up, the size, distribution and duration of benefits within welfare programs determine the level of political participation. Welfare programs can come from both the private and public

[22] Ibid.

sources. In this study, the data is limited to welfare provisions provided primarily by the government.

2.3.3 Program Interpreters: Political and Administrative Elites

Program interpretation is a third significant characteristic of the impact of policy. The political and administrative elites are the major interpreters of the public policies and convey meaning about the policies to the general public. They influence the mass public's perceptions of viable policy alternatives. Consequently, the "interpretive" choices tend to become locked in because policies foster their own sets of norms and values. Furthermore, the interpretation has ripple effects in shaping constituents' broader views of government and their willingness to participate in democratic processes. Over time citizens come to expect certain things from their welfare states.

In this dissertation, I look at the political and administrative elites for their interpretation of Reservation Policies. I hypothesize that *beneficiaries' political attitudes and behaviors* tend to be influenced by *the interpretation of these elites.*

2.3.4 The Process of Policies towards Politics

A more detailed analysis is needed to explain how the above three aspects of the the impact of policy affect the recipients' engagement toward politics. The recipients' political engagement is a process started with their understanding of the existing policies. The extant programs can be sources of political information. This is particularly true for universal, richly-funded and well-organized programs. These programs are supported in an institutional setting in which information can be conveyed by program personnel or by interest groups that may develop around policies. Related to political information is "political learning". It is the lesson that programs convey (through political information) about program recipients' role in the political system. The programs that are implemented with well-publicized and justly administered rules convey the lesson whether the programs are fair and the governments are responsive. Through the process of political learning, the recipients have a better idea of how responsive the governments are towards their demands; they have more of the capabilities and confidence to deal with the government. The more responsive the programs are towards the recipients' demands, the more they feel capable and confident to involve themselves in politics, and the more likely the recipients tend to participate actively.

Furthermore, political interest may be shaped around the relevant policy areas; to a larger extent, group identities may be shaped as well. Whether interest groups develop around a given program depends on the preexisting characteristics of beneficiaries and the nature of the benefit conferred. It is also a function of program designs. As Walker (1991) contends, interest group formation is often a consequence of government policy rather than a cause of it. Those programs with universal, well-funded and rational-bureaucratic characteristics can define groups and create identities. They can foster groups to self-mobilize or be mobilized by extant interest groups, political parties, and bureaucracies. There are some programs designed explicitly to develop group identity. For example, India's reservation quota policies enhanced the extant caste group identities and promote the identity politics.

Interest groups, as the mobilized groups around the public policies or as those mobilizing the policy recipients, can encourage public support/resistance of the programs and the larger governments. On one hand, they interpret the political information about the policy choices and affect the perception of these policies. On the other hand, they play roles in mobilizing around policy threats or opportunities, and shape the breadth of the participation. In one word, interest groups act as an important medium over which public policies influence political participation.

2.3.5 Participatory and Ideological Outcomes

Through the political learning process, programs can influence both political attitudes and political participation. Political preference can be shaped from a number of sources: the extant political culture, early political socialization, and group dynamics, among others. Program designs can influence political preferences as well. These preferences include the weakening/enhancing role the state should play, the trust the program recipients have in governments, and so forth. It is argued that universal programs, compared to the targeted programs, foster more trust and support in governments. In addition, the designs of public policies can affect the political ideology and partisanship of the program recipients. It is mentioned above that universal welfare programs invite more state intervention and tend to push the recipients further left on the ideological spectrum.[23] A similar reasoning is that program designs could affect partisanship as well. The idea is that universal programs build support for the parties that created them – such as the left political parties that were the architects of the welfare state in many West European countries. For example, Esping-Andersen (1985) asserts that universalistic welfare state programs have become a "power resource" for social democratic parties in Scandinavia countries, enabling these parties to secure their political dominance. Where welfare state programs are less universal, left parties have a harder time maintaining political power, and support for the welfare state also decline. In other words, the belief system of the program recipients and probably the broader public can be transformed in the process of pursuing certain policies. If sufficient people accept one certain party ideology, the party system can be characterized by the dominance of that political party over the others.

Outcomes of political participation can be affected as well. I classify the participation outcomes of the program recipients into three kinds: pre-program participation, post-program participation, and program-specific participation. Pre-program participation concerns to the political participation of the program recipients before the relevant programs are made, i.e. their "normal" level of participation in the electoral politics. This is a function of their preexisting characteristics (before the programs take place), including socioeconomic status and all other effects they receive except the programs. Post-program participation refers to the level of these recipients participate in politics after the programs take place. Program-specific participation emphasizes the effects of the specific programs on the participation of the recipients. It points

[23] Social security in U.S. may be an exception since U.S. seniors tend to vote Republicans.

directly to the political engagement with regard to their program, such as whether they vote or make campaign contributions on the basis of their programs.

The latter two kinds of participation are strongly correlated. Social Security and Medicare are the examples with high levels of program-specific participation and post-program participation. The program-specific participation is high not only because universal programs cover large numbers of people, but also because these recipients can be mobilized easily around the programs. The post participation level is high as well because of the cumulative participatory effects produced by the program-specific participation. In contrast, targeted welfare recipients participate at low rates in general because they lack politically-relevant resources to begin with, and the program does not provide a compensatory amount thereafter. Unorganized, welfare recipients also engage in little program-specific activities, which leads to the general low participatory rate after the program is implemented. The pre-program participation is a reference point for comparison. It helps understand both the comparison of the same policy effects on different groups of people; and the comparison of the different policy effects (universal/targeted) on the same group of people.

2.4 More Methodological Consideration

The last section aims to build a theoretical framework and identify the specific process in which program characteristics influence the recipients' political preferences and participation pattern. Designs of the government programs shape the capacities of and opportunities for the recipients to participate in politics generally. Beyond the general understanding of the policy approach, there are more methodological aspects deserving careful consideration. First issue is "spillover effects". Under what conditions can programs inspire extra participation in addition to the narrow program-specific participation? The post-program participation cannot be a simple total of pre-program participation and program-specific participation. It is possible that universal programs, compared to targeted programs, have stronger "spillover effects" which increase the participation of recipients groups on one hand, and on the other hand create the participation of non-recipient groups based on its generous resource effects and multi-channel interpretive effects.

Second issue concerns the effects of participation and attitudes on subsequent policymaking. Skocpol (1992) argues that prior policy influence subsequent policy choices. The discussion thus far has focused on the ways in which programs influence the political ideology and especially the political participation of relevant groups. This part of "policy - political behavior – policy" cycle is emphasized since the policy-as-explanatory-variable is a relatively unexplored phenomenon. Nonetheless, much remains to be learned about the second part of the cycle – how the various political activities and ideas influence subsequent policymaking through a feedback mechanism. Reservation welfare for the lower castes and tribals in India, which will be discussed in the following chapters, shows the relevant spending has increased tremendously over time in some states rather than in others. Thus, the complete studies that trace the entire cycle add the most to our understanding of the implications of government program design for participatory democracy and subsequent policy choices.

Moreover, it is also crucial to understand how designs of public policies change over time. In the *liberal* form of *globalization*, many welfare states in both developed and developing world have begun reducing the role of public provision. Even those welfare states not engaging in wholesale retrenchment are restructuring the programs in fiscal, administrative and targeting terms. The design changes may have profound effects on interest group mobilization. For example, the recent pension policy restructuring in India increases the role of private insurance so that pension program will change from a universal program to the one in which senior recipients are split into different programs. This accordingly divides the relevant constituency. The weakened constituency may be less able to fend off the retrenchment in this or other programs. In one word, adding this dynamic element helps increase our understanding of the factors behind political behavior.

2.5 Policy Approach and the Indian Case

To sum up, "Policy produces politics" where policies are independent rather than dependent variables, has successfully been employed to explain the political phenomena. Its importance cannot be overlooked since it presents an opportunity for significant methodological innovation. Studying public policy and its designs provides the possibility to bring together the behavioral and institutional schools in a methodologically productive way. Moreover, it enriches the historical institutional research by including the mass public, together with the tradition's emphasis on state and elite actors. It may also solve the problem of the historical institutional approach by analyzing the changing the impact of policys and the "spillover effects". Therefore, the crucial policy factor can provide a fuller picture of the forces behind political behavior.

An additional benefit of applying a policy approach is the freedom of employing a greater variety of methodologies to the questions at hand - qualitative and quantitative methods. Quantitative methods can be applied in analyzing the variables as recipients' participation in the electoral politics, the spending design and targeting design of the specific programs. Meanwhile, the recipients' feelings about the programs from which they benefit and the administration patterns through which welfare provision is delivered are probably best captured by qualitative methods such as in-depth interviews, participant observation, and ethnographic fieldwork. Policy approach may corroborate both the qualitative and quantitative methods to test and develop various hypotheses.

The next chapter concerns the Reservation Policies in India. The reservation policy study raises important considerations about the appropriate means of performing such research. There has been growing popularity of cross-national comparative analysis of various social policy effects. This enables exploration of policy similarities and differences and their outcomes. However, cross-national comparison shows a methodological weakness: one can hardly control for alternative explanations for attitudinal and behavior patterns, such as cultural, institutional and social differences. For instance, the comparison of affirmative action policies between the U.S. and India can be methodologically difficult. The lower castes in India are culturally and socially different than their counterparts (the blacks, Hispanic and American Indians) in the U.S. Thus, a policy research could be better undertaken in a region where the cultural and social setting is commonly shared. More importantly, comparing different designs of one policy that serve the similar recipients in this region controls for even more competing hypotheses.

Besides, it is also important to seek the appropriate administrative level at which social policies are designed and implemented. In this dissertation, I focus on the state-level policy research in the case of India instead of studying the cross-country comparison. As a federal country, it is the state governments rather than the central government that make the social policies and create the bulk of expenditure on social sectors. Designs (spending distribution, beneficiary targeting and administrative pattern) of all kinds of programs are decided at the state level governments.

Therefore, I adopt a comparative analytical framework complemented by three states in India - *Tamil Nadu, Uttar Pradesh and West Bengal-* for intensive case-study analysis. Although all these three states have designed Reservation Policies (RPs), the RPs in these three states evolved in three very different directions. The relatively meager reservation benefits in Uttar Pradesh has emphasized Scheduled Castes (SCs) and Scheduled Tribes (STs); while in Tamil Nadu, reservations have been relatively generous and universal (covering SCs/STs/OBCs). West Bengal has the poorest welfare provision history for the lower castes and tribals among the three states. These are the states with similar deserving population, but the impacts on political participation and attitudes have significantly diverged over time. Such divergence is expected to be produced by policy contrasts. Overall, this research sets out to investigate the evolution and character of state-level welfare policies and their effects on the participation of lower castes and tribals. The ultimate goal is to ascertain whether and to what extent it constitutes a distinct "Indian model" of welfare provision.

Chapter 3

Reservation Policies in India

Executive Summary: This chapter reviews the history of India's Reservation Policies, especially for the Other Backward Classes (OBCs) in the post-Independence period. In this chapter, I analyze the disparity of quota politics at state level and hypothesize that it is partly resulted from impacts of Reservation Policies.

3.1 Introduction

If one has to pick a policy research in India that helps understand my proposition that "policy influences politics", the notion of positive discrimination probably comes first among the range of choices. Positive discrimination has entered Indian politics, especially mass politics, for three decisive reasons. First, three fourths of the Indian population (Scheduled Castes account for 16%, Scheduled Tribes for 8% and Other Backward Classes for another 50%) have been affected by the policy. Second, the policy is directly targeting and influencing the lower castes and tribes in India's hierarchical society because it isolates a few social groups on an ascriptive basis. Third, the affected people have been politically conscious and well organized around the policy in the forms of the voluntary groups (such as caste associations) or ethnic/multiethnic political parties (such as the Bahujan Samaj Party in Uttar Pradesh, the Dravida Munnetra Kazhagam in Tamil Nadu). As Ashutosh Varshney (1999) contends, the more direct the effect of a policy, the more people are affected by it; and the more organized they are the greater potential for mass politics.[24]

Positive discrimination refers to preferential policies that promote equal opportunities for the selected underprivileged ethnic groups. Positive discrimination, or affirmative action, or

[24] Varshney, Ashutosh. "Mass Politics or Elite Politics? India's Economic Reforms in Comparative Perspective." In *India in the Era of Economic Reforms*, by Ashutosh Varshney, Nirupam Bajpai Jeffrey D. Sachs. New York: Oxford University Press, 1999.

compensatory discrimination, or preferential policies, or Reservation Policies, as these policies are variously called, are one kind of government intervention. It refers to "laws, regulations, administrative rules, courts orders, and other public interventions to provide certain public and private goods, such as admission into schools and colleges, jobs, promotions, business loans, and rights to buy and sell land on the basis of membership in a particular ethnic group." (Weiner 1983, p.35)

I address Reservation Policies (RPs) in India, one form of positive discrimination, which favors the disadvantaged ethnic groups by giving them reservations in employment, education and even in the political assemblies. These caste group members share involuntary and rarely alterable ethnic identity. They are Scheduled Castes (SCs/Untouchables/*Dalits*), Scheduled Tribes (STs/*Adivasis*) and "Other Backward Classes" (OBCs).[25] Due to their average low socio-economic status, they are generally under-represented in the political arena and obtain fewer educational and working opportunities as compared to the rest of the society. RPs are designed to address these inequalities that attributed to a person's social group identity.

In this chapter, I first review the historical origins of Reservation Policies in India, which can be divided into two major phases: the pre-Mandal phase and the post-Mandal phase. In the pre-Mandal period, the emphasis of RPs stayed with SCs and STs.[26] Such RPs has attained broad public support at state and federal level. After the establishment of the Mandal Commission in 1979, especially after the reopening of the Mandal Report by the V. P. Singh government in 1989, a continuous and intense debate has been undergoing in terms of the extended reservation for "Other Backward Classes" (OBCs). Subsequently I offer some observations about the state-level *mass politics* arising from the issue of extending reservations for OBCs. Uttar Pradesh, Tamil Nadu and West Bengal will be the three reference states, which represent the, northen, southern and north-eastern regions of India respectively. I will focus attention on the spheres of

[25] In the Hindu society, *varna* model shows four orders: *Brahmins*, Kashatriyas, *Vaishyas* and *Shudras* plus its Untouchables. SCs are the Untouchables, OBCs represent the *Shudras* population while the STs are the aboriginal people in India. They are defined as SCs, STs and OBCs in Indian Constitution.

[26] Reservation Policies are not applicable to Muslims at national level and in many states.

employment and education in the following chapters, where positive discrimination has proved to be most controversial.

3.2 Pre-Mandal Reservation Policies

The Scheduled Castes (SCs) total about 167 million people or 16 percent of Indian population (Census Data 2001, India). They have been seen as "untouchable" for centuries because of their allegedly polluting status in the Hindu hierarchical society. The idealized caste system consists of the *varna* model with its four orders -*Brahmins* (scholars, teachers, priests), *Kshatriyas* (warriors, kings, administrators), *Vaishyas* (agriculturists, merchants) and *Shudras* (artisans, service providers) - and "untouchables". The first three *varnas* (categories) are the "twice born" castes and are often called forward castes. The *Shudra*, or the intermediate castes are mostly peasant proprietors and will be discussed in the next section. The "untouchables" or *Dalits* are positioned out of the caste system. They share a low socio-economic status across India. The same is true for the Scheduled Tribes (STs), the aboriginal peoples of India most of whom lived in isolated areas. Their number has arrived at approximately 84 million or 7 percent of the population (Census Data 2001, India). Most of the SCs and STs are among the most deprived people in India and are often "depressed class" or "Most Backward Class" (MBC).[27]

As early as the late nineteenth and early twentieth century, the history of Reservation Policies (RPs) began in the form of anti-Brahmin movements in the southern India. The aim was to increase the non-Brahmin quotas in public service and in educational institutions. The participants were the non-Brahman groups, including the SCs and STs as well as relatively well-off Hindus from the middle castes.

---

[27] For Background, see Glanter, Marc. *Competing Equality Law and the Backward Classes in India* Berkkeley: University of California Press, 1984. Or Joshi, Barbara R. *Democracy in Search of Equailty Untouchable Politics and Indian Social Change* New Jersey: Humanities Press Inc., 1982.

The 1920s saw efforts undertaken for the good of these "backward communities" in both the western and southern regions of India. In Madras Presidency (directly under the British rule), systematic endeavors were made to improve the positions of non-*Brahmins*. In response to the plea of the anti-Brahmin Justice Party which won the election in 1920, the British rulers agreed to increase the representation of various non-Brahmin communities both in the bureaucracy and in the assemblies. For instance, specific quotas were established in 1926 for public appointments. Among every fifteen appointments, two to "backward" (i.e. OBCs) Hindus, six to other Hindus, two to "depressed" (i.e. SCs) castes, two to Brahmans, the other three to Anglo-Indians, Christians and Muslims. The RPs also took place in western India. In Bombay Presidency in 1925, the positions were reserved in public service and in higher educational admissions for the SCs and STs.

RPs created a center of attention throughout India in the 1930s. The historic debate took place between Mahatma Gandhi and Bhim Rao Ambedkar over the issue of separate electorates and seats for the SCs. The most revered Dalit leader, B. R. Ambedkhar, strongly advocated establishing separate electorates and seats for the depressed communities. Mahatma Gandhi, on the other hand, was opposed to any kind of separation of the "*Harijans*"[28] from the rest of the Hindu community. The debate eventually reached a compromise in the form of 1932 "Poona Pact". Over one fifth of India's legislators (both at central and state level) would be ensured of scheduled origin. But the SC and ST candidates for these seats would be elected by general electorates instead of separate "untouchable" and tribal electorates. As it was incorporated into the Government of India Act of 1935, the reservation for SC/STs for the first time gained its countrywide legitimacy.

[28] *Harijan* is a term Gandhi created for the untouchables. It literally means people of God.

The positive discrimination in favor of SCs and STs was officially written into the 1950 Constitution.[29] Despite of its tendency to focus on equal individual right and freedom[30], the 1950 Constitution targeted three groups for special advantages and protections, SCs and STs and potentially other "weaker sections" or "backward classes" as well. In Article 46 of the "Directive Principle of State Policy", it asserts: "The State shall promote with special care the educational and economic interests of the weaker sections of the people and, in particular, of the Scheduled Castes and Schedule Tribes, and shall protect them from social injustice and all forms of exploitation."[31]

More specifically, there are several provisions of the Constitution pertaining to the positive discrimination in the political, employment and educational spheres. Articles 330, 331, 332, and 334 address the political reservations. According to these Articles and amendments, in some parliamentary constituencies at both the central and the state level, SC/ST representatives would be elected by all eligible voters with the number of reserved seats proportional to the SC/ST population in that constituency. The period of such reservation is limited to twenty years; but an additional ten year period has regularly extended. Regarding the public service jobs, Section 4 of Article 16 permits the state to make "any provision for the reservations of appointments or posts in favor of any backward class of citizens which, in the opinion of the State, is not adequately represented in the services under the State". In addition, Article 335 calls for a certain percentage of jobs for SCs and STs in the civil and technical services, in state-run and semi-autonomous enterprises, and in the private as well as public technical institutions. In the educational arena, a new provision to Article 15 asserts that nothing in the Constitution "shall prevent the State from making any special provision for the advancement of any socially and educationally backward

[29] The Constitution was drafted under the aid of the famous Dalit leader B.R. Ambedkar who was the chairman of the Constitution drafting committee. Jawaharlal Nehru named B.R. Ambedkar as law minister and chairman of the constitution drafting committee of the Constituent Assembly.

[30] Such as the guarantee to all citizens of equality before the law (Article 14), the prohibition of discrimination on grounds of religion, race, caste, sex, or place of birth (Article 15), and the assurance of equality of opportunity in matters of public employment (Article 16).

[31] "Constitution of India." Lucknow: Eastern Book Company, 1981. p.17

classes of citizens or for the Scheduled Castes and Scheduled Tribes."[32] The office of Commissioner of Scheduled Castes and Scheduled Tribes was established in federal and state government administrations, in order to enforce and oversee these RPs. In a word, reserved seats for SC and ST members in elective legislative bodies are mandated, whereas reservations in employment and education are authorized and encouraged.

3.3 OBCs and the Mandal Recommendations

Beyond the constitutional provisions, the Indian governments at the central and state level have developed an array of further protective legal devices and "uplift" welfare for SCs and STs. While the SC and ST members benefited from more and more privileged programs, a debate was undergoing in terms of who belong to the third category of disadvantaged people as the potential "weaker sections" and "backward classes" mentioned in the Constitution, and in terms of what reservation benefits they should receive.

The "backward classes" are broadly equated to the Hindu lower castes, explicitly the "Other Backward Classes" which refers to the castes between the "forward" castes and the SC/STs. As compared to the SCs and STs, OBCs present a more complicated picuture. They are situated above the untouchables but virtually below the "twice born" castes (including *Brahmins*, *Kshatriyas* and *Vaishyas*). They constitute the bulk of *Shudra*s, the last *varna* of the classic Hindu arrangement. They include upwards of 600 million people who account for almost half of the Indian population. These numerous low caste Hindus demand similar reservations on the grounds that their communities were no less socio-economically disadvantaged than those benefiting from positive discrimination.

[32] The new provision was following the two Supreme Court decisions that rejected discrimination in educational admissions.

However, identifying those belonging to the OBCs and deciding the extent of their reservation benefits, have led to great controversy.[33] The expansion of reservation granted to "Other Backward Classes" has experienced many twists and turns. In 1961, the Nehru government rejected creating an all-India list of backward castes, which was prepared by the first Backward Classes Commission.[34] Under the Janata Party, which defeated the Congress Party in 1977 and won the national election, a second attempt was made by B.P. Mandal and the new Backward Classes Commission in 1978 to formulate an all-India policy for OBCs.[35] The Mandal Commission recommended reservations for OBCs in both employment (in central government services, public sector enterprises and educational institutions) and education (OBC student reservations in scientific, technical and professional institutions). As regards who were qualified for these Reservation Policies (RPs), the Mandal Commission prepared a list of castes who were estimated at 52 percent of the total population. Since a limit of 50 percent on national reservation set by the prior Supreme Court, only the 27 percent quotas were designated to the OBCs, bringing the overall percentage of reserved seats in public employment to 49.5 percent. That means, almost half of the population in India is now eligible for reservations of one kind or another. However, the Mandal Commission report was shelved for almost one decade until 1990 when the Janata Party lost power in 1979 and the subsequent Congress Party administrations showed no interest in pursuing the reservation issue. Only in the late 1980s and early 1990s, the recommendations of the Mandal Commission were resumed by the then Prime Minister, V.P. Singh (1989-91), and its new coalition government led by the populist Janata Dal.

---

[33] Glanter, Marc *Competing Equality Law and the Backward Classes in India* Berkkeley University of California Press, 1984 pp 154-281

[34] In 1953 the Nehru government appointed the first Backward Classes Commission under Kaka Kalelkar A list of 2,399 backward castes (116 million people, 32 percent of the total population) was prepared in the 1955 report Kalelkar himself expressed doubts about the caste criterion to define "backward"

[35] In 1978, the second Backward Classes Commission was established under the chairmanship of B P Mandal, who was appointed by the Janata Party After two year research, a long list was prepared of 3, 248 castes comprising roughly 350 million people or 52 4 percent of the population of India

3.4 Inter-State Disparity of Reservation Policies

Unlike the reservations for SCs and STs, the reservations for OBCs have a weak constitutional base. There were no clear ways of defining the proportion of the Indian population which belongs to the "backward class". This not only provides a weak legitimate base for designing relevant policies, but technically creates the difficulties of targeting the OBCs in the process of implementation. Due to the failed efforts of the central government to develop a uniform set of criteria, each state government has its own criteria for OBC reservations. As a consequence, while SC and ST members are given reservations in the central services and in centrally run educational institutions and public service, the OBCs reservation are confined to state and locally run educational institutions and administrative services.

Nevertheless, the India's Reservation Policies (RPs) for OBCs have found its legitimacy at state level. When the Nehru government refused to create an all-India list of backward castes in the early 1960s, it advised the state governments to choose their own criteria. In the absence of the uniform policy, the criteria for inclusion led to a one-for-all definition of the whole group of OBCs. Amebedkar had argued in the Constituent Assembly Debate that "A backward community is a community which is backward in the opinion of the government". The state governments were given the discretion to grant reservations to the most deserving groups. Consequently a wide variety of policies and practices developed in the states by the early 1970s. The demands from the OBCs met with some positive responses in some states rather than the others.

By contrast with the general acceptance of SC/ST reservations in the early 1950s, the Mandal announcement in the 1990 has brought up vehement controversies over the quota policies. The "caste polarization" around Mandal spread to all parts of India. On one hand, strong opposition to V.P.Singh's Mandal announcement in 1990s was widespread and has been mainly triggered from the middle and upper caste Hindus, especially in north India. On the other hand, the Mandal report has also highly raised the political consciousness of lower castes. "For the first time, lower caste people have started to vote en mass for leaders belonging to their own milieu."[36] Their movements are broadly named the "second democratic upsurge" in the history of Indian democracy.

However, the actual contention and conflicts have been at the state level as a result of the Mandal Report since the late 1970s. Reservations for OBCs in some states have enjoyed strong support among their beneficiary communities, while in other states OBC reservations have not found it's legitimacy due to mounting opposition from the urban upper/middle castes and from the OBCs, such as the recent issues in Rajasthan, where the high court turned down the plea for special reservation to Gujjars in government jobs citing the lack of quantifiable data that could demonstrate the backwardness of the community at the end of 2010. [37] There are still other states where neither support nor opposition took place. In some parts of southern India (such as Tamil Nadu and Karnataka) many OBCs had long been favored by forms of positive reservations in education and employment. A visible and strong political pressure came from these caste groups demanding even more favorable Reservation Policies (RPs) for the OBCs. In western India (such as Gujarat and Maharashtra), where the SCs gained ground early due to the efforts of Jotirao Phule and B. R. Ambedkar, strong opposition was brought along by the upper and middle castes.[38] The most violent reaction to the Mandal Report came from the northern region of India (including Rajasthan, Bihar, UP etc), where the Mandal Reports led to the most serious cleavage between the upper castes and lower castes, and within lower castes. In the north-eastern state West Bengal, where there were no OBC programs in the pre-Mandal period, there were few relevant political activities. The Communists and their allied political parties were very reluctant to take caste into account. They hold the view that this social category was bound to be

[36] Jaffrelot, Christophe "The Rise of the Other Backward Classes in the Hindi Belt " *The Journal of Asian Studies* 59, no 1 (2000) 106

[37] Cited from *Are Gujjars any less backward than Jats in Rajasthan?* December 25, 2010 http //articles timesofindia indiatimes com/2010-12-25/india/28218277_1_jat-community-jat-reservation-obcs

[38] Jyotirao Phule was known for his criticism of the Indian caste system in the 19th century He argued that education of the lower castes and women was a vital priority in addressing social inequalities

submerged by that of class. For a long time in the history, the Socialists in West Bengal only consider the lower castes as subcategory of the whole class concept.

3.5 Design Possibilities of Reservation Policies

Different from other policies dealing with the inequality, Reservation Policies (RPs) is more explicit in support of groups than individuals. Under RPs, individuals are given special benefits not because they have a poor socio-economic status, but because they belong to a particular social category- a caste, tribe and religion, which, on the average, have fewer accesses to education and employment than other caste groups, and are defined as historically disadvantaged.

The reasons that I take positive discrimination as the subject for policy research are as follows. Firstly, since RPs are firmly grounded on a constitutional basis, the RPs were designed in a significantly state interventionist way. It is the government authority that recognizes beneficiary groups. Only the governments can make their own judgments about which groups are disadvantaged and deserve RPs. For instance, the certification of beneficiary status is an official government process, handled by officials in the locality where the individual was born and/or raised. Another example is that many of the details of RPs are dependent on the judicial interpretation of the Constitution. Thus the Indian courts have played a significant role in shaping the way in which these policies are implemented. Moreover, the reservations (in jobs and educational admissions) are mandated throughout most of the public sector, such as the government services, public sector undertakings, and government funded colleges and universities. RPs also have had an impact on the views of upper castes who form a vast majority of students/teachers at private institutions.

Different from the centralized welfare programs (such as education, healthcare and pension), the Reservation Policies (RPs), especially the RPs for OBCs, is mainly under the authority of state governments. The designs of spending, targeting and administrative arrangement are all defined and planned at the state level, which will be explored in subsequent chapters.

It was mentioned above that the RPs in India have been mainly focused in the fields of political legislatures, public employment and educational admissions. Positive discrimination in educational admissions is practiced mainly at the level of higher education. It is usually at the more selective and prestigious higher educational institutions that positive discrimination preferences are systematically applied. Positive discrimination is manifested in various forms, such as the reserved seats for under-represented groups, scholarships, subsidized living quarters and meals, special programs, and textbook loans etc. All these programs were provided and funded by the governments at central and state levels. In the political domain, seats are reserved for SC/ST/OBC representatives in central and state legislative assemblies. The reserved seats have enabled *Dalits* (Scheduled Castes) and *Adivasis*(Scheduled Tribes) in constituencies where those groups form a relatively significant part of the population.

Chapter 4

Constructing New Caste Identities

Executive Summary: This chapter puts an emphasis on the formation of identities. The state, such as legalized identification, information provision, financial means, as well as institutional operations, has helped construct the political identities of marginalized ethnic groups in a much systematic way. Studying the CSDS Post Poll Survey Data, as well as the legislative debates and Caste Certificate issuance, I argue that the new political identities are a construction originated in or strengthened by the positive discrimination policies. The formation of such identities is irreversible.

4.1 Introduction

"Deprived sections of society in different parts of the world have organized themselves into protest movements to fight against discriminations of various kinds based on color, religion, caste and tribe. Their problem, however, has been one of establishing a new identity – the kind of image that they want to protect in order to gain self-respect, honor and status."[39] Many social scientists agree with the idea that identity is not a primordial given, but a social construction which is hard to change once constructed. They also agree that the state, through its policy-making power to dominate discourse, seize on financial sources and manage administrative deliveries, is one key agent in the process of identity construction. The Indian case is illustrative.

Only after the Independence, did the Untouchables and Aboriginal Tribes at pan-Indian level become aware that they share an identity naturally. Not until very recently was the identity of "Other Backward Classes" created. All these new identities were formed as a basis of compensatory and welfare policies in order to promote the social, political and economic status of the backward. As M. S. A. Rao argues, "the problem of identity is crucial in the formation of protest groups and for collective mobilization." [40] An important question thus would be: how did the Indian state, in a relatively short period of time, carry out its mammoth task of identifying the

[39] Rao, M.S.A. "Social Movements among the Backward Classes and the Clocks: Homology in the Source of Identity." In *Social Movements in India*, by M.S.A. Rao, Delhi: Manohar, 1984. PP.191-2
[40] Ibid.

beneficiaries of affirmative action? A more crucial question then would be: how did the identification lead to incentives/resources.

This chapter attempts to model the identification mechanism of Reservation Policies for Other Backward Classes (OBCs), especially at the state level. How did the British transform the discriminatory practices by mapping and enumerating caste groups across geographic India? How did the independent Indian government and state agencies seek to define, bound and even invent "the backwardness"? To what extent has the targeting created space within which the beneficiaries are bound to see/involve into the "state"?

Starting from the literature on state and caste identities, I clarify the causal effects of reservation policies on caste-based identity building. I address the moves made by constituent members, government agencies, jurists and politicians in the decades after 1947, exploring the impact of targeting process on the formation of political identities of the lower castes, its implications for their demands in various issue domains, as well as for the shifting political party system at state level. OBC certificate issuance is chosen to understand how the OBC identification was designed.

4.2 Literature on State v.s. Caste-based Identification

The existing literature shares a few insightful analyses on caste identities and the constructivist role of state. As early as 1960s, there were discussions over the government's role in the making of the caste system in colonial India. Postmodern scholars regard the caste system as a construction originated by the modern state in British times. Bernard Cohn (1968) argues that colonial policies and laws were instrumental in fashioning caste and caste identity in India. Edward Said's Orientalism (1978) and Benedict Anderson's Imagined Communities (1983), one decade later, more systematically criticize the views of the essentialists who see caste identities as a given character of the Indian society since time immemorial. In their analysis of identification mechanism, people under the British rule were registered as imaginative social categories by the colonial Census. Then the vested interests were created and nurtured as belonging to these categories because castes, once recognized and listed, increasingly became the beneficiaries of group-specific policy and law.

The claims of constructivist theory are not limited to the past events. When it comes to recent developments in the post-Independence period, the constructivist dissertation may explore a more sophisticated model of identification with new factors involved. Indeed, after the independence, the project of affirmative action prepared by the government of India for the "backward classes" is strikingly similar to the British colonial project. The process of selecting and registering the beneficiaries of affirmative action bears strong resemblance to the British colonial Census of India. However, political leaders after independence did not simply imitate the image of caste that British rulers had created. First, the new category of "Other Backward Classes" (OBCs) was introduced in addition to "Scheduled Castes and Scheduled Tribes" (SCs and STs). Reservation in governments and education was extended for them. Particular welfare initiatives and relevant social expenditure were also applied to the extended sections.

Moreover, construction theory could be enriched by looking into the political behavior of these new identities. Since the 1970s there has been a political rise of the OBC groups who demanded collectively for proportional representations in state machinery and educational institutions. Christophe Jaffrelot (2003) and Ashutosh Varshney (2000) trace the political mobilization of lower castes (OBCs as well as the Scheduled Castes) especially in north India. Jaffrelot emphasizes caste as a "building block" of the OBCs politics in the north India. Varshney, on the other hand, contends that the SC elites, as products of affirmative action, promote further mobilization.

However, who are these "backward"? It has been hard to identify the qualified reservation recipients in India's context. "In theory, when it came to the mechanics of listing, counting and naming, these "Other Backwards" should have been all but impossible to identify."[41]

4.3 Construction of the New Caste Identities

Since caste became a category in the Census of India, the discriminatory practices began to transform in favor of the historically disadvantaged caste communities, the *Dalits* and *Adivasis* in particular. Beginning in the 1930s, the British Census systematically translated the multiplicity of the local caste practices into India-wide statistics. The term of "Scheduled Castes" was coined by the British officials in 1935 when they prepared a separate schedule for the different castes that had been historically discriminated against. In addition to Scheduled Castes (SCs) and Scheduled Tribes (STs), the notion of "Backward Classes" was introduced in the Constitution at Independence with a view to providing equal opportunities to one and all.

These official caste categories reflect the state's imagination of caste. For instance, the colonial administration from the mid 19th century realized the divisive potential of castes and religions. Thus an ethnological mapping was done for effective social control. The caste hierarchy as defined in Census of India, as David Ludden contends, was not based on the social truth but based on "imperial utility" such as collecting taxes and controlling the population of India.[42] The Constitutional debate on affirmation action was due to the differences among the political leaders about their differing ideas of "equality" and "development".

Nevertheless, the tangible effects of affirmative action often differ from what the state predicts. Despite of the secular objectives of "equality of opportunity for all citizens in matters of

---

[41] Bayly, Susan. "State Policy and "Reservations": the Politicization of Caste-Based Social Welfare Schemes." Chap. 7 in *Caste, Society and Politics in India from the Eighteenth Century to the Modern Age*, by Susan Bayly, 286. Cambridge: Cambridge University Press, 1999.

[42] "Orientalist Empiricism· Transformations of Colonial Knowledge." In *Orientalism and the Postcolonial Predicament Perspectives on South Asia*, by D.C. A. Breckenridge and P van der Veer Ludden, 250-278. Philadelphia: University of Pennsylvania, 1993.

public employment"[43], the prolonged attempts ever since independence to construct the "backward classes" were to reinforce the caste system and casterization of politics. "The backward classes never emerged as a viable identity. What emerged instead was a multiplicity of castes."[44] The all-level commissions/committees on backward classes and the administrative procedures on the lower castes have contributed to the different versions of "the Other Backward Classes" (OBCs) across India, as well as the crystallization of localized OBC politics.

Unlike SCs and STs, "the socially and educationally backward classes" is not a clearly defined category in the Constitution. It is necessary to understand the extent and mode of identification of the Backward Classes. The rest of the chapter attempts to suggest answers to the following two questions. 1) How did these new identities come into being? 2) How did the reservation policies provide resources for mobilization of these new identities?

4.3.1 Notion of Backward Classes and Constitutional Debates

It is commonly accepted that the notion of "Backward Classes"[45] was created in south India in the late 19 century. Thereafter the central administration gradually moved in the same direction and tried to unite and standardize the local classifications. Continuous efforts were made by the central government to identify these particular caste groups. The affirmative action programs were progressively extended to them all over India.

In the 1870s, the term "Backward Classes" was first used by the Madras government in the framework of reservation policies favoring the under-educated. The list of the "Backward Classes" was lengthened as the various caste communities claimed to be included in the welfare package of affirmative action. In 1925, "Backward Classes" were differentiated by the Madras government between "Depressed Classes" (Untouchables and Tribals) and "Castes other than

[43] Draft of Rao, B. Shiva. "Report of the Sub-Committee on Fundamental Rights to the Advisory Committee." (3 April 1947) In *The Framing of India's Constitution – Select Documents*, by B. Shiva Rao, Bombay: NM Tripathi, 1967. P.171.

[44] Zwart, Frank de. "The Logic of Affirmative Action· Caste, Class and Quotas in India." *Acta Sociologica* 43, no. 3 (2000): 235-249.

[45] "Backward Classes" is a term referred as a social group (caste) instead of class.

Depressed Classes".[46] In the 1935 Government of India Act, the "Untouchables" were designated as "Scheduled Castes"(SCs) and the Tribals as "Scheduled Tribes"(STs). The denomination since then was spread throughout India. However, "Castes other than Depressed Classes", referred to as "Other Backward Classes"(OBCs), has not been elaborated further except once Nehru Jawaharlal used the term during a speech on December 13, 1946. In his Objectives resolution before the Constituent Assembly, Nehru announced that special measures were to be taken in favor of "minorities, backward and tribal areas and depressed and other backward classes".[47]

In the making of the Constitution, debates were raised over the definition of "Backward Classes" and reservation issues. There was one consensus and two differences about the debate. The members of Constitutional Assembly came to a consensus over the role of state in preventing discrimination against "any backward class of citizens". Reservation policies are designed to compensate for the under-representation of the backward classes in the posts of public service. However, over the question of "who are the beneficiaries of the reservation policies" there came the first difference. This question was easy in the case of the SCs and STs because SCs are characterized by social segregation and STs can be identified through spatial isolation. More directly, their number had been translated into statistics in the Indian Census.

Yet SCs and STs are not the only "backwards", not even most of the "backwards". The other backward classes consist of a heterogeneous category who faced discrimination. Discussions were carried among some of the Constituent Assembly members concerning whether or not to use explicit terms instead of the vague notion of "Backward Classes". Differences were between the members from northern and southern India.[48] The former, as compared to the latter, had little clue of "the Other Backward Classes" and suggested the term of backward classes be replaced by the

---

[46] P.Radhakrishnan. "Backward Classes in Tamil Nadu, 1872 -1988." *Economic and Political Weekly* 25, no. 10 (1990): 509-517.

[47] "Constituent Assembly Debates." Vol. 1. New Delhi: Lok Sabha Secretariat, 1989. P.59.

[48] Jaffrelot, Christophe (2003) in his book "India's Silent Revolution, the Rise of the Lower Castes in North India" has detailed the north-south discussion over "Other Backward Classes".

clearer expressions of "Depressed Classes" or "SCs". But the discussions did not lead the members anywhere to clarify this notion.

The second difference was from the political leaders over the question -"what are the criteria for identifying backwardness". B.R.Ambedkar, Chairman of the drafting committee of the Constitution, systematically emphasized that caste was responsible for social backwardness. In the debate on the first amendment to the Constitution, Ambedkar claimed that the definition of the "Backward Classes" was "nothing else but a collection of certain castes".[49] Nehru was reluctant to take "caste" as the major factor of backwardness though. He referred to a much broader concept of backwardness which crossed educational level, economical conditions and social status. "…There are groups, classes , individuals, communities…who are backward in many ways-- economically, socially, educationally - sometimes they are not backward in one of these respects and yet backward in another." [50] The divisive effects of castes, together with religions and regions, conflict with his idea to build a united and powerful India. In his opinion, backwardness can only be eradicated by economic modernization.

As the consequence of the debates, the Constitution only provides the legislative principles rather than specific solutions. Article 15(4) and 16(4) prescribe the fundamental rights in favor of "the advancement of any socially and educationally backward classes." Yet no uniform criteria are disclosed to identify who are the "socially and educationally backward classes". Affirmative action programs, as mandated by the Constitution, are assigned to the SCs and STs. Reservation benefits are made for seats in the legislatures, in government employment and in educational institutions, in proportion to their strength in the population. For the Other Backward Classes (OBCs), there are no constitutional provisions entitled directly to them.

---

[49] Parliamentary Debates, vol. XII -13 (Part II), col. 9006

[50] Jaffrelot, Christophe. 2003. India's Silent Revolution, the Rise of the Lower Castes in North India. New York: Columbia University Press. P.286.

4.3.2 Caste Criteria and the OBC List

Although the Constitution does not clarify the notion of backward classes, it suggests the need to determine backwardness by adopting suitable identification criteria. The Articles 340(1), 340(2) prescribes that a commission may be appointed by the President, to "fit to investigate the conditions of socially and educationally backward classes", then to "present to the president a report setting out the facts as found by them and making such recommendations as they think proper."

In accordance, two commissions– Kalelkar Commission in 1950s and Mandal Commission in 1980s –were appointed by the Central government, with the main agenda to determine the criteria for identifying all those who come under this category. The First Backward Classes Commission was appointed on January 29, 1953 under the chairmanship of Kaka Kalelkar. This was the first India-wide attempt to identify the Other Backward Classes (OBCs). After more than two years' research, the commission came up with a list of 2,399 eligible castes, which comprises roughly 32 percent of the population of India. These beneficiaries were selected on the basis of social, educational, representational and economic criteria (Table 5). Castes were (and still are) applied to be the key criterion of selection instead of individuals. However, the recommendation of this commission - creating an all-India list of OBCs- was rejected by the Nehru government which was reluctant to recognize caste as the major criterion for affirmative action.[51],,

The second all-Indian effort to identify the OBC communities was made in 1979 when the Second Backward Classes Commission, chaired by B. J. Mandal, came into existence. More confirmed than its predecessor, this commission insists that "[c]astes are the building bricks of the Hindu social structure [and] in the traditional Indian society social backwardness was a direct consequence of caste status."[52] After two year research, 11 criteria of backwardness were adopted

[51] Even so, the Nehru government had provided reservation benefits to SC/ST castes.

[52] *Report of the Backward Classes Commission.* Government of India Press, New Delhi: Government of India, 1980.

to identify 3,743 caste groups as OBCs, who consist 52 percent of the total population.[53] A vast majority came from Hindu peasant castes. A reservation of 52% in education and government jobs accordingly was recommended. Under the direction of the Supreme Court, 27 percent reservations for the OBCs were formally approved in 1990 by the then Prime Minister V. P. Singh.

To support a standardized Central list of OBC, the Government of India adopted a principle of Commonality in 1993. According to it, the castes/communities which were commonly found in both the Mandal list and the State Government lists can be included in the Central list of that state. This process was phased over three year period (1993-1995) because only 14 states had prepared their own list of OBCs before 1993', with the rest of states and Union Territories not finished till 1995.[54] After issuance of different notifications in the three phases, total of 1990 caste/communities were included in the central list from 1993 to 1995 (Table 6).

In short, the Constitution has left a great deal of ambiguity with respect to the OBCs –in laying down criteria for identifying the beneficiary groups, in specifying reservation benefits, and in making provisions for implementing and monitoring affirmative action. Consequently, two central commissions were appointed in the 1950s and 1980s to deal with these issues. Caste was firmly taken as the major criteria of selection. A Central list of OBCs was also processed to standardize the identification system in the mid-1990s. However, a more accurate list has largely been left to the discretion of the respective state governments. As Ambedkar explained in the

[53] 11 criteria are grouped under social, educational and economic headings. Of these three groups, separate weightage was given to indicators of each group. A weightage of three points each was given to all the social indicators. Educational indicators were given two points each. Economic indicators were given one point each. All these 11 indicators were applied to all the castes covered by the survey for a particular state. All castes which have a score of 50 per cent of the total (i e, 11 points out of 22 points) can be listed as socially and educationally backward.

[54] In 1993, at the time of the Supreme Court judgement, 14 states prepared with their own OBC lists. They are Andhra Pradesh, Assam, Bihar, Goa, Gujarat, Karyana, Himachal Pradesh, Karnataka, Kerala, Madhya Pradesh, Maharashtra, Punjab, Tamil Nadu and Uttar Pradesh. In the second phase, 1994, another four states were included : Orissa, Rajasthan, West Bengal , Trpura, as well as 3 Union Territories: Dadra and Nagar Haveli, Daman and Diu and Pondicherry came up with their own state lists of OBCs. Delhi, Jammu and Kashmir, Manipur, Sikkim were included in the third phase in 1995.

making of Constitution, "we have left it to be determined by each local government. A backward community is a community which is backward in the opinion of the government."[55]

4.3.3 State-level Versions of OBC Identification

When the Nehru government shield away from creating an all-India list of backward castes in 1955, it advised the state governments to choose their own criteria. In the absence of the uniform policy, the criteria for inclusion led to the considerable differences caused by the state governments. Thus there has been a wide variety of policies and practices developed in the states as the state governments were given the discretion to grant reservations to most deserving groups.

Based on the social, educational, representational and economic criteria set by the Kalelkar report, states formed local versions of positive discrimination for the OBC communities. In point of fact, after the First (Kalelkar) Backward Classes Commission, most state governments set up their own Commissions/Committees in the late 1960s or early 1970s dealing with identification of backwardness and recommendations on compensation. These are mostly the states in the northern and western tiers of India, namely Bihar, Uttar Pradesh, Punjab, Haryana, Jammu and .Kashmir, Maharashtra and Gujarat. Despite an early history of non-Brahmin movements, Maharashtra did not set the criteria until the 1960s. In the mid-1970s, Gujarat and Maharashtra in the west and Uttar Pradesh in the north began to extend reservations to the OBCs. But the extent of benefits was quite moderate in these states. Compared to their massive strength in the population, the OBC reservations in public services are only 10 per cent in Gujarat, 14 per cent in Maharashtra, 15 per cent in Uttar Pradesh.[56]

However, the story is quite different in the south (Andhra Pradesh, Karnataka, Kerala, and Tamil Nadu). The reservations for the OBCs (beyond the SC and ST quotas) in these four states have existed, in one form or the other, for over half a century. The extent of reservations has reached the point of saturation, covering almost their proportional strength in the population. In

---

[55] "Constituent Assembly Debates." *supra* (Book1) 3, no. 10 (April 1947): 702.

[56] According to the National Sample Survey (2005-06), OBC population stands at 31.7% of the total Maharashtra; 34.2% in Gujarat, and 50.4% in Uttar Pradesh.

Karnataka since the 1960s, almost half of the state government jobs have been reserved for OBCs. In Tamil Nadu, the OBC quota was 25 percent in 1951 which was increased to 50 percent three decades later. Kerala has been 40 percent while OBC quota reached 25 percent in Andhra Pradesh. In contrast, there are other states, such as Rajasthan, Madhya Pradesh, Orissa and West Bengal etc., have left much behind in the map of reservation expansion. In these states, similar commissions were not established until the 1980s. For instance, West Bengal, governed by CPIM-led left front for over three decades, is one of the very few states which had neither established the list of OBCs nor introduced quotas for them till the 1990s.

4.4 Reservation Policies in Tamil Nadu and West Bengal

This section focuses on the identification process of the Other Backward Class reservation policies and its impact on the state-level politics. Shown in last section, Tamil Nadu and West Bengal, in varying periods and to a varying degree, have introduced the tasks to identify the new caste generation: the Other Backward Classes (OBCs). What new elements have been injected into the India's mass politics during the new round of reservation distribution?

This dissertation concerns several observations about the identification mechanism of affirmative action policies. Firstly, there is a discrepancy between the eligible population and the limited amount of quotas owned by the governments. More than half population qualifies for the OBC reservations, but reservation percentage cannot exceed 27 percent according to the Mandal judgment made by Indian Supreme Court. The fact that not all the eligible people can obtain the welfare benefits has led to politics of contest, namely, caste groups contest for the limited reservations.

In the mid-seventies the Backward Classes Commissions appointed by many of these states started identifying the non-SC and non-ST backward classes. This process has driven up the nation-wide demands from the lower castes for inclusion. The descendants of people who campaigned as recently as the 1940s and 1950s for recognition as upper caste *Kshatriyas* have been fighting the last 30 years to remain on the lists of low-status "backwards". As a result of the longer OBC lists and the increased quotas for the lower castes, the competitive politics has not only been displayed among the low castes but also between the high castes and low castes. Indeed, the reports submitted by the state-level commissions for creating quotas have driven the anti-reservation agitations by the "forward castes" and elite Hindus, which began in the late 70s in Bihar and spread to other parts of the country. The upper castes showed agitation against the reservations, when the proposal was made to extend quota benefits have extended to private education institutions and private enterprises with higher standards and more fiercer competition for the rest. In a word, the identification process of reservation policies has added new caste elements in the overloaded "demand polity".[57]

Secondly, the affirmative action policy lacks firm rules for defining eligible OBCs collectivities that politicians approached the issue of reservations to the maximize support among these populous lower castes. "As soon as government created the machinery to provide named 'communities' with electoral and material assets, the way was open for reservations schemes to become an instrument of competitive party politics."[58] To attract those caste communities with profit from affirmative action policies, the political parties either turned to build allies with the politically powerful caste-based interest groups, or to define themselves as a collectivity apart from the rest and demanding separate quotas. This may lead to the fissions or coalitions of interest groups in quota politics, i.e. the volatility in politics.

Susan Bayly emphasizes that the politicians have "routinely built" *Jati* and *Varna* "into their populist appeals." The disintegration of Congress party system in the late 1970s has seen the

---

[57] Rudolphs(1987) argue that India has transformed from a "command polity" to a "demand polity"

[58] Bayly, Susan "State Policy and "Reservations" the Politicization of Caste-Based Social Welfare Schemes " Chap 7 in *Caste, Society and Politics in India from the Eighteenth Century to the Modern Age*, by Susan Bayly, Cambridge Cambridge University Press, 1999 P 278

rising regional rivals.[59] The political profile of the OBCs has thus been raised in various forms by different regional parties which consistently pursued the populist credentials. For instance, the 1996-97 anti-BJP United Front in UP brought the Samajwadi Party (SP) and Bahujan Samaj Party (BSP) together to deny power to the upper caste Congress and the BJP [60] However, due partly to the ground-level OBC-*Dalit* hostility, the SP-BSP coalition did not last long. Besides the regional parties, the Congress Party and its national opponents (Janata Party in 1960s, BJP after 1980) espoused the popu3list strategies which emphasize the *Jati* and *Varna* basis of classification.

Thirdly, the benefits of affirmative action have been unequally distributed among the people who fall into the eligible categories. This implies that the new definitional category of "Creamy Layer" was created to identify those within castes who economically did not deserve benefits but who were eligible because of caste membership. The identification criteria, the subsequently created caste-name lists and other data used in the identifying exercises have flaws in themselves. Among the 11 indicators of backwardness, greatest weight is disproportionately allotted to social backwardness on group basis and the least to economic backwardness. As a matter of fact, if one scores high on the social backwardness criteria, educational and economic backwardness need not come into the picture at all.[61] Apparently group caste status prevails over economic status in recognizing the OBC groups. Therefore, the comparatively well-off OBC families (due to the previous generations' educational and economic advances), among all the OBC groups, became the major beneficiaries of the OBC identification process.[62] "Those who have gained comparatively little from the process are the members of the very poor non-*Harijan* groups-the

[59] The Congress returned to power in the 1967, though with a significant reduced electoral support compared with the first three polls of election after Independence.

[60] SP represent the non-elite "peasant"/OBC castes and the BSP is organized for the purpose of the welfare for the Scheduled Castes/Dalit populations.

[61] Of a maximum of 22 points only 11 are needed to qualify as the backward. It is not at all difficult for a particular caste to score on each of indicators in the social category, earn 12 points, and thus qualify as an OBC.

[62] These were the people who also claimed themselves as part of the large-scale 'middle peasant' caste clusters. More specifically, these are the Koiri, Kurmi and Ahir-Yadv in Bihar. Vokkaligas and Lingayats in Karnataka, *Jats* and Kanbi-Patidars in Gujarat, Kammas or Reddis in Andhra.

small 'backward' specialist populations associated with 'traditional' services or artisanal occupations".[63]

The process of identification on caste criteria has created not only a new social category of "Creamy Layer", but the "Creamy Layer" phenomena in the political sphere.[64] For instance, the *Lingayat* and *Vokkaligga* communities made attempts to exclude their state's rival *Kisan* (peasant) clusters from the OBC listings in the 1960s and 1970s. Some scholars (Kaul 1993, Kohli 1987, and Manor 1989) agree on this point that the disproportionate gains for these "clean-caste" groups through the reservations have crowded out the benefits for smaller middling-status caste clusters who have a weaker voice in state-level politics.

The following sub-sections will introduce the identification process for OBCs by the state governments in Tamil Nadu and West Bengal, analyzing how the quota redistribution among the OBCs featured the state politics.

4.4.1 Tamil Nadu

To identify the OBC groups is a socio-political process even though the OBC population has been conveniently treated as non-Upper-SC-ST residual.[65] Tamil Nadu is a state with long history of OBC reservation that started in 1921 and also has the highest percentage of OBC population in the country at 72%. Accordingly the reservation quota has worked out to be 69% as mandated by the state law with that of OBCs standing as high as 50%.

The more-than-50% quota policy for the OBCs was not shaped in one day (See Appendix 4.1). In 1951, Tamil Nadu government introduced totally 41% reservation for the lower castes, with 16% Reservation for SC/STs and 25% for OBCs. The first Tamil Nadu State Backward Classes Commission was appointed in 1969 by the Dravida Munnetra Kazagham (DMK)

---

[63] Bayly, Susan. "State Policy and "Reservations": the Politicization of Caste-Based Social Welfare Schemes." Chap. 7 in *Caste, Society and Politics in India from the Eighteenth Century to the Modern Age*, by Susan Bayly. Cambridge: Cambridge University Press, 1999. PP.293-4

[64] "Creamy Layer" is not a separate caste group but defined as a category of well-off caste groups that have benefited from the reservation policies.

[65] The Mandal report estimates the OBC communities account for 52 percent of the total population in India, with the SCs and STs 22.5 percent and the Forward Castes 25.5. percent.

government under M Karunanidhi. This commission was supervised under the chairman A N Sattanathan, with the aim to identify the backward classes and suggest the compensative measures for the backwardness. According to the recommendations, the DMK government increased the OBC reservation from 25% to 31%[66], which was again increased to 50% from 31% in 1980 by the then DMK government which made consistent efforts to enhance its pro-reservations image. "Tamil Nadu's DMK, political heirs to the anti-Brahman ideologies of the Madras Justice Party, came to power in the state in 1967....KMK erected an edifice of caste-welfare provisions which perpetuated the use of *Jati*and *varna*-based classifications in state politics."[67]

After two-year investigation, the commission introduced two important concepts and the relevant recommendations: 1) that of "Creamy Layer" and its removal from the list of beneficiaries for the good of "the real disadvantaged section of the lower castes"; 2) "Most Backward Classes"(MBCs) and their separate educational and employment reservation from the rest of Backward Classes (BCs).[68] The Sattanathan Commission based its recommendation on the observation that MBCs had a very small presence in state services and professional colleges as they were clubbed together with other castes. Having defeated the AIADMK in the state election of 1989, the DMK government finalized the separate reservation for MBCs by splitting the OBC reservations with 30% for OBCs and 20% for MBCs. The total reservation thus increased to 69%, far outnumbering the percentage limitation of 50%. This bulk of Tamil Nadu population includes more than 252 caste groups, the longest reservation list of all other states.

"Creamy Layer" is defined by the Sattanathan Commission in 1970 as "some castes have taken full advantage of the state's protective measures and made rapid strides, while many others

---

[66] Meanwhile, the reservation for SC/ST to 18% from 16%. Total reservation thus stood at 49%.

[67] Bayly, Susan. "State Policy and "Reservations": the Politicization of Caste-Based Social Welfare Schemes." Chap. 7 in *Caste, Society and Politics in India from the Eighteenth Century to the Modern Age*, by Susan Bayly. Cambridge: Cambridge University Press, 1999. P.292.

[68] In 1971, the Sattanathan Commission altered the reservation percentage for Backward Classes to 16% and separate reservation of 17% to Most Backward Classes (MBCs).

continue to trail behind and are still in the lower stages of stagnancy."[69] With the increasingly long list in favor of backward classes, the exclusion of creamy layers from the reservation list became politically impossible. "In fact, state-level election manifestos routinely feature competing pledges to expand the reservation system is beyond the old arenas of college admissions quotas and pubic service posts." The "Creamy Layer" in Tamil Nadu are the families of salaried persons whose annual income exceeded Rs 9,000, landowners with more than 10 acres of land and business people with taxable income exceeding Rs 9,000. The then DMK government did not follow the recommendation of the Sattanathan Commission to eliminate the creamy layer. One decade later, M G Ramachandran (MGR) and his AIADMK government that issued the Government Order of Creamy Layer exclusion faced the restive protests by the DMK and other Opposition parties; and even the electoral loss in the 1980 Lok Sabha election. As a result, MGR not only withdrew the order but increased the reservation for the Other Backward Classes (OBCs) from 31 % to 50 %.

The "untouchable" creamy layer issue in Tamil Nadu incited the interference of the Central government and the Supreme Courts. The criteria for identifying the Backward Classes, as a result, were reset in the early 1990s in Tamil Nadu. With regard to the extension of reservation for the OBC groups, the Supreme Court reiterated that Reservation percentage cannot exceed 27% and "Creamy Layer" should be excluded from the Reservation benefits. Under the directions of the Supreme Court, the second Tamil Nadu State Backward Classes Commission came into existence on March 15, 1993. It was formed to examine and recommend upon the requests relating to inclusion and exclusion from the list of BCs and MBCs. For judgment, three major factors were designed to identify a caste group as backward: social backwardness, economic backwardness and educational backwardness.[70] The weightage allotted is 50 per cent for social

[69] "Creamy Layer" is used two ways: 1) an economically well-off part of a caste; 2) a full caste that has become relatively well-off than other castes in the same *varna*.
[70] Backwardness is defined as a worse or less advanced condition. In India's circumstances, backwardness is employed to describe the social, economic and political status of the lower castes who have historically been in disadvantaged conditions.

backwardness, 40 per cent for educational backwardness and 10 per cent for economic backwardness. "If any class/caste or segment of the Society secures 50% and more, but below 65%, such class or segment will be identified as a backward class. Above 65%, it qualified to be Most Backward Class."[71] (see Appendix 4.2 and 4.3) In 2006, Supreme Court again asked Tamil Nadu Government to exclude Creamy Layer from Reservation benefits.

4.4.2 West Bengal

Compared with Tamil Nadu, West Bengal has historically been characterized by the relative weakness of the Other Backward Classes (OBCs) who were at the forefront of the construction of caste-based political identities in Tamil Nadu. Firstly, th =e middle castes (i.e. the OBCs in West Bengal) are characterized by their great fragmentation. With the exception"…[of the *Mahishyas*, the *Sadgops*, the *Goalas* and the *Kurmis* in South Western Bengal], none of the other [middle] castes numbered more than 3 per cent of the population in any district".[72] Secondly, West Bengal has been characterized by the hold of upper castes on the political leadership after Independence.

There were historical moments of demanding reservations for the low-born people, though reservation for OBCs in West Bengal was largely an "imported" issue. "The Communists, they were very reluctant to take caste into account, holding the view that this social category [OBCs] was bound to be submerged by that of class. For a long time the Socialists were the only ones to consider the lower castes as a pertinent social and political entity."[73]

It was in the late 1960s that the leadership of Biplabi Bangla Congress had mobilized the *Antayaja* (low born) peasants and *Namashudra*s in Calcutta in order to demand a certain percentage of reservations in jobs.[74] Such political move to consolidate the base of the party among the lower castes could not hold the ground for long. After 1969, the Communist Party of

---

[71] Cited from the website of Tamil Nadu Department of Backward Classes and Most Backward Classes and Minorities Welfare. Most Backward Class is defined as the most backward part of the OBCs.

[72] Partha Chatterjee. 1998. The Present History of West Bengal. Delhi: Oxford University Press. P.74

[73] Jaffrelot, Christophe. "The Rise of the Other Backward Classes in the Hindi Belt." *The Journal of Asian Studies* 59, no. 1 (February 2000): 86-108. P.88

[74] Namasudra (Namassej) is the name of a Hindu community originally from certain regions of Bengal, India. They were traditionally engaged in cultivation and as boatmen but lived outside the four tier ritual *varna* system.

India (Marxist), or CPI(M), mounted a systematic attack on its social base. To maintain the Marxist image and character, the left government in West Bengal was not ready to concede its class-based ideology till very recently. In order to avoid any identification on caste lines the CPI(M) leadership was tactfully pursuing the line that OBCs did not exist in the State. For instance, Chief Minister Jyoti Basu has denied the existence of any OBC in the State. In addition, the Left Front government had made it clear that identification of OBC should not be on caste lines, but be based on the life pattern and poverty.

As late as in the 1990s, the Mandal Commission Action Committee (MCAC), headed by chairman of the State Forward Bloc, Bhakti Bhusan Mandal, has emphatically claimed that at least 50 per cent of the total population of West Bengal belonged to the other backward classes group. It brought out a comprehensive list of 177 castes belonging to OBC group.

4.5 Caste Certificate Issuance

Caste Certificates are the proofs of one's belonging to a particular caste, especially in case one belongs to any of the backward classes, as specified in the Indian Constitution. The case study of caste certificate issuance is to attest the identification mechanism of reservation policies. Who are entitled to the reservation benefits and who are successfully targeted? Are the targeted beneficiaries more politicized than others? To answer these questions, I use the data collected from the government agents in West Bengal and from intensive interviews with 35 OBC villagers, government officers, school teachers and researchers in New Delhi, West Bengal, Maharashtra and Tamil Nadu.

In order to certify the identities while allocating welfare goods and grants, Indian governments issue various certificates. Besides the basic certificates, such as birth certificates, marriage certificates, there are various certificates for particular uses. For instance, employment cards are issued to the low-income Indians that confirm their eligibility to work under the government-funded employment programs, such as Employment Assurance Scheme (EAS). Caste certificates are available to the members of SCs/STs/OBCs who are entitled to the benefits of affirmative action. These cards or certificates can only be available after the official information is collected from the "household unit" or "caste cluster" instead of individuals. EAS cards, for example, are to be allocated to the members of "registered laboring households", and it is households that are defined as Below Poverty Line (BPL) on the basis of periodic forays into the countryside by government officers.[75] The similar case is with caste certificates. The "castes" in government publications like the Census of India or the OBC lists used for affirmative action are mostly regional- or state-level caste clusters.

Official construction of caste identities is a continuous process which can be tracked back to the colonial India. Governments recognize the targeted social categories by following the criteria of identification and a series of administrative procedures. Above all, citizens must register in order to qualify for the material rewards - jobs and education - that make these constructions real in their consequences. In the colonial period, the British rulers established a registration system and collected caste-wise information related to the lower castes, especially Scheduled Castes (SCs) and Scheduled Tribes (STs). Such registration system has been continuously used by the Government of India after Independence.

In the post-Independence period, the reservation benefits extended to the population of the Other Backward Classes (OBCs). The accurate estimates of OBC population are the basis of formulating sound policies on affirmative action in the country. But, the official figures on OBC population and data on their social, economic and educational indicators are lacking. The latest figures on OBCs, which was used by the Mandal Commission to estimate the OBC population in 1980s, were collected in 1931 and have not been updated yet.[76] Therefore, state governments established state-level commissions/committees to frame the state-specific OBC lists. According

[75] Stuart Corgridge, Glyn Williams, Manoj Srivastava and Reve Veron. *Seeing the State: Governance and Governmentality in India.* UK: Cambridge University Press, 2005.

[76] Various surveys like National Sample Survey (NSS) and the National Family Health Survey (NFHS) have their own estimates of India's OBC population.

to the recommendation and criteria of selections, the state governments assign the targeting tasks to local governments. In the Indian case, the authorities competent to issue the OBC certificate are at the district level. For a qualified certificate, two signatures must be presented. One is from the District Magistrate and the other from Sub-Divisional Officer of the area where the candidate and/or his family resides.

Most of the states in India follow a very similar administrative procedure to issue caste certificates. In the case of Tamil Nadu, the system of issuing permanent Community Certificate was introduced in the year 1988, while issuance of OBC certificates was started dated back in 1994 in West Bengal, and it was introduced in 2001 in Uttar Pradesh. The applicants for OBC certificates living in Block areas go to the concerned Block Offices, and the applicants living in municipal areas within a Sub-Division go to the concerned Sub-Division Officers. Usually there is no fee charged for the service and applications are to be disposed of from one week (Uttar Pradesh) to eight weeks (West Bengal) from the date of its submission.

4.6 Summary

Caste, wrote the noted social anthropologist M N Srinivas, "is so tacitly and so completely accepted by all, including those most vocal in condemning that it is everywhere the unit of social action". Caste as a factor in Indian politics is not new, though the resurgence of the OBC movement is of comparatively recent origin. In this chapter, I trace the history of identifying OBCs and examine whether and how the targeted beneficiaries have been grouped as a new caste generation.

The constructivist dissertation holds that the caste identities produced either in the Census of India, or defined in Constitutions, or judged in Courts, correspond only loosely to social reality at first, but become increasingly real in its consequences once policies are fashioned upon it. The reservation policy, with its particular structural features, helped to "materialize" this fiction of state.

The identification mechanism based on the criteria of backwardness has some far-reaching implications. First of all, the caste criterion adopted by both center and state-level commissions implies that state, through its legislative process and administrative practices, has been shaping new social categories, like Scheduled Castes (SCs), Scheduled Tribes (STs) and Other Backward Classes(OBCs). The process of identification and reservation benefits, administered by the state organs, reconstructed the caste system in a secular and modern way. For instance, the India-wide investigation that the Kalelkar Commission had finished not only framed the targeted communities officially but also consulted representatives of the new categories in question which helped to refashion each group's particular identity.[77] Reservation formula, in the imagination of state, can provide the new caste identities with equal opportunities to the forward castes.

Yet, the imaginary state did not go hand in hand with social changes, especially in the liberalizing economy. The continuous use of the same standards or the incorrect standards of caste recognition, has caused the rigidity of state treating a changing caste system in a capitalist economy. On one hand, the figures of caste-wise population in Indian Census, as the foundation for the uplift of OBCs, have not been updated since 1931.[78] On the other hand, a number of OBC caste members have become economically successful as a result of *Zamindari* abolition, the Green Revolution and the recently rapid economic growth. These "Creamy Layer are easily found among *Jats, Gujars, Kurmies, Yadavs.* Still they are qualified for affirmative action. In 1992, the Supreme Court announced that "Creamy Layer" should be excluded from reservation benefits. In 2006, the Supreme Court again asked Tamil Nadu government to exclude "Creamy Layer" from reservation benefits. "Creamy Layer" are the relatively wealthier and better educated members of the Other Backward Classes (OBCs) and are not eligible for reservation benefits. But cutting

[77] Jaffrelot, Christophe. *India's Silent Revolution: the Rise of the Lower Castes in North India.* New York: Columbia University Press, 2003. P.229

[78] The population of OBCs, according to the Mandal report, is derived by subtracting from the total population of Hindus, the population of SC and ST and that of forward Hindu castes and communities. It works out to be 52 per cent.

"Creamy Layer" out of the OBC groups has not been implemented at all-Indian level. As a matter of fact, the creamy layer plays a leading role in the OBC politics, with many more accesses to the affirmative action schemes. Chapter 7 will discuss the "Creamy Layer" issue in details.

Secondly, with its rigid caste-based identification and reservation benefits, a state has constructed and maintained casteism in the political landscape. As Susan Bayly contends, the caste-based uplift schemes have created "incentives for Indians to affirm their caste origins since aid-seekers must proclaim ritually inferior birth in order to qualify."[79] The First Backward Classes Commission fermented the political assertiveness among the masses. In order to understand the needs of the OBCs, the Kalelkar Commission sent a detailed questionnaire to various representative organizations and received strong responses -3,344 memoranda as well as 5,636 interviews.[80] These actions opened the window of hopes for the backward castes that their social and economic conditions can be improved. Collectivities were thus mobilized among them claiming for recognition as backward classes. "[T]he result of our inquiry," Kalelkar writes in his letter, "is that caste consciousness, caste loyalties and caste aspirations, have increased throughout the country." The increasing caste consciousness, loyalties and aspiration could be further canalized into political activities for the uplift of the lower castes.

A new political consciousness has also been shaped among the upper/middle castes and well-off Hindus against the Reservation Policies for OBCs. Social tensions arising out of such disparities manifest themselves in the movements both for and against the extension of reservation for the OBCs. By contrast with the general acceptance of SC/ST reservations in the early 1950s, the Mandal announcement in 1990, together with previous similar recommendations, has brought up vehement controversies over the quota policies. Its retention of "caste" as the most important criteria for the backwardness has sparked off agitations and protests between the lower castes and the well-off Hindus and upper /middle castes. The "caste polarization" around Mandal

---

[79] Bayly, Susan *Castem, Society and Politics in India from the Eighteen Century to the Modern Age* Cambridge: Cambridge University Press, 1999.P.277

[80] Glanter, Marc. *Competing Equality Law and the Backward Classes in India* Berkkeley: University of California Press, 1984 P.170

can be sensed across India. On one hand, strong opposition to V. P. Singh's Mandal announcement was widespread and has been mainly triggered from the middle and upper caste Hindus, especially in the northern India. On the other hand, the Mandal report has also highly raised the political consciousness of lower castes. "For the first time, lower caste people have started to vote en mass for leaders belonging to their own milieu."[81]

[81] Jaffrelot, Chritophe. 2000. The Rise of the Other Backward Classes in the Hindi Belt. The Journal of Asian Studies 59, no.1. P.106

Chapter 5

Resource Effect of Reservation Policies:

An Explanation of Lower-Caste Demand Politics

Executive Summary: This chapter looks at the lower-caste version of demand politics. Starting with a policy approach, I analyze the origins of this "upsurge" of lower caste groups and consider the possible consequences of the unequally and insufficiently distributed benefits of the Reservation Policies. Through the comparative case study in Tamil Nadu and Uttar Pradesh, I argue that policy and policy choice opens institutional space to lessen the conflicting political participation among the lower castes.

5.1 Introduction

Resources empowering social movements have long intrigued students of political science. An emphasis on resources provides insight into ways in which discontented social groups solve collective action problems and successfully mobilize. Arguably, a commitment of public resources yields not only social and economic effects, such as increased education; but also sheds some effect on democratization itself. Andrea Campbell (2000) demonstrates that certain social policy in the United States has constructive effects on the political participation among the beneficiaries from low to moderate income backgrounds, as greater dependence on program resources makes them more inclined to be involved.[82] Such phenomenon can also be seen in India, yet in different forms.

According to the Rudolphs, India began to see the rise of demand politics in the mid-1960s which was caused by security, political, and economic events.[83] More recently, the demand

[82] Campbell, Andrea Louise. "The Third Rail of American Politics: Senior Citizen Activism and the American Welfare State." *Ph.D. dissertation.* University of California, Berkeley, 2000.

[83] Ruldophs introduce the twin concepts of demand polity and command polity in their analysis of Indian politics."Legitimacy in demand politics depends on the state's capacity to provide short-run equitable treatment of citizen's demands. Legicimacy in command politics depnds on the credibility" Cited from Rudolph, Lloyd I. Rudolph

politics of India has intensified and gained great substance due to the newly emerging caste, religion and regional movements. The next three chapters attempt to elaborate how and why the Mandal issue and Reservation Policies (RPs) in the 1990s encouraged the wave of political demands among the lower castes. With an analysis of the policy effects of RPs, this chapter elaborates the political conflicts among the demand groups who struggled for more political space. The next chapter will analyze the issue from the perspective of political elites, and the chapter after the next will specifically study the "Creamy Layer" groups who are the direct products of RPs.

Many scholars have identified the rise of the lower-caste groups in politics. Roderick Church (1984) argues that the patterns of politics in different states could be understood in terms of the extent and mode of political participation of the lower castes around the early-middle 1980s.[84] Based on his study, John Harriss (2000) tries to develop a comparative framework to analyze lower-caste politics at the state level in India. He measures regime differences based upon the degree of upper caste dominance and challenges to the lower castes/classes. Yogendra *Yadav* (2000) introduces the idea of the "second democratic upsurge", directing the movements of the lower-caste and other disadvantaged people in the Hindi belt.[85] Christophe Jaffrelot (2003) named this upsurge as "India's silent revolution" and detailed the development of the lower-caste mobilization in the northern states.[86] In other words, the political arrival of the lower castes can come in many ways – through the party politics or regional politics. Starting with a policy approach, I shall analyze the origins of this "upsurge" and consider the unequally and insufficiently distributed benefits of the RPs. It is true that reservations only touch a fraction of

---

and Susanne Hoeber. *In Pursuit of Lakshmi The Political Economy of the Indian State* Chicago: University of Chicago Press, 1987.P.212.

[84] Church, Roderick. "Chapter 9: Conclusion: The Pattern of State Politics in Indira Gandhi's India." In *State Politics in Contemporary India Crisis or Continuity?*, by John R. Boulder and London: Westview Press, 1984

[85] *Yadav*, Yogendra. "Reconfiguration in Indian politics: State Assembly Election 1993-95." *Economic and Political Weekly* 31, no. 2 and 3 (January 1996): 95-104.

[86] Jaffrelot, Christophe. *India's Silent Revolution: the Rise of the Lower Castes in North India* New York: Columbia University Press, 2003

the political participation among the backward classes, but the RPs provides a new institutional channel for us to understand the lower caste politics.

The first section of this chapter focuses on the theoretical analysis of political conflicts that might continuously occur. In the second section, some observations are noted about the demand politics of Indian lower castes. The third section provides a general study on the policy impacts of Mandal issues, suggesting the effects of political empowerment and economic development by analyzing the political reservations and fiscal spending issues. In the fourth section, a state-level comparative study of Tamil Nadu and Uttar Pradesh is developed.

5.2 Interest Groups and Political Contention: A Theoretical Consideration

When making and carrying out public policies, governments use their authority to allocate the benefits and costs of living among the different individuals and groups However, the allocation may never be equal. Some segments of the society receive more of the benefits and rewards while other segments bear more of the governmentally imposed costs and burdens. The inequality usually leads to the surging political demands and even conflicts over who will have more and who will have less of what governments allocate. Pursuit of political power has become one of the major channels to enable the disadvantaged segments of the society to reshape the content and direction of public policy. Thus, the government's unequal distribution of resources is the primary source of competition for political power.

Government policies and programs have a variety of feedback effects on clients. Pierson differentiates them into resource effects and interpretive effects.[87] He argues that these effects, on one hand, are relevant for the political participation of target groups, like the politically-relevant resources, political engagement, and mobilization opportunities they can confer, on the other hand, they influence attitudes among clients, such as their orientation toward government,

[87] Pierson, Paul. "When Effect Becomes Cause, Policy Feedback and Political Change." *World Politics*, 1993: 595-628.

ideological self-placement, and partisan identification. This chapter mainly focuses on the resource effects, suggesting the effects of unequal resource distribution due to the Reservation Policies (RPs).

Under a competitive, constitutional democracy, different groups and organizations within the society are able to engage in political competition for political power. A political interest group, or a pressure group/demand group comes into being when its members, sharing common interests and views in a single area of public policy, focus their attention, energy, and resources upon that particular policy area and seeks to acquire and exercise political influence therein. A political interest group develops and wields political influence through such activities as: supporting party leaders in the elections; staging mass demonstrations that catch the attention of the news media; filing suit in a court of law to prevent enforcement of a decision of the legislature or of the executive branch; lobbying members of the legislature and officeholders in the executive branch of the government; forming associations/committees which contribute money to the election campaigns of candidates for government office.

If two interest groups have differing and conflicting interests and views in a single area of public policy, namely, the common interests and views of one group in the particular policy area clash with the common interests and views of the other group in the same policy area, the contending groups will compete with each other for the capacity to influence and mold government governmental decisions in that specific policy area. As mentioned above, this happens often when the decision or action taken by the government is likely to be favorable to some segments of the society and detrimental to others. Hence, there would be continuing political conflict within the society, continuing conflict among different segments of the society over who will have more and who will have less of what the government allocates. In other words, democracy can result in a competition between different segments of societies over political and economic resources.

5.3 Demand politics, Political Contention and Lower Castes in India

The Rudolphs conceive of interest groups as encompassing two forms: organized interests and demand groups. Compared with organized interests that develop "elaborate organizational infrastructure" and work formally in institutionally defined policy arenas, demand groups in India are defined as "a more spontaneous and less formed type of collective action." By raising new issues and mobilizing support for them, demand groups try to gain bargaining advantages and transform public policy. "They perfect democracy and promote more equal bargaining by mobilizing voters and lower constituencies slighted or ignored by organized interests."[88]

The Rudolphs clearly define the demand groups in India in the following terms:

"The demand group is a form that interest representation can take in competitive, open democracies when political mobilization of mass publics outstrips or overflows the formal institutions of the political process. Demand groups are an expression of movement and issue politics. They do not replace organized interests so much as they incorporate and transcend them."[89]

The Rudolphs argue that demand politics in India surfaced in 1965 for both domestic and foreign reasons. It rose again in 1977 when the Janata party unexpectedly won an election victory. This resurgence of demand politics, "...persists after a Gandhi Congress government returned to power in 1980."[90] The early 1980s saw the farmer agitation for remunerative prices. In 1984, labor unrest reached an unprecedented levels. A more recent peak of demand politics took place in the late 1980s. V.P.Singh, the then Prime Minister, announced the Mandal issue and reservation quotas for the Other Backward Classes (OBCs), a development that signaled the emergence of a new constituency for demand politics. In the early 2000s came the stagnation of the democratic upsurge. Suhas Palshikar and Sanjay Kumar (2004) ascribe this stagnation partly

---

[88] Rudolph, Lloyd I. Rudolph and Susanne Hoeber. *In Pursuit of Lakshmi The Political Economy of the Indian State* Chicago: University of Chicago Press, 1987. pp.247-56.
[89] Ibid *P 252*
[90] Ibid. P.240.

to a relative slowing down of the expansion of the participatory phenomenon among the *Dalits* and the OBCs.[91] The ups and downs of the demand waves can be seen from the vote turnout in the Lok Sabha. From 1952 to 2004, the vote turnouts in the Lok Sabha rose above 60 percent in 1967, 1977, 1988, 1989 and 1998, 1999 while dropping again in the early 1970s, 1980s, 1990s and 2000s.(Table5.1)

Table5.1: Lok Sabha Election Turnout (1952-2009, %)

1952	1957	1962	1967	1971	1977	1980	1985
45.7	47.7	55.4	61.3	55.3	60.4	57.2	64.1
1989	1991	1996	1998	1999	2004	2009	
61.9	55.9	57.9	62.1	60	58.3	56.97	

Source: part of the data comes from Suhas Palshikar and Sanjay Kumar, Thursday, May 20, 2004, the Hindu

The demand group which we focus on here is lower castes: Other Backward Classes (OBCs)- a newly created social category in the 1970s and a new participant in the demand politics that escalated in the late 1980s. With the increasing population of lower caste, the rate of strikes, lower caste unrest in addition to the vote turnout also increased dramatically. In this chapter, I show how policy monopoly enables the state to manipulate an increasing number of weaker units in the society. Focusing on the OBC demand groups, I emphasize the pronounced resource effects of Mandal Recommendations and Reservation Policies on the lower castes who competed for limited quotas of reservations.

The OBC groups are probably the last social stratum to be brought into India's electoral politics. It is a common observation of Indian politics that political participation has been expanding downwards to include ever lower social strata. The Scheduled Castes and Tribes (SC/STs), the poorest and most oppressed segments of the India population, received the special recognition and privileges at Independence. By the 1960s, the only people excluded from a share of political representation and policy benefits were the castes below the middle castes and above the SCs. They wanted a larger share of state power and its rewards due to their numerous

[91] Suhas Palshikar and Sanjay Kumar observed the stagnation of India's democratic upsurge in their article Kumar, Suhas Palshikar and Sanjay. "How India Voted -- Verdict 2004." The Hindu, May 20 (Thursday), 2004.

populations. "This is evident in new levels of violence and corruption, in populist appeals to the "poor," in calls for law and order, in the emergence of regionalism, in struggles over reservations for the "BCs," and in the efforts of political parties to recruit representatives from the lower castes."[92]

5.3.1 Political Rising of the OBC groups

The term "OBCs" has become a relevant category for the lower-caste mobilization because they have come to self-identify with it. The Mandal Commission Report, which recommends reservations for OBCs in employment in central government services and public sector enterprises as well as educational opportunities in educational institutions, has helped the OBC groups to coalesce. "The OBC phenomenon helped the lower castes to organize themselves as a 'demand group', outside the vertical, clientelistic Congress-like pattern."[93] This coalescence enabled the OBCs to benefit from their massive numbers during elections. These lower-caste voters began to vote for candidates from their own social categories and their own regional parties. For instance, in the Uttar Pradesh Assembly (1980-2002), the share of OBC MLAs has been increasing from 16.91% in 1980, reaching the peak of 32.67 % in 1993, Although dropping a little in 1996, the percentage of OBC MLA increased again to 27.52% in 2002.

In the ninth general election in 1989, voters turned out in unprecedented numbers to protest poor economic performance and to vote in favor or government's Reservation Policies (RPs). According to Javeed Alam (1999), the inner composition of voting also changed as voting rose among the poor and lower castes but dropped among the upper castes and well-off Hindu elites. Alam observed from the CSDS surveys that "in 1996, as against 1971, there were more poor,

---

[92] Church, Roderick. "Chapter 9: Conclusion: The Pattern of State Politics in Indira Gandhi's India " In *State Politics in Contemporary India: Crisis or Continuity?*, by John R. Boulder and London: Westview Press, 1984. P.231

[93] Jaffrelot, Christophe. *India's Silent Revolution the Rise of the Lower Castes in North India* New York: Columbia University Press, 2003 P 349.

illiterate, Dalit, OBC, rural based people, and Muslim sections."[94] Yogendra *Yadav* (2000) made a similar argument that the lower castes tended to vote more than upper castes and there was a large-scale political mobilization and empowerment of poor and traditionally disadvantages social groups.[95]

Meanwhile, OBC groups also have occupied an increasing number of seats in the legislature. It is a bumpy and contentious process, but the trend was evolving at the expense of the upper castes. Jaffrelot (2003) has studied the voting behavior of the OBCs in the Hindi belt, where these groups became dramatically mobilized and the **number of OBC MPs was increased sharply in the late 1980s.** As the Congress share of parliamentary votes and seats dropped, especially when it lost power in 1989, the percentage of OBC MPs "...doubled from 11.1% 1984 to 20.9% in 1989…the proportion of upper castes MPs thus feel for the first time below 40%... the share of OBCs among MPs continued to grow in the elections in 1991 and in 1996. This trend was evolving at the expense of the upper castes, because all the political parties were now giving a larger number of tickets to OBC candidates."[96]

5.3.2 Tensions and Violence against Mandal, Case of Student Protests

The reactions to the Mandal across the north India were unprecedented in their scope and intensity. The initial violence began in Bihar and spread from Orissa into the east to western Uttar Pradesh and into New Delhi. These developments paralleled the ballooning of student enrollment in higher education and the student unrest that accompanied it. Incidents of student indiscipline grew phenomenally after the announcement of Mandal issues.

The Mandal Commission elucidated caste as a sensitive political issue. Castes were consolidated in two camps right after the Mandal report was announced by the central

---

94 Alam, Javeed. "Is Caste Appeal Casteism? Oppressed Castes in Politics." *Economic and Political Weekly* 34, no. 13 (March 1999): 757-61.
95 *Yadav*, Yogendra. " Understanding the Second Democratic Upsurge." In *Transforming India Social and Political Dynamics of Democracy*, by Francine Frankel, 120-45. Delhi: Oxford University Press, 2000.
96 Jaffrelot, Christophe. *India's Silent Revolution the Rise of the Lower Castes in North India* New York: Columbia University Press, 2003. pp.349-352.

government: forward castes and backward castes. Forward Caste in India, defined by Dipankar Gupta, constitute the communities and castes who do not qualify for reservation benefits, which set quotas of education benefits, government jobs and political representation for Other Backward Classes, Scheduled Castes and Scheduled Tribes.[97] Backward Castes, correspondingly, consist of Other Backward Classes (OBCs) and SC/STs who are eligible for Reservation Policies (RPs). Caste polarization between forward and backward castes, therefore, was brought to the centre stage of the Indian politics in the early 1990s. "The cleavage between upper castes and lower castes had suddenly been reinforced by a collective, open hostility from the former and even by the unleashing of violence."[98] The forward castes "feared that their hopes of government patronage would be thwarted by a coalition of lower castes".[99] Among the forward castes, the upper caste students have been playing a pioneer role. They came out against the former Prime Minister V.P. Singh's decision to implement the Mandal Commission report in the late 1980s. There is a zero sum nature to issue quotas to lower castes when upper castes have been expanding opportunities in private enterprises for the past decade and a half.

The upper caste students mobilized organizations soon after the implementation of the Mandal commission Report. The anti-Mandal Commission Forum was set up in Delhi University when the Mandal recommendation was approved. The student protests spread across India. North India, where upper castes still have deep roots, became the epicenter of this campaign. "In Uttar Pradesh, the Arakshan Virodhi Sangharsh Samiti(Committee for the Struggle against Reservations) and the Mandal Ayog Virodhi Sangharsh Samiti (Committee for the struggle against the Mandal Commission) were founded by students who were mainly from the upper castes…"[100] They campaigned with the aim of abolishing "all reservations including reservations

---

[97] Gupta, Dipankar. *Caste in Question Identity or Hierarchy?* New Delhi: Sage Publications, 2004.

[98] Jaffrelot, Christophe. *India's Silent Revolution the Rise of the Lower Castes in North India* New York: Columbia University Press, 2003. pp.347-8

[99] Hasan, Zoya. *Quest for Power Oppositional Movements and Post-Congress Politics in Uttar Pradesh* New Delhi: Oxford University Press, 1998.P.155

[100] The lower middle class is referred as the OBC communities in Hasan, Zoya *Quest for Power Oppositional Movements and Post-Congress Politics in Uttar Pradesh* New Delhi· Oxford University Press, 1998. P.155

for the SCs".[101] In Varanasi, the city of Uttar Pradesh, almost all the students of academic institutions including Banaras Hindu University (BHU), Mahatma Gandhi Kashi Vidyapeeth (MGKV), Sampurnanand Sanskrit University (SSU) and all the intermediate schools participated in the anti-Mandal agitation.[102]

The student agitation started in Delhi where it soon turned violent. The former Delhi University Students' Union (DUSU) president, Rajiv Goswami, who was the first student to set himself ablaze during the anti-Mandal agitation in 1990, had sparked off a series of self-immolations by students. One hundred and fifty-two people followed suit, of which sixty three succeeded.[103] The self-immolation student movement further spread throughout the country, to a variety of degrees. As table 5.2 shows, the most serious self-immolation movement took place in the Hindi belt. Madhya Pradesh, Delhi, Uttar Pradesh and Haryana ranked highest among other states, with more than 20 students attempting to suicide by self-immolation during the anti-Mandal agitation. The southern and western states, such as Maharashtra, Andhra Pradesh and Tamil Nadu, experienced it to a much less extent, with fewer than 3 students involved. (Table 5.2)

Table5.2: Cases of Self-Immolation, Suicides and Casualties of Police Firing During Anti-Mandal Agitation

	Self-immolations(includes unsuccessful attempts)	Suicides (includes unsuccessful attempts)	Persons killed in police firing
Delhi	20	3	5
Haryana	22	32	6
Uttar Pradesh	25	28	16
Madhya Pradesh	27	5	-
Gujarat	10	3	-
Bihar	8	12	12
Chandigarh	7	8	-
Rajasthan	12	8	1
Punjab	6	30	9
Himachal Pradesh	9	13	-

[101] Ibid. P.155

[102] Cited from the article "Mandal Memories Revived." *The Hindustan Times.* April 9, 2006.

[103] Cited from The India Today, October 15, 1990. P.15.

Andhra Pradesh	3	6	-
Tamil Nadu	2	-	1
Jammu & Kashmır	1	1	1
Maharashtra	-	-	7
Orissa	-	-	7
Assam	-	1	-

Source cıted from Indıa's Sılent Revolutıon whıch cıtes from natıonal Maıl 12 Jan 1991

The anti-caste-based-reservation protests that reoccurred in 2006 across India were in opposition to the decision of the Indian government to reserve new OBC quotas of 27 percent in central and private institutes of higher education.[104] Like the anti-Mandal agitation in the early 1990s, massive protests proceeded. The protesters claimed that the government's proposal was discriminatory and driven by "vote-bank'" politics.

5.3.3 Caste Alignments, Break-ups and Realignments at Post-Mandal Elections

After the intense protests against the announcement of the Mandal report, the subsequent developments were characterized by caste alignment, break-ups and realignments within lower castes groups and between upper castes and lower castes. Firstly, the strengthened hostility between the upper castes and the lower castes over the Mandal issues "…made the crystallization of an OBC political identity much easier. The lower castes began to share a common political identity that was expressed in terms of the OBCs v.s. the upper castes: caste had become the building block of a larger, social coalition."[105] It seemed that the consolidation of OBCs as a social group reduced the tension between the OBCs and the Scheduled Castes (SCs), as both stood for reservation quotas. As the anti-reservation agitation at most places ıs shared by both set of castes, they are coming closer to each other.[106]

[104] The Supreme Court of Indıa ın 2008 upheld the law whıch provıdes a quota of 27 per cent for candıdates belongıng to the Other Backward Classes ın Central hıgher educatıonal ınstıtutıons that ıncludes the Indıan Instıtutes of Technology (IIT's) and the Indıan Instıtutes of Management (IIM's)

[105] Jaffrelot, Chrıstophe *Indıa's Sılent Revolutıon the Rıse of the Lower Castes ın North Indıa* New York Columbıa Unıversıty Press, 2003 P 349

[106] The allıance between the OBCs and SCs, however, lack structural unıty accordıng to Chrıstophe Jaffrelot (2003)

Take Uttar Pradesh (UP) as an example, the OBC groups attempted to ally with Scheduled Castes and Tribes in order to obtain a larger influence In the mobilizing process, they chose to join or ally with the political parties, such as Samajwadi Party (Socialist Party; SP) or Dalit parties such as Bahujan Samaj Party (BSP, Party of *Dalits*) For instance, the BSP has increasingly absorbed OBC candidates, from 23.7% in 1993 to 50.5% in 1998. "Benefiting from the support of OBC castes such as the *Kurmis* and the Kacchis, the BSP is definitely more than a Dalit party in Vindhya Pradesh."[107]

The BSP and the SP joined hands in the 1993 Assembly Elections because they had common interests of opposing the upper castes who still have a large political influence in northern India.. This SP-BSP alliance has won them 67 seats in the 425-member Assembly. In the 1990s, caste conflicts are a reaction to the emergence of the political rise of lower castes in Uttar Pradesh. "...local *Brahmins* sponsored a Sa*varna* Samaj Party (Party of the Community of the Upper Cates) whose leader polled 13.43% of the valid votes in Rewa constituency in the 1996 general elections. In this context, *Kurmis* and Kachhis also forcefully identified themselves with the *Dalits* and the Ambedkarite discourse..."[108]

The fragmented and newly politicized OBC communities, however, did not hold the *Dalits*' attention for long. The SP-BSP short-lived alliance lasted less than two years when the Dalit party BSP pursued the stronger allies that can take it to power. After falling out with the SP in 1995, the BSP allied with the upper-caste dominated parties, BJP and Congress alternatively, to improve its vote share.[109] The BSP, which primarily attracted votes from *Dalits* and most Backward Castes, rotated its alliances with different parties till very recently in 2011 in order to enlarge the "Sarvjan vote bank" (vote bank for all people). It successfully owned Brahmin votes

---

[107] Jaffrelot, Christophe *India's Silent Revolution the Rise of the Lower Castes in North India* New York Columbia University Press, 2003 P 406

[108] Ibid P 406

[109] The BSP joined hands with the BJP in 1995 which did not last for one year In 1996 Lok Sabha and Assembly Elections it joined hands with the Congress, from which the BSP won 20 6 percent with 6seats in 1996 compared to8 7 percent and no seat in 1991 The BSP-Congress alliance fell through as none of the parties won sufficient Assembly seats (The Congress got 33 and BSP 67 seats only) Then, the BSP got back to the BJP and arranged a pact of'six-month rotational chief ministership" In the 2002 Assembly elections, the party joined hands again with the BJP but the government fell again after one year

in the 2007 elections, especially when the *Brahmins* had been disillusioned with the Congress and the BJP for the past 20 years. Prepared for the 2012 Assembly election of UP, the BSP again took actions to woo all the caste communities to its folder. The caste committees were reconstituted soon after being dissolved by the BSP chief following the 2009 Lok Sabha elections In 2011, the BSP began to reconstitute the Brahmin Bhaichara at the booth and constituency level. [110] In another northern state Bihar, the upper caste voters have also been courted in Bihar 2010 assembly election by Rashtriya Janata Dal (RJD, "National People's Party") and Lok Janshakti Party (LJP) that have primarily focused on the support of backward and minority voters. [111]

5.4 Resource Effect of the Mandal Issue

It is true that Mandal policy is an ambitious plan to promote the social and political positions of the subaltern Indians. The overall percentage of reserved seats in public employment had been added up to 49.5 percent specifically for the lower castes. The deliveries of quotas, however, became a difficult problem for a populous country like India.

5.4.1 A Swelling OBC List

The listing of OBCs across India has remained one of the most complicated tasks for the government. The term of "Other Backward Classes" (OBCs) has never acquired a definite meaning at all India level. It had come to mean different things in different places because its implementation has been left to state governments. Marc Glanter (1991) specifies ten such denotations of the term "OBCs", which he categorizes into two major species: 1) as the most inclusive group of all those who need special treatment; and 2) as a status higher than the untouchable but nonetheless depressed. This double usage continues even today: the former in the

[110] Srivastava, Piyush *2012 UP Polls Mayawati Government to Woo Displeased Brahmins, Lucknow* November 8, 2011 http //indiatoday intoday in/story/mayawati-government-brahmin-community/1/159084 html

[111] Jha, Giridhar "Upper Caste Voters Gain Prominence as Frantic Parties Woo Them with Sops " *India Today* October 24, 2010 http //indiatoday intoday in/story/upper-caste-voters-gain-prominence-as-frantic-parties-woo-them-with-sops/1/117559 html

usage of Backward Classes in the wider sense (including SCs and STs) and the latter in the usage as equivalent to OBCs (social status higher than SC/STs, lower than intermediate castes and upper castes).[112] Either usage offers large space for creating a list of OBCs as these "residue" populations are defined in various uncertain terms.

How did a swelling list of OBCs come into being in practice? The OBC groups had been identified and scheduled by the states/UTs until 1992 and thereafter also by the Central Government. In order to incorporate all the eligible members, the lists recommended by national Kalelkar and Mandal Commissions contain as many as 2399 and 3743 OBC communities respectively. The officially accepted OBC list contains a total of 2176 communities that have been scheduled as the OBCs by the central government. There are several considerations involved in this "large number." First and foremost, most OBC communities generally pursuing the same occupations are known by different names in different states/UTs.[113] Moreover, the number of OBCs of the same occupational and other cultural traits has come to be counted many times under different names over the swelling OBC lists.

Apart from the anomalies of numbers, there are other listing drawbacks. Some states have sub-divisions of OBCs, such as Bihar, Tamil Nadu, Andhra Pradesh and Kanataka. Yet sub-divisions are not of the same variety in each state. In Bihar and Tamil Nadu, the list is sub-divided into OBCs and MBCs. In Andhra Pradesh and Karnataka, OBC lists are subdivided into group/category of A,B,C,D. Reservations are apportioned among the categorized sub-groups in proportion to their respective population among the OBCs. In these four states, "some categories of communities that should have logically gone into the list of SCs and STs have actually been

[112] Glanter, Marc *Competing Equality Law and the Backward Classes in India* Berkkeley University of California Press, 1984 Paperback edition with new preface in 1991, New Delhi Oxford University Press
[113] There are very few pan-Indian OBC communities called by the same name across the country For example, Kurmi and Ahir are two OBC communities that are scheduled in quite a few states

included among the OBCs".[114] There are various measures of categorization in the remaining states, yet all of them are treated at par officially. (See Appendix 5.1)

The OBC lists also include some such communities that are not socially and educationally backward and are adequately represented in the government services. Their population size or political importance, however, has enabled them to gain entry or remain in the list..[115] Some entries were made before 1992 when there has not been a unified national list for OBC groups. Still, other entries were made after 1992.[116] Take the cases of *Jats* in Uttar Pradesh and *Lingayats* of Karnataka as examples. In Karnataka, whether *Lingayats* are backward still remained unresolved after discussions at state Backward Classes Commissions. *Jats* in Uttar Pradesh have successfully been included in the state OBC list, even if the petition of *Jats* to be included in the central list of OBCs was rejected by the National Commission for the Backward Castes. The *Jats* who are not an economically disadvantaged community are currently enjoying the benefits of Articles 15(4) and 16(4) in Uttar Pradesh.

5.4.2 Empowerment and Development of the OBCs

There is a large discrepancy between the number of the eligible OBCs and the number of real reservation recipients. Firstly, those OBCs who directly benefit from the reservation of legislative bodies and of government jobs constituents are only a small fraction of the backward classes. They are far outnumbered by those who are eligible for a vast array of special schemes for education and economic uplift.[117] Secondly, a breakdown of plan expenditure reveals a continuing emphasis on SC and STs. Financial allocations for these skeletal few schemes were

---

[114] Sujatha, V.S. " Chapter 4 OBCs: Composition, Decomposition, Characteristics and Empowerment Tasks." In *The OBCs and the Ruling Classes in India*, by Hs Verma. Rawat Publications, 2005. pp.105-6

[115] This concept will be further studied in the later chapters.

[116] The case of Vokaligas in Karnataka belongs to the first category whereas the inclusion of *Jats* in Uttar Pradesh and Rajasthan belongs to the second category.

[117] OBCs share some of the educational and economic welfare programs with SCs and STs. Some educational programs, such as provision of meals, supplies, and hostels etc., are intended primarily for these groups. In addition, a lengthy catalog of measures to improve the economic status: allotments of (and subsidies to purchase) agricultural land; installation of irrigation wells; provision of livestock, seeds and tools, encouragement of cottage industries by the provision of training, supplies, and equipment; support for agricultural and craft cooperatives. Finally, there are schemes for providing housing, roads (in tribal areas), drinking-water wells, health clinics, legal aid, and nursery schools.

meager and some secured no allocations at all. In social sector expenditure (SSE), the welfare spending for backward castes is incorporated with that of SCs and STs, which accounts for somewhat 6 percent of the total SSE. (Table 5.3)

Table5.3: Composition of Social Service Expenditure, State Governments, as Percent to Social Service Expenditure* (1990-2011)

Years	1990-91	2000-01	2010-11 (BE)
Social Service Expenditure	100	100	100
(a) Edu., Sports, Art & Culture	55.5	57.4	50.1
(b) Medical &Public Health	16.4	12.3	10.6
(c) Family welfare	-	2.3	1.8
(d) Water Supply& Sanitation	5.9	5.3	2.9
(e) Housing	1.3	1.3	1.8
(f) Urban Development	2.3	2.6	8.0
(g) Welfare of SC/ST/OBCs	6.4	6	6.8
(h) Labor & Labor Welfare	1.6	1.2	1.2
(i) Social Security & Welfare	4.9	4.8	10.4
(j) Nutrition	1.9	2.4	4.1
(k) Natural Calamity Relief	3.1	3.8	1.4
(l) Others	0.7	0.7	0.8

Note: * BE=budget estimate
Source: Fieldwork

In the early 1990s, many of those groups that had been classified ritually within the Hindu *varna* system as *shudras*/intermediate castes began to internalize their new administrative classification as OBCs. They adopted this new identity mainly in order to derive political and economic benefits from it. However, on neither front was the state able to meet their requirements. Reservations in the government employment were one of the major demands of the backwards, yet the underrepresentation of the OBC groups has not been improved as required. Table 5.4A shows that the OBCs' representation was even worse than the Scheduled Castes and Tribes (SC/STs) in 1979-80. Totally, the share of OBCs in government positions accounted for only 12.55%, as against 68.74% of high castes and 18.71% of SC/STs. Over the period of 25 years, the OBCs' representation is drastically reduced from 12.55 to 4.51%, while the already-dominant upper caste representation has further improved.[118] (Table 5.4A and B)

Table5.4A: SC/ST/OBC and Upper Caste Representation in Public Employment (1979-80)

Category of Employment	Total Number of Employees	SC/ST %	OBC %	Upper Caste % (Derived)
Population %		22.56	52.00	17.58
Class I	1,74,043	5.68	4.69	89.63
Class II	9,12,786	18.18	10.63	71.19
Class III & IV	4,84,646	24.40	24.40	51 20
All Classes	15,71,475	18.71	12.55	68.74

Source Mandal Commission Report I & II, 9 48, Page 41, 42)
(30 Central Ministries, 31 Attached Offices and PSUs under 14 Ministries)

Table5.4B: SC/ST/OBC and Upper Caste Representation in Public Employment as on January 1, 2004

Group	Total Number of Employees	SC %	ST %	OBC %	Upper Caste % (Derived)
Population %		15.05	7.51	52.00	17.58
A	80,011	12.2	4.1	3.9	79.80
B	1,35,409	14.5	4.6	2.3	78.60
C	20,40,970	16.9	6.7	5.2	71.20
D	8,02,116	18.4	6.7	3.3	71.60
Sweepers	91,601	64.76	5.86	3.65	25.73
Total	31,50,107	18.44	6.52	4.51	70.53

Source Ministry of Personnel, Public Grievances & Pensions

The minimal OBC representation is generally proved to be notional because of their total absence in some of the key government departments such as the police headquarters, judiciary and the direct employment recruit agencies.[119] Furthermore, the State Government Secretariat set up, where the real state power rests, is still controlled by the *Brahmins* and other "twice born" castes. H.S. Verma emphasize that one of the strategies of upper caste bureaucrats consisted in "keeping a large number of positions outside the scope of reservations' and that direct recruitment was limited generally to Class II positions and that higher positions were filled with promotion.

[118] It is probably the impact of "Creamy Layer" that squeezed out the qualified OBCs

[119] H S Verma, R A Singh and J Singh, "Power Sharing Exclusivity and Exclusion in a Mega State ", cited from Jaffrelot, Christophe *India's Silent Revolution the Rise of the Lower Castes in North India* New York Columbia University Press, 2003 pp 343-4

Besides, most quotas were not fulfilled."[120] Moreover, the reservation benefits were unequally distributed in favor of the "Creamy Layer" of the lower castes while the real needy have been kept out usually due to lack of qualification. Chapter 7 will take a detailed look at this issue.

It is noteworthy that OBC political empowerment in southern and western India has developed one hundred years earlier than its counterparts in the north and east. As mentioned in the previous chapters, more than half of the positions in the state legislature and government branches were reserved for the subordinated caste groups in Karnataka, Tamil Nadu, Andhra Pradesh and Kerala in the early 1950. By contrast, some northern and eastern Indian states have not made their own state OBC lists until the 1990s.

Besides political empowerment, economic development promised by Indian policy-makers has offered great economic opportunities to a large number of socially backward groups. But economic development in the present structure does not move at the speed and in the direction that the policy-makers would wish. In advanced industrial democracies, anywhere from 30 to 60 percent of GNP is filtered through government programs, which simply does not compare to a large-size developing country like India.

The plan provisions for OBCs have followed an irregular course owing to the controversy about the membership of that category. Very few specific schemes have been directly addressed to the OBC categories. Welfare for OBCs, which is under welfare for SC/ST/OBCs, is a newly created category and the development of the OBCs has been regarded as some alterations here and there or some humanistic ameliorations. It was only in the ninth plan that that some semantic attention was paid to this requirement. The central government has been deliberately ignoring the task of development of the OBCs. Until very recently, the Working Group Report (Feb-April, 2001) was seen as a qualitative departure in viewing the OBC development seriously.

The state-level spending on the OBC groups has been as varied as the state-level OBC empowerment history. Indicated from Table 5, the welfare per capita for the SC/ST/OBCs were

[120] Ibid. P.344

much better in southern and western states than the northern and eastern states. The western states, such as Maharashtra and Gujarat, have expended their spending on the SC/ST/OBCs around 5 times from 1991 to 2001, compared to the all-Indian average of triple increase. (Table 5.5) This probably is due to the faster economic development in these states and a total increase of state expenditure on social sector.

Table5.5: State-level Welfare of SCs/STs/OBCs Per Capita (1990-2001)

WELF p.c.		
State	1990-91	2000-01
Andhra Pradesh	61.13	171.15
Bihar	14.46	27.56
Gujarat	33.89	134.71
Haryana	13.53	27.79
Karnataka	40.99	142.85
Kerela	23.17	84.77
Madhya Pradesh	67.07	195.55
Maharashtra	25.54	138.19
Orissa	26.65	76.84
Punjab	18.07	34.37
Rajasthan	9.03	19.23
Tamil Nadu	22.09	83.10
Uttar Pradesh	10.67	47.83
West Bengal	22.43	72.03
All-India	27.76	89.71

Source: Fieldwork

Identification does not guarantee the successful delivery of public goods and service to the lower caste and poor communities. The allocation through the Indian administration has been ineffective and costly. The cost of the general state administration (including interest payments on state borrowing) makes up 30 percent of Total Expenditure.[121] Regarding social spending on education for lower castes, "less than half of the spending can be delivered to ground because of the costly administration fees and corruption."[122] For instance, all the *Dalit* families at Rattu Bigha, a Maha *Dalit* hamlet in Bihar, since June 2008, "has received regular supply of foodgrains on its yellow (Antyodaya Anna Yojana) card which entitles it to 25 kg of rice or wheat at Rs. 2

[121] The number was calculated by the author using the states finances database, which was compiled by the World Bank from annual publications of the Reserve Bank of India Bulletin, and various state statistical abstracts.

[122] Interview note with a IAS officer at the Ministry of Social Justice and Empowerment of Indian Central Government.

(for 10 kg rice) and Rs. 3 (for 15 kg wheat). The coupons are lying with the villagers, as the dealer is claiming "shortage of foodgrains" and keeping the shop closed for most of the time."[123]

In other words, economic development and political empowerment have been stymied by an unbridgeable chasm between the rhetoric of Reservation Policies and the ground realities of implementing these policies. In this context of unequal distribution of the Reservation Policies, an important impediment has been the nature of the redistributive capabilities of the state.

5.5 Understanding the Lower Caste Mobilization in the Post-Mandal Period: A Comparative Study of Tamil Nadu and Uttar Pradesh

Mandal Policy, which was introduced in favor of Other Backward Classes (OBCs), consolidated the OBCs as demand groups in its direct effects. Take Uttar Pradesh (UP) as an example, the Backward Castes consolidation has helped the Samajwadi Party (literally the socialist party) get near-total support from *Yadav*s and *Lodhs* and substantial backing from Other Backward Classes such as *Kurmis* and *Keoris.* Even within the BJP and the Congress Party, "supporters from among the Backward Classes ended up supporting SP candidates at the local level."[124] Beginning with the 1996 assembly elections, the parties, including the national parties BJP and Congress Party, have realized that their vote bank could not expand without gaining supports from the Backward Classes.

In order to earn better economic and status interests, the OBCs chose to mobilize politically in several ways. One is straightforward appeal to their economic interests. In this circumstance, the lower castes usually see themselves as "the poor" and recognize their affinity with "*Kisan* groups" (peasant groups) who have a somewhat similar economic position. For instance, the

[123] Banerjee, Shoumojit. "Bihar hunger deaths: lower level bureaucracy apathetic." *The Hindu.* The Hindu, Auguest 23, 2009.
[124] Pai, Sudha. "Electoral Identity Politics in Uttar Pradesh: Hung Assembly Again." *Economic and Political Weekly* 37, no. 14 (2002): 1334-41.

OBCs in Uttar Pradesh, the major constituents of Samajwadi Party, demanded subsidized electricity and unremunerative agricultural goods.

In order to pursue economic and political interests, the OBC groups also linked with SC/STs, intermediate castes and even upper castes. The OBC-*Dalit* alliance, as practiced by the SP and the BSP, has featured the UP politics in the early 1990s. However, coherent actions taken by these OBCs seemed difficult. For instance, the "caste politics" of the SP and the BSP turned out to be short-lived coalitions.[125] Due to caste-based mobilization, the parties that confined to their narrow sectarian bases have been unable obtain majority support and form stable governments. The SP has given tickets to Upper Castes besides *Dalits*, as has the BSP.

The intermediate castes in some Indian areas acknowledge common interests with the lower castes in order to mobilize "the larger number" to win elections. For instance, the *Maratha-Kunbi* elite, the populous intermediate caste groups in Maharashtra incorporated leaders from the lower castes such as *Malis, Dhangars, Telis, Lingayats, Vanjaris, Mahars* among others into Congress Party and the local institutions, such as the cooperatives and the Panchayati Raj were organized.[126] Such political accommodation in some cases works as a successful mobilizing strategy that attracts the supports from these caste-based communities. Another attempt is to emphasize the regional community. To share broader community identification can be sometimes successful by blaming outsiders for the economic difficulties of a region and the poor. For example, regional identities such as *Telegus* or *Tamils* can grant the lower castes an equality of status which they have not traditionally had.

Although a tendency of caste coalitions can be seen between different sub-groups among the lower castes in the post-Mandal period, such alliances were usually short-lived when the political parties sought maximum electoral support. To understand the variety of caste mobilization, a comparative study of Uttar Pradesh (UP) and Tamil Nadu (TN) will be explored in the following

[125] It is due to the economic or political conflicts between the OBCs and SCs; such as land. OBCs owned land that the SCs also wanted.

[126] Jadhav., Vishal. " Elite Politics and Maharashtra's Employment Guarantee Scheme." *Economic and Political Weekly*, December 2006: 5157-5162.

sub-sections. In Uttar Pradesh where the upper castes had dominated, with the middle castes in a secondary role, and OBCs and SCs in a still more subordinate position, the lower caste mobilization came on a large scale as late as the late 1980s. In Tamil Nadu, one of the four southern states where the earliest anti-Brahmin movements took place, the pattern was different. Here large landlords were less common, the proportion of the upper castes was lower, and anti-Brahmin movements had already forced *Brahmins* to the sidelines. This left the regional parties (DMK and ADMK) in the control of the lower castes, mainly OBC castes –or, more accurately, in the hands of elite segments of these castes.

The two states have followed quite different political trajectories. Firstly, the caste compositions are quite different in both social and political terms. In UP, the upper castes represent a much larger proportion of the population than they do in TN. According to the census of 1931, the upper castes represented 20 percent of the population.[127] In TN, the upper castes represented merely 4 percent of the population. The large numbers of non-Brahmin castes (mainly OBCs, including SC/STs) had successfully led Dravidian Politics even before the Independence. Although the OBCs and SCs constitute more than half its population in UP, it is the 20% upper castes that have been dominating UP society and politics until the very recent entry of OBCs and SCs into the political system in 1970s.

Secondly, the political mobilization of lower castes across the two states also greatly differs. In the former, i.e. Tamil Nadu, the upper caste elite lost power due to the effective collectivity of the anti-Brahmin movements since the early 1920s. In UP, though, the lower castes were almost as numerous as those in TN, they were more fragmented and more submissive, partly because the Brahmin population is larger in this region and has been in power longer than in the south.

Thirdly, the party systems in UP and TN show a differentiating picture. The two-party system in Tamil Nadu has been stabilized since the late 1960s between Dravida Munnetra

[127] The *Brahmins* were 9.2 percent, the highest percentage of *Brahmins* in any Indian state, and the Rajputs 7.2 percent, with Banias accounting for the remainder.

Kazhagam (DMK, or Dravidian Progress Federation) and All India Anna Dravida Munnetra Kazhagam (AIADMK/ADMK, or All-Indian Dravidian Progress Federation), both of which are lower-caste-orientated parties and pursue substantial benefits for the poor and the backward castes. In UP, the lower-caste parties like the Samajwadi Party (SP, Socialist Party) and the Bahujan Samaj Party (BSP, Party of *Dalits*) have not been able to retain its power without alliances with other parties. For instance, BSP have allied with the upper-caste-oriented party Bharatiya Janata Party (BJP or Indian People's Party), in order to remain in office during the late 1990s and the early years of the 21st Century, and there are deep Upper Caste-Dalit alliance in the Congress. As seen in the Chart 1, multiple parties, such as BJP, Congress Party, BSP and Janata Dal (JD) had to compete intensely in the Uttar Pradesh assembly elections since 1988. (Figure 5.1)

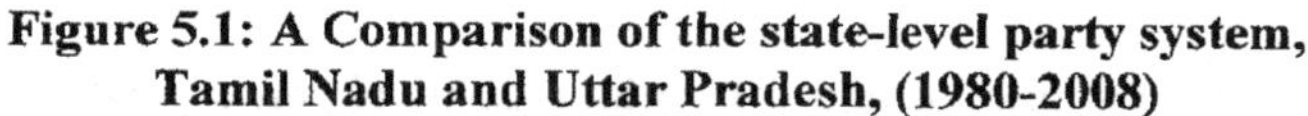

Figure 5.1: A Comparison of the state-level party system, Tamil Nadu and Uttar Pradesh, (1980-2008)

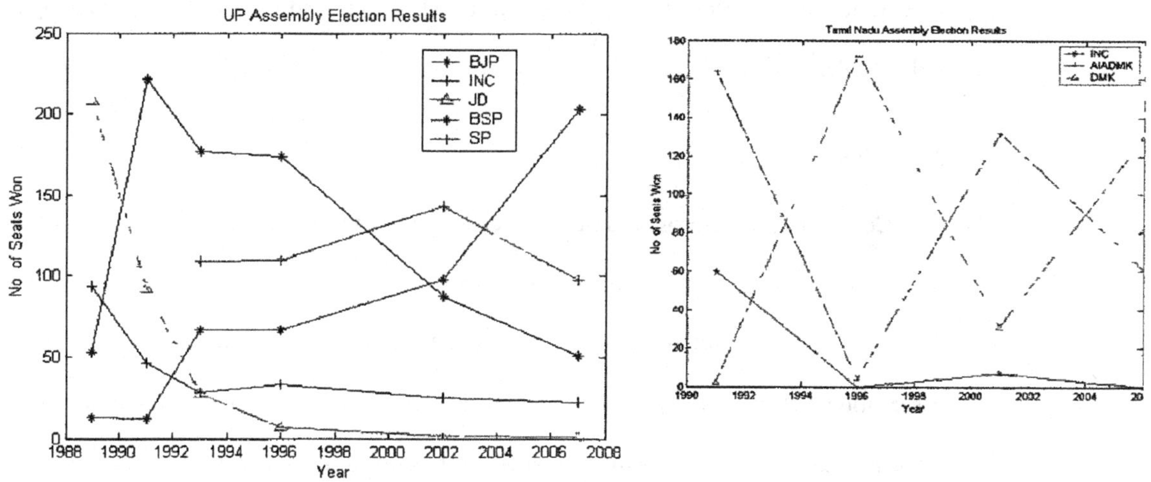

Fourthly, the social conflicts directly related with Reservation Policies became much more violent in UP than they did in TN. When the reservation protests hit northern India in 1990 and again in 2006, a contrasting quiet serenity was noticed in Chennai, the capital city of Tamil

Nadu.[128] Later, as the anti-reservation lobby gained in visibility most of northern cities, Chennai saw quiet street protests demanding reservation. Doctors in Chennai, including a doctors' association for social equality were in the forefront expressing their support for reservation in institutions of higher education run by the Central government. The contrasting responses indicate a great difference of the effects the Reservation Policies had in the two areas, partly due to earlier resolution of caste issues in the south.

There are thus some important questions to ask. Why have the lower castes and the interests of the poor been mobilized in a more collective matter in TN than in UP? Why does it proceed more smoothly, with less violence and turmoil, in TN than in UP? If certain institutional channels are available for lower castes in quest for support and power, can the political mobilization of OBCs come less violently? In the latter part of this chapter, I contend that Reservation Policies, through its resource effect, help shape such institutional channels. In other words, institutional channels, such as pro-reservation organizations, political parties, and administrative agencies, determine how the interests of the lower castes are articulated with/without producing a crisis in public order.

5.5.1 Uttar Pradesh

Considering their profound differences in caste composition and the contrasts between the state-level political environments in which they operate, I attempt to explain the different political mobilization effects in Uttar Pradesh (UP) and Tamil Nadu (TN) from the perspective of reservation history. In the post-Independence period, the Government of India directed the state governments to prepare their own OBC lists after rejecting the report of Kalelkar Commission to recommend communities to be listed as the OBCs. Various state governments set up committees/commissions to identify the OBCs. However, not all the states formulated their OBC lists despite legitimizing mechanisms of the committees/commissions. Marc Galanter (1991)

[128] The protest became much less in 2006 as higher castes have found more career opportunities in private enterprises.

notes a regional variation in the listing and also in the range of benefits granted to the OBCs. He emphasized the difference between the Dravidian states (Andhra Pradesh, Karnataka, Kerala, Tamil Nadu) where a major segment of population were listed as OBCs and those states including Uttar Pradesh and Bihar where the listing had a communal base initially, but the benefits to the OBCs have been minimal.[129]

In Uttar Pradesh, though the social profile of the political leadership has undergone the transformation in the late 1980s as the non-elite groups became increasingly represented in the legislative assemblies and in the government, the lower-caste representatives have hardly reached the deserved proportion. As Jaffrelot and Zerinini-Brotel state, the caste profile of UP's MLAs has undergone a great transformation. OBC MLA increased from 13.7% in 1980 to 29.9% in 1993 and 24% in 1996, as indicated in the table 6 (1980-1996). As a consequence, the representation of OBCs in the UP assembly rose and peaked at higher levels when the Mandal recommendation was approved.[130] The proportion of upper-caste MLAs, however, did not decrease as expected in the same period because the increase of OBC MLA was at the expense of Muslim and independent competitors (Table 5.6).

Table5.6: Caste and Community in the Uttar Pradesh Assembly, 1980-2002 (%)

Caste & Communities	1980	1985	1989	1991	1993	1996	2002
Upper castes	42.40	39.45	39.24	41.77	33.42	37.67	35.38
Intermediate castes	2.21	3.23	2.28	2.78	2.74	3.18	4.67
OBCs	**16.91**	**20.84**	**24.56**	**26.58**	**32.67**	**24.40**	**27.52**
SCs	22.06	22.33	21.77	22.28	22.19	23.61	21.87
Muslims	11.76	12.41	10.13.	5.82	7.73	10.08	10.57
Sikhs	1.23	0.99	0.25	0.25	0.50	0.27	-
Unidentified	3.43	0.74	1.77	0.51	0.75	0.80	-
Total	100	100	100	100	100	100	

Source Field work by Šumit Ganguly, Larry Jay Diamond, Marc F Plattner (eds) 2007 The state of India's democracy The Johns Hopkins University Press

[129] Glanter also points to the third group of states (West Bengal and Orissa, across Madhya Pradesh and Rajasthan), where OBCs have not emerged as a relevant category until 1992 when the central list of OBCs was established

[130] Zerinini-Brotel, Christophe Jaffrelot and Jasmine ""Post-"Mandal"" Politics in Uttar Pradesh and Madhya Pradesh " In *Regional Reflections Comparing Politics Across India's States* , by Rob Jenkins New Delhi Oxford University Press, 2004 P 362

However, the rising share of OBCs in government employment and in elected bodies does not endow the lower castes with decision powers. Jaffrelot concludes from his fieldwork study that "93.8% of the principal secretaries and secretaries to the government (in UP in 1984) were from the upper castes (including 56.3% *Brahmins*) and this was also the case for 86.6% of the heads of departments and 93.2% of the section officers. At the local level, 78.6% of the District Magistrates were from the upper castes in 1985, including 41.1% of *Brahmins* and 25% of Kayasths. In the public state units, 94.5% of the managing directors were from the upper castes in 1984. "[131] Moreover, a higher representation of OBCs in the UP assembly has yet to cause a larger spending for the numerous lower castes.[132] Instead of expanding the public expenditures for the marginal caste groups from the 1985-1995 (the period that saw the upsurge of lower-caste mobilization), Uttar Pradesh retrenched the spending proportion of welfare for SC/ST/OBCs to Social Sector Expenditure from 4.81% in 1985 to 3.46 % in 1993, with a marginal increase in 1994 and 1995. (Table 5. 7)

Table5.7: Proportion of the Expenditure of Welfare for SC/ST/OBCs on Social Sector Expenditure, Uttar Pradesh (1985-1995, %)

Year	1985	1990	1995
Uttar Pradesh	4.81	3.17	4.77
All-India	5.70	5.67	5.96

Source Fieldwork

Reservation Policies created the OBCs as a new category in order to provide group equality in India's hierarchical society. However, the state resource can't be reallocated enough and equally as it suggests especially in a society with hierarchical Hindu culture. It seems that underrepresentation of the lower castes in UP politics has given them incentives to politically mobilize. The OBCs were no longer simply an administrative category. On one hand, the caste

[131] Christophe Jaffrelot 2003 Chapter 10 The Janata Dal and the Rise to Power of the Low Castes, in Jaffrelot, Christophe *India's Silent Revolution the Rise of the Lower Castes in North India* New York Columbia University Press, 2003

[132] It is probably because of the tensions between the SCs and OBCs

polarization between the upper and lower caste communities has been intensified over the question whether the OBCs are qualified for the reservation benefits. The violence of the upper-caste Hindus reaction against reservation quotas further initiated the hostility of OBC groups who demanded that the State's upper-caste bias should be forcibly dismantled. On the other hand, the increasing tension between the upper castes and lower castes further helped the OBC political movement to coalesce. The OBCs of north India, including UP, started to fight collectively for reservations and, beyond that, to concentrate their votes on the parties representing their interests. Political parties also organized around OBC identity to ratchet up their mobilization efforts to an unprecedented level. Occasionally, the OBCs were joined by other social groups such as SC/STs or agrarian groups, but there are structural reasons there is broader cooperation between these two sets of groups.

In UP, the OBC groups and the *Jats* (who consistently requested being included in the OBC lists) made their first inroads into power in the 1960s in the form of peasant movements under the leadership of Charan Singh and his political party. The peculiar trend of agrarian politics in the state has contributed to setting it on a different path of OBC political mobilization. This development of peasant movements–under the aegis of Charan Singh –did not focus on caste, but projected itself as the true advocate of the *Kisan*s (farmers) generally. The OBC groups, who formed the bulk of the cultivating castes, acted an important role under the coverage of peasant instead of castes. "The Chaudhury's movement could not be characterized as an OBC political force. It was spearheaded by members of non-OBC castes and, moreover, did not rely on caste as the basis for political mobilization."[133] Yet, in a very important respect it sowed the seeds for the OBC movement unleashed by the implementation of the Mandal report more than 20 years later.

A real OBC mobilizing experience was led by Rammanohar Lohia and his Socialist Party. Influenced by Marxism, Lohia looked at the eradication of caste as the primary objective of any

[133] Zerinini-Brotel, Christophe Jaffrelot and Jasmıne. ""Post-"Mandal"" Politics in Uttar Pradesh and Madhya Pradesh." In *Regıonal Reflectıons Comparıng Polıtıcs Across Indıa's States* , by Rob Jenkins. New Delhı: Oxford University Press, 2004. P.150

socialist programme. He emphasized political empowerment of the lower castes, demanding quotas in the administration and elected bodies. In his opinion, the protected quotas in the education system, though desirable, were not put on the top list. "In 1959 the third national conference of the Socialist Party expressed the wish that at least 60 percent of the posts in the administration be reserved for OBCs…To show the way, the SP nominated a large number of candidates from non-elite groups, and the socialists had a larger number of OBC MLAs elected than did any other political party in UP and Bihar."[134]

In other words, the OBC groups in UP have been mobilized under two differing mobilizing strategies. Charan Singh focused on defense of the peasants, allied with the lower castes (cultivating castes) with the aims to eliminate the domination of landlords and to demand for fairly priced electricity and unremunerative agricultural goods. Lohiaite socialists more directly asked to promote the political status of OBC communities. They demanded for larger protected quotas in the elected bodies and public offices. These mobilizing strategies involved the OBC groups into the intense UP politics. Yet, both have failed to provide real and direct policy benefits to them.

5.5.2 Tamil Nadu

In the southern states, reservation for the OBCs has been in vogue for a long time. Tamil Nadu has long history of reservations and had powerful social movements propelled mainly by the OBCs. The "communal quotas" were introduced by the Justice Party in the 1920s that led the cause of the backward castes in the pre-Independence period. The Sattanathan Commission (1970) identified 105 communities as OBCs using caste as a criterion. The Ambasankar Commission (1982) gave separate OBC lists for the purposes of Articles 15(4) and 16(4) on the basis of socio-economic and educational conditions of the population of the state.

[134] Ibid. P.150

The reservation system in Tamil Nadu is much in contrast to the rest of India, not only by the longer listing for the lower castes but by its history India) succeeded in attaining the reservation quotas and to a great extent weakened the dominance of *Brahmins*. As early as in 1927, the backward movement (or called Dravidian movement in southern After independence, the quotas for the backward castes expanded continuously in Tamil Nadu, reaching 25 percent in 1951 and increasing to 69 percent three decades later.(Figure 5.2). Compared with UP, these backward castes were much more empowered with decision making powers. As shown in table 5.8, the OBCs in the positions of empowered Secretariat and "Collectorates" in Tamil Nadu in 1970 accounted for over 20 % of the gazetted posts and around 40 % of non-gazetted posts (Table 5.8). By comparison, "93.8% of the principal secretaries and secretaries to the government were from the upper castes (including 56.3% *Brahmins*)."[135]

Figure 5.2: Tamil Nadu Reservation Timeline (1951-1997)

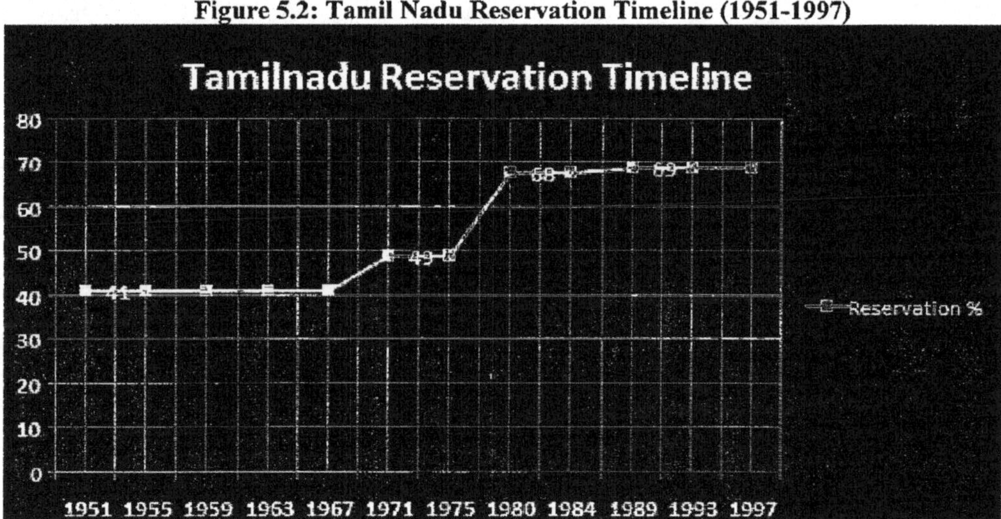

Table 5.8: OBCs in the Secretariat and in the "Collectorates" in Tamil Nadu, 1970 (%)

	Non-gazetted posts	Gazetted posts
Secretariat	39.8	20.8
"Collectorates"	47.5	24.8

Source: Adapted from Sattanath, Report of the Backward Classes Commission, pp.140; cited from Christophe Jaffrelot. 2003. India's Silent Revolution: The Rise of the Lower Castes in North India. New York: Columbia University Press. P239

[135] This is due to the better education that these Upper Castes can access. Cited from H.S. Verma, R.A. Singh and J. Singh, "Power Sharing: Exclusivity and Exclusion in a Mega State.", cited from Jaffrelot, Christophe. *India's Silent Revolution. the Rise of the Lower Castes in North India* New York: Columbia University Press, 2003. P.343

The issues of empowerment, though providing backward castes with political benefits, have not had immediate relevance for the majority of voters. In the area of preferential quotas, Tamil Nadu has been a pioneer in providing generous welfare spending as well as educational and job opportunities with the backward castes. Welfare and social reform policies played an important role in winning electoral support among a larger pool of the poor since the 1930s. Tamil Nadu has long been noted for the measures aimed at providing minimum levels of social insurance to the "poor-in general". All political parties in Tamil Nadu competed with each other to promote welfare schemes.

The first case with social insurance content was introduced in the 1930s by the Congress Party, which again introduced some important general social welfare policies in the 1950s and 1960s when Kumarasami Kamaraj was in power. The DMK led by Muthuvel Karunanidhi also added similar policies aiming at specially targeted population after it came to power in the late 1960s. DMK under Maruthur Gopalan Ramachandran (MGR) signaled a marked shift in favor of more broad-based measures aimed at women and vulnerable occupational groups that was promised by the MGR before he came to office. The universal measure became irreversible when the second Karunanidhi government of 1989-91 failed to retrench the tight state budgets by substituting a few highly visible and selective measures with the old universal and generous programs. Continuous delivery of welfare goods toward the broad-based poor in the areas of social insurance, prohibition, and food and nutrition polices, have won electoral support for any political party that was in power.

Contrasts in the social composition of TN and UP partly explain the different level of political tension in the two states. More importantly, the use of broad caste labels denoting "the common people", including "non-*Brahmin*" and "Backward Classes", the introduction of reservations for employment for these groups, in Tamil Nadu, have helped reduce subsequent conflicts over internal differentiation among the Other Backward Classes (OBCs). Lastly, the gradual transition from upper castes to the OBC power made the transition relatively peaceful in the southern states. By contrast, the greater speed introduced a higher degree of tension in the north.

At an Early Stage: Backward Castes Empowered

How did the reservation policy impact the mobilization in Tamil Nadu? Tamil Nadu (along with Kerala) was one of the first states to witness mobilization of lower castes and substantial changes which reached its peak between 1949 and 1967, when the political party Dravida Munnetra Kazhagam (DMK) which led the Dravidian movement, won control of the government of Madras (later called Tamil Nadu).

In November of 1916, the Justice Party was formed, aiming to redress the imbalance between the *Brahmins*, who processed a monopoly of power, and the non-*Brahmins*, who demanded more equitable treatment in political and economic terms. The Justice Party marked the formal birth of the Dravidian movement, and of the non-*Brahmins*' electoral competition with the upper-caste dominated parties. As the electoral expression of a non-Brahmin movement, the Justice Party actively challenged the Indian National Congress for political hegemony in Madras Presidency from the late 1910s to 1930s. During this period, the most notable development was the enactment of fixed quotas for lower caste groups in government employment, as well as establishment of control over the fiscal management of Tamil Nadu's large well-endowed temples, the elected local boards of which had become important centers of patronage, almost exclusively for *Brahmins*. With the growing non-Brahmin electoral support granted by the Reservation Policies and political reforms of 1920, the Justice Party won elections and formed provincial governments in every triennial election from 1923 to 1934 but one –that of 1926.[136]

[136] Swamy, Arun R. "Parties, Political Identities and the Absence of Mass Political Violence in South India." In *Community Conflicts and the State in India*, by Amrita Basu & Atul Kohli. Delhi: Oxford University Press, 1998. P 113

However, the Justice Party began to lose its significance in the late 1920s. On one hand, the Self-Respect movement of Periyar E. V. Ramasami emerged in the 1920s as a more radical version of the non-Brahmin movement. It regarded the Justice Party as the representative of the elite non-*Brahmins* (such as the Vallalas) and believed the political quotas were distributed unfairly without considering the real poor Dravidians. In 1944, Periyar went further toward the secessionist phase of the Dravidian movement by founding the Dravida Kazhagam (DK) or Dravidian Association which demanded an independent state in southern India for the Dravidians. On the other hand, the Congress came back during the 1930s with an expansive base by emphasizing the real economic issues such as land taxes etc that the Justice Party ignored. Also, the political rise of non-Brahmin K. Kamaraj in the Congress and in Tamil politics largely defused the charge that Congress was a Brahmin vehicle of credibility. Therefore, the Congress won 74% of the seats in the province elections of 1937, following the expansion of the franchise in 1935 (refer to Brown 1985: 287). Consequently, many Justice Party politicians joined the Congress while the rest were absorbed by Periyar's movement that had challenged the Justice Party and its elite strategies in the late 1930s.

In the Post-Independence Period: the DMK and Economic Development

The DK had faded out of existence as the redrawing of state boundaries along linguistic lines underplayed its rationale for secession. Following Independence in 1947, the DMK emerged under Periyar's principal lieutenant Annadurai, as the electoral vehicle of Tamil nationalism. The DMK learned the lessons from the Justice Party and the DK that political empowerment of the lower castes itself udoes not guaranteed a stable political victory.

The DMK grew its influence since it contested elections in 1957 and became the principle challenger to the Congress in the state.[137] In order to challenge the dominating position of the Congress Party in Tamil Nadu, the DMK took a pragmatic attitude to undermine the latter's claim

[137] The DMK began to increase its influence from winning less than 13 percent in 1957 to win over a quarter of the vote in 1962.

to represent Tamil aspirations and the poor. To search for more power, it began to ally with different minor parties in Tamil Nadu, such as Communist Party in 1959 and even with the Brahmin-led Swatantra party in 1962. In the economic arena, the DMK began to emphasize distributional issues, notably the welfare policies for backward castes, to expand its base. Between 1980 and the death of Maruthur Gopalan Ramachandran (MGR) in 1987, Tamil Nadu experienced better rates of growth in per capita income and human development indices in almost all aspects. The record of the MGR government and his DMK party showed that Tami Nadu had delivered material benefits in the form of growth and poverty alleviation considerably better than that of most Indian states. As Arun Swamy simply put it, this suggests that "the absence of political violence in the state is ultimately the result of at least some of the attributes of good government, themselves the product of competition."[138]

MGR's accession to power marked a shift in the politics of Tamil Nadu from one characteristically associated with issues relating to upward mobility to one in which social welfare policies became the hallmark of the state. A great shift from the past of the social policy in the state lies in that it was much more broadly based. MGR government, on one hand, began to target a few more subordinate social groups beyond the backward classes. A massive feeding programme has been successfully implemented toward all the children that came to be known as the Noon Meal Scheme. The extended social security provisions aimed at some particular groups such as poor women and widows, fishermen, rickshaw pullers etc. Even when the DMK split in 1972, the party and its electoral opponent, the ADMK, have been competing with each other on the Reservation Policies and relevant social policy issues.[139]

[138] Swamy, Arun R "Parties, Political Identities and the Absence of Mass Political Violence in South India " In *Community Conflicts and the State in India*, by Amrita Basu & Atul Kohli Delhi Oxford University Press, 1998 P 147

[139] Historically, there has been a rural/urban split between two groups

5.5.3 Summary

The 1980s and 90s has seen two transformations in the politics of UP: the upsurge in participation of the marginal groups, especially the lower castes, struggling for further political empowerment and the increasing dependence of various political parties on caste appeals to facilitate participation. It is interesting to see a similar version of lower-caste based demand politics in Tamil Nadu in the earlier years (from 1920s to 1960s). The emergence of this similar outcome, despite the different inheritances of the *Dalit* and OBC movements in these two states, can be explained by an analysis of the resource effects of the Reservation Policies in these two states. On one hand, the identification of OBCs as a new administrative category has created a necessary condition for gathering these communities as a single identity for mobilization purpose. The underrepresentation of these numerous groups in government and educational institutions, on the other hand, provided a major cause of political contest between the upper castes and lower castes.

However, Tamil Nadu has a relatively ordered lower-caste mobilization that is clearly missing in UP. Zoya Hasan emphasizes that the opening up of the institutional space to greater participation by marginal groups is vital. It is equally critical how this can be achieved.[140] Assuming that institutionalization could be enhanced by having competing parties with the prospect of their alternating in power, there are two routes that can be imagined through the policy effects. One route focuses on empowerment effect. By providing newly mobilized voters with a political identity and positions in the government and legislature for their aspiration, Reservation Policies have proved an institutional channel of incorporating new waves of voters. The 69% of the legislative seats were reserved for the backward castes in Tamil Nadu, within which Backward Class, Most Backward Class (MBC), Backward Class Christian, Backward Class Muslim, as well as Scheduled Castes and Tribes accounted for 23%, 20%, 3.5%, 3.5%,

---

[140] Hasan, Zoya. "Representation and Redistribution: The New Lower Caste Politics of North India ." In *Parties and Party Politics in India*, by Zoya Hasan. New Delhi: Oxford University Press, 2002.

17% and 1% respectively according to their population proportion in the state. (Table 5.9A) The reservation for the OBCs had already reached 25 percent in 1951 in TN while the first Backward Class Commission in Uttar Pradesh was held to identify a state-level OBC list more than twenty years later.[141] (Table 5.9B)

Table5.9A: Proportion of seats reserved in TN in Present Day

No.	Category	Percentage
1	Backward Class (BC)	23
2	Backward Class Christian (BCC)	3.50
3	Backward Class Muslim (BCM)	3.50
4	Most Backward Class (MBC)	20
5	Scheduled Caste (SC)	17
6	Scheduled Tribe (ST)	1
7	**Total**	**69**

Source: Govt. of Tamil Nadu

Table5.9B: Proportion of Seats Reserved in TN in 1951

No.	Category	Percentage
1	Open Competition	60
2	Scheduled Castes	15
3	Backward Classes	25

Source: Govt. of Tamil Nadu

The second route focuses on development effect. To adopt a development strategy by expanding spending on the welfare of backward castes not only helps improve the economic status of targeted beneficiaries but politically unify those with different caste and social backgrounds around the universal programmes. Today's Tamil Nadu has inherited much from an old tradition of promoting spending on the broad-based marginal groups that is clearly missing in

[141] The first Backward Class Commission in Uttar Pradesh , or Uttar Pradesh State Sarvadhik Pichhada Varg Ayog, was held from 1975 to 1977 with Sh. Chhedi Lal Sathi as Chairman.

UP.[142] The relatively generous and universal programs in Tamil Nadu, such as education scholarship for the populous lower-caste students and economic loans for the lower-caste businessmen, provide institutional avenues to meet the needs from cohesive SC/ST/OBC beneficiaries. Consequently, the Tamil Nadu government tends to see fewer social conflicts when compared with its counterpart in Uttar Pradesh where there are deep tensions between SC/STs and the OBCs. Bihar is another stronghold of OBC politics in the north. Like Uttar Pradesh, the politically empowered OBC groups belong to the upper strata of the OBCs who did not take any economic and social measures in favor of the non-elite categories. Actually, the south was several decades earlier than the north tackled the demand of lower castes and worked out solutions to these demands. That's probably why it was yet to see an orderly OBC movement in Uttar Pradesh and Bihar.

5.6 Conclusion

To some extent, the caste version of demand politics in India has instigated political contention about resource distribution. Lower castes became increasingly vocal in politics through the system of reservations, which guarantee seats in government, access to educational institutions and employment in the administration for selected segments of society.

The particular group rights and benefit allocation remain a source of conflict between those who support them and those who oppose them On one hand, the reservations are perceived as creating fission and conflicts among the caste groups who protested for political and economic benefits of the Reservation Policies (RPs). The Mandal recommendations approved by the central government had consolidated castes in two camps of forward and backward. Caste polarization

[142] According to Dreze and Sen (1989), promotive measures in social policy refer to the expansion of basic capabilities of population, and will have to be seen primarily as a long-run challenge It can be compared with protective social policies which are concerned with protection from a decline in living standards as might occur in unexpected circumstances, such as economic recession or famine Dreze J and Sen, A K *Hunger and Public Action* Oxford University Press, 1989

became fierce.[143] On the other hand, the system of reservations on a caste basis were seen as a matter of social justice for victims of the Brahmin dominated caste system and thus provide a coalition link among various non-Brahmin caste communities. The new caste polarization has provided a basis for cooperation between the OBCs with other subordinate caste groups such as SC/STs, though in north the level of cooperation has been relatively low.

The term of "Other Backward Classes" has been successfully created and was substantially used in the politics of India. *Yadav* argues that "the expression "OBC" has [...] travelled a long way from a rather less bureaucratic nomenclature in the document of the Constitution to a vibrant and subjectively experienced political community."[144] This newly created political demand group manifested itself in different mobilizational forms at state level. In some circumstances, it developed at expense of other mobilized groups; under other conditions, it facilitated the process otherwise.

Tamil Nadu manifests a pattern of caste region relationship. The non-Brahman movement dealt with the issue of regional identity right from the beginning of 1920s. Just as this movement sought to effect a fusion of many non-Brahman castes, it also aspired to build a "southern" identity opposed to "north".[145] Thus, caste-region interaction in Tamil Nadu strengthened an exclusionary regional nationalism. It also sought to delegitimize Brahmans not only from their superior caste position, but also from the scope of regional identity. In Uttar Pradesh, "...this silent revolution ...was based on the quota strategy, an incremental approach to social change that eventually prevailed at the expense of *Kisan* politics."[146] V. P. Singh and his logic to "transfer of power from elite groups to the subalterns" were unwelcomed by Charan Singh and his disciples because it can lead to the possible divisions between the rich farmers, represented by the Jat

---

[143] The consolidation is only to an extent

[144] *Yadav*, Yogendra "Reconfiguration in Indian politics State Assembly Election 1993-95 " *Economic and Political Weekly* 31, no 2 and 3 (January 1996) 95-104 P 102

[145] Partly this was due to non-Brahmin identity Both were the descendents of Aryan northern Indians, and this larger issue untied all castes across the forward and backward communities

[146] Jaffrelot, Christophe *India's Silent Revolution the Rise of the Lower Castes in North India* New York Columbia University Press, 2003 P 350 This incremental approach is much faster than Madvas and with adult franchise (i e more lower caste votes)

community, and the lower agricultural class as well as exacerbate differences between the better-off OBCs and SC/STs.

In north India in the late 1980s and 1990s, the OBC and SC/ST leaders, such as Mulayam Singh *Yadav*, Laloo *Yadav*, Kanshi Ram and Mayawat, began to rise from below, often in competition with each other. Nonetheless, these and other lower caste leaders often make or break coalitions in power. In the three national elections held between 1996 and 1999, the various parties explicitly representing lower castes, in the aggregate, received between 18 to 20 per cent of the national vote, as against 20-25 per cent for the BJP, and 23-29 per cent for the Congress party. However, the ambiguity of the Reservation Policies on identification of OBCs also provides chances for the political parties and elite lower castes to manipulate. The next chapter will take a look at the interest groups and party politics in India with the analysis of the Reservation Policies and its interpretative effects.

Chapter 6

Interpretive Effect of Reservation Policies:

The Elites' Role in the Lower-Caste Mobilization

Executive Summary: In this chapter I examine the hierarchy of interpretative privilege within the judiciary, administrative and political arenas in regards to Reservation Policies. I especially look at the political elites and political parties. The case studies from West Bengal and Tamil Nadu indicate the varied outcomes of the various mobilization strategies of the political parties. All in all, I argue the mobilizing pattern of the OBCs relies on the interpretation of the elite groups on the targeting, distribution and administrative process of Reservation Policies.

6.1 Introduction

Access to the public resources depends largely on whether a person has some knowledge of the complex structures and processes of decision-making and implementation. Those who are aware and have access to the political system all held positions to use it to their advantage than those who are ignorant of them. The awareness of mass publics about Reservation Policies (RPs), in the case of India, has been largely manipulated by the political elites.[147] This chapter mainly focuses on the interpretative effect of political elites over the reservation issue.

Post-Mandal scenario brought a remarkable change in the assertion of the politics of Other Backward Classes (OBCs). Identifying with their newly created category and realizing the significance of their numerical strength, the OBCs became actively involved in the voting process against the upper-caste dominance in politics. This helped them to transform themselves into an interest group. "Now that every party is wooing the deprived classes, with every round of

[147] The elite-dominance in India has become much less after the democratic upsurge in the 1980s.

elections more and more representatives of the deprived sections will be elected. This will ultimately be reflected in the social composition of the local bodies, state governments, and the central government. A silent transfer of power is taking place in social terms."[148]

Yet, the political reality was much more complicated than what V. P. Singh envisaged. In last chapter, resource effects of RPs were analyzed through the logic: you give us benefits, we give you votes. With the emergence of caste politics, lower castes increasingly influenced the political system. More specifically, the scarce and unequally distributed government benefits have contributed to the political contention in India. Policies to benefit the poor were usually stillborn or administered in such the way that they help the better-off strata of the poor. Politicking over scarce resources was controlled under the dominating patterns of the elites. "The openness and competitiveness of the political arena worked primarily to ensure that different segments of the elite could get a share of state resources and build their patronage networks."[149]As a result, whether or not the resources can be delivered to the real mass public relies on the interpretation of these elite groups over the targeting, distribution and administrative process of certain public policies.

This chapter is organized as follows: Section II outlines the theoretical thinking over the interpretative effects of public policies on the political behavior of the masses. In section III, the Indian context is introduced in which the Reservation Policies(RPs) were designed and implemented. The role of the political parties is specially emphasized in the context of divisive politics of India. Section IV explores the interpreters of RPs in three arenas: the court system, the state administration as well as the political party system. The behavior and characteristics of the interpreters are explored in these three arenas that secure the manipulation over political participation of the backward castes. In section V, the mobilization strategies of some major

[148] V P Singh "Power and Equality –Changing Grammars of Indian Politics", cited from Jaffrelot, Christophe *India's Silent Revolution the Rise of the Lower Castes in North India* New York Columbia University Press, 2003 P 350
[149] Church, Roderick "Chapter 9 Conclusion The Pattern of State Politics in Indira Gandhi's India " In *State Politics in Contemporary India Crisis or Continuity?*, by John R Boulder and London Westview Press, 1984

political parties are introduced. Section VI is about the case studies of Tamil Nadu and West Bengal to compare the political ideologies of caste-based and class-based political parties. I examine how the political party elites dealt with the OBC identification and benefit distribution along caste or class lines from which the voters formulate preferences across political parties. In the conclusion section, I reemphasize the influencing chain of elite interpretation on the political behavior of the mass publics.

This chapter draws essentially from a double set of quantitative data. The first set is provided by the Election Commission of India. I used the data to examine the voting patterns for some states at the constituency level. The second set originates from the National Election Study (NES), conducted by the Centre for Study of Developing Societies (CSDS). Some segmented qualitative analyses, combined with the electoral data from CSDS and Election Commission of India, are provided to crosscheck some hypotheses on this topic.

6.2 A Theoretical Consideration on the Interpretation Effects of Public Policies

In chapter 4, it is argued that the identification of Reservation Policies (RPs) has an impact on group formation based on the analyses of the constitutional articles and government-assigned commissions. In this chapter, the process of identification is further explored through the political practices of elite groups who are the major interpreters of the RPs.

Pierson (1993) states that interpretive effects of public policy can inform the mass public of their place in the political system, alert them to their stake in policy matters, and shape their feelings of political efficacy.[150] The literature on social construction of target groups also state that policies convey messages to the public about their worth as citizens and their role in the democratic polity.[151] Gramsci (1971) emphasizes the hegemonic role of the messengers of the

[150] Pierson, Paul. "When Effect Becomes Cause, Policy Feedback and Political Change." *World Politics*, 1993: 595-628.
[151] Schneider, Helen Ingram and Anne. "The Social Construction of Target populations: Implication for politics and policy " *The American Political Science Review* 87, no. 2 (1993): 334-347.

policy effects. He reasons that so long as the economically powerful had control over the cultural means of a society – its language, education and arts – they could establish hegemony over the subaltern sections of the society and essentially obfuscate the subalterns about their own interests.[152]

Among all the elite interpreters that have impacts on the political actions of the mass publics, the role of party leaders is the most direct. How do the benefit-seeking voters choose between competing political parties vying for their vote? "..the voting decision…is characterized by severe information constraints. These information constraints…induced voters and politicians to favor co-ethnics in the delivery of benefits and votes."[153] Faced with a choice between parties, voters, especially the lower-caste voters make decisions based on whether the party can represent their "own" caste category and whether it can distribute generously to its supporters both material and status benefits. The party leaders, therefore, should design and explain well the electoral propagandas and party ideology in order to obtain as many supporters as possible. For example, Mayawati, UP Chief Minister and the leader of Dalit party BSP sensed discontent in the Brahmin community ahead of the 2012 UP assembly elections. In order to woo the community back into BSP's fold, Mayawati wrote letters in the mid-September of 2011 to Prime Minister Manmohan Singh, demanding for constitutional amendment for introducing reservation for poor members of the upper castes and Muslims. She not only attempted to enlarge the coverage of Reservation that includes poor upper castes and Muslims, but also strived to promote quotas in private sector and other government or semi-government services as well.[154] Mayawati's behavior is being seen as an effort to strike a balance in her "Sarvjan vote bank" (all people vote bank) which comprises *Dalits*, most backward classes as well as *Brahmins* and Muslims.

, Ingram, Anne Schneider and Helen *The impact of policy for Democracy* University of Kansas Press, 1997

[152] Gramsci, A 1971 Selections from the Prison Notebooks In Q Hoare and G N Smith (eds), London Lawrence & Wishart

[153] Chandra, Kanchan. *Why Ethnic Parties Succeed* New York Cambridge University Press, 2004 P 12

[154] Mayawati writes to PM, demands quota for upper caste poor *The Statesman* September 19 , 2011 http //thestatesman net/index php?option=com_content&view=article&id=383795&catid=36

Uttar Pradesh is not the only case in the northern states that seemed obsessed with the Mandalization of politics over the past two decades. In Bihar, Lalu Prasad's Rashtriya Janata Dal (RJD, "National People's Party") and Ram Vilas Paswan's Lok Janshakti Party (LJP) promised 10 percent reservation of government jobs for economically backward upper caste members in their joint manifesto for the state's assembly polls in 2010. [155]

In this chapter, I focus on the political and administrative elites and their interpretive roles in the Reservation Policies (RPs) for the Backward Classes (BCs). I summarize the interpreters' characteristics that secure the manipulation over political participation of the backward castes. I mainly explain the interpreters' behavior in three arenas: judiciary system, the government agencies, and the political party politics. Because voters have limited information about government efforts, the elites can manipulate the contents and flow of policy information for their own interests.

Then I apply the model to the case studies in Tamil Nadu and West Bengal in India, with an emphasis on the political party elites. I focus on the regional parties (the Dravida Munnetra Kazagham (DMK) and All India Anna Dravida Munnetra Kazhagam (AIADMK)) in Tamil Nadu and the Communist Party of India (Marxist) (CPM) in West Bengal. These two states have shown widely diverging patterns over the interpretation of the RPs. The former state was dominated by the regional parties which consistently promoted the Dravidian Movement and preferential policies for the lower-caste electorate for many decades. The Left party CPM and its alliance in West Bengal also constantly worked on the welfare of the subaltern sections of the society, yet tended to target them along the class lines instead of castes. Both were successful in promoting their agenda in the past elections.[156]

---

[155] Jha, Giridhar. "Upper Caste Voters Gain Prominence as Frantic Parties Woo Them with Sops." *India Today*. October 24, 2010. http://indiatoday.intoday.in/story/upper-caste-voters-gain-prominence-as-frantic-parties-woo-them-with-sops/1/117559.html.

[156] After 34 years of uninterrupted Marxist rule, the CPM in West Bengal was defeated in the 2011 election by the Trinamool Congress partly due to its ignorance of farmers' needs in the Singur and Nandigram movements.

6.3 Divisive Politics and the Reservation Policies

In India, the act of voting has always been characterized by the identities of the citizens – along the lines of religion, caste or language. Although the elections after 1990s appeared to be moving India towards a bi-polar polity at center, the fragmentation process of the electorate and party system is still progressing, "partly and firstly by the distorting effect of the majoritarian electoral system, as well as by the growing propensity of various social groups to vote according to regional and ethnic identities."[157]

It is argued that reservation provisions for lower castes are an attempt to create a permanent division in the political society on caste lines. Before Independence, the British rulers had devised a system of separate electorates based on religion, caste and region, thereby intensifying the division of Indian society and weakening the Independence movement. Although the framers of the Indian Constitution aimed to enhance integrity of the nation and secularism, the reservations for the new categories such as "OBCs", "SCs" and "STs" have had a long-term divisive impact even after one hundred years. The problems relating to caste and religion have become so acute that no political leaders or parties dare to contest the election without maneuvering caste groups in the constituencies.

However, the Reservation Policies came into play through the intermediate variable -the political parties. After Independence, the use of caste as a vote catching device during elections has continuously played an important role in deciding the fate of the candidates in elections. For instance, the Congress Party, which once enjoyed the support of almost all the communities due to their leadership in the freedom movement. The party leaders thus had to search for alternative measures beyond the "all-inclusion" strategy. The Congress Party developed a crack on caste lines, giving rise to factionalism that reflected a contest among a set of elite leaders. In 1957 in

---

[157] Verniers, Christophe Jaffrelot and Gilles. "India's 2009 Elections: The Resilience of Regionalism and Ethnicity." *South Asia Multidisciplinary Academic Journal, 3*, 2009: http://samaj.revues.org/index2787.html .

Bihar, for example, the defeat of A.N.Sinha, a *Rajput* by Dr.S.K.Sinha of *Bhumihar* caste during a contest for the leadership of Congress Legislative Party in Bihar Assembly divided the party to such an extent that the *Rajputs* started deserting the party, even though both came from the higher castes. Later K.B.Sahay belonging to *Kayastha* community and B. N. Jha, a Brahmin aggravated the factionalism in the party.

The "caste" card was played prevalently in the 1990s.[158] V. P. Singh, who aimed to transfer political power from the elite groups to the subalterns through the Mandal affairs, ignited the "caste war" again across India. During the elections in the post-Mandal period, all the major political parties had to release more seat tickets to the lower castes. They began selecting candidates from the subordinate castes, with goal of gaining votes among the lower-caste groups in the constituencies. For instance, till 1984 elections in Bihar, it had been the *Bhumihars, Rajputs, Kayasthas* and *Brahmins* (economically dominant upper caste groups) who manipulated their political hegemony. Now it is the turn of the Backward Castes (usually who have acquired access to money and land) under the leadership of dominant OBC *Yadavs* who have a prominent voice in policy. The OBC leaders have entered the politics across India. For example, the OBCs in the eastern U.P. and *Jats* in the western U.P., *Patels* and *Rajputs* in Gujarat, Marathas in Maharashtra, *Reddys, Khammas* and *Kapus* in Andhra Pradesh, *Lingayats* and *Vokkaligas* in Karnataka, *Thevars, Vanniyars, Pallars* in Tamil Nadu are the dominant caste groups and they have gained /are gaining and maintaining the political hegemony during elections.

Although the political parties had to continuously make efforts to capture caste votes in the pro-reservation environment, they still have autonomy to interpret the policy to make it more compatible with their political ideology and vote-getting strategies. In the languages of divisive politics, public policies can be interpreted differently along the lines of region, religion and caste according to the needs of various political parties.

---

[158] "Caste"cards have always been played. Difference in the 1990s is the appeal to lower castes.

In the Constitution, OBCs are described as "socially and educationally backward classes", and the government is enjoined to ensure their social and educational development. The political parties, at different points of history, also have different ways of dealing with this obscurely termed caste group. Prime Minister Nehru's Congress Party refused to consider OBC reservations in northern and western India in the 1950s, fearing the creation of divisions of the national politics. However, under the leadership of Indira Gandhi in the 1960s and 70s, the Congress (I) governments in northern and western states such as Gujarat and Madhya Pradesh began to appoint commissions to establish OBC reservations. To attract OBC votes became especially obvious after the Congress lost votes from both the *Brahmins* and the *Dalits*. On the other hand, the Socialists always made a special appeal to the backward castes on the ground that the interests of castes and classes coincide. Rammanohar Lohia initially recognized that caste, more than class, was the huge stumbling block to India's progress. Later he became the proponent of affirmative action, comparing it to turning the earth to foster a better crop. He urged the upper castes "to voluntarily serve as the soil for lower castes to flourish and grow". But he failed because caste was the major source of identification for most Indians.

In the following section, the interpreters of the Reservation Policies in three arenas – judiciary system, government agencies as well as political party system –will be examined. These elite groups are the major sources of the interpretation of the Reservation Policies, based on which the subaltern people shaped their perception and political behavior.

6.4 Reservation Policies and the Interpreters

The elite groups can most effectively influence perception and political behavior of the mass publics. According to the elite theory, the political elites can influence the policy decision of governments and secure their interpretive power over the implementation of the policies, because they have personal resources, such as intelligence and skills, and a vested interest in the government.

In the Indian context, the interpreters have a larger manipulating space in the arena of Reservation Policies. The Independence movement has produced many organized interest groups, who are now in ruling positions, including urban capitalists, bureaucrats, intellectuals and professionals. The independence movement, however, did little to organize the interests of the poor peasant and landless laborers. While the government has been made as an arena for the politically powerful, it continues to be the "paternalist regime" for the less articulate and less politically forceful communities. In this situation, those who benefit from the exclusive access are likely to see the stability and perpetuation of the caste structure of inequality. For instance, the high Marathas show a substantially greater ability to get familiar with the electoral procedures, and access to government system in comparison with the low Marathas, Mahars and SCs.[159] The powerful elite groups, as introduced in the following subsections, have all play roles in interpreting the Reservation Policies with the aim to stabilize their existent "paternalist regime".

6.4.1 Judiciary System and it's Interpretative Power

In the case of identifying the beneficiaries of Reservation Policies (RPs), what the states do is increasingly subjected to the examination of the courts. Courts have thus become the "official" interpreter of the constitutional articles as they are supposed to be related to the "Backward Classes". It has been the Supreme Court rather than the central government that have the unifying and limiting influence over this controversial term. Presumably any new central policy pertaining to the compensatory discrimination has to be shaped in light of the judicial predominance.

According to the Constitution of India, the Supreme Court is at the apex of India's unified, hierarchical judiciary, with the power influencing the decisions of the High Courts and through

[159] Lele, Jayant. *Elite Pluralism and Class Rule. Political Development in Maharashtra, India* Toronto: University of Toronto Press, 1981.

them to all inferior courts.[160] It is the guardian of the Constitution and has a limited original jurisdiction, notably to issue writs to prevent violations of Fundamental Rights. At state level, the High Court exercises an extensive jurisdiction to review the lower courts.[161] "The Indian judicial structure, as we have seen, is more unified, more pyramidal, and more heavily weighted at the top than, for example its American counterpart."[162]

The higher judiciary in India enjoys enormous respect, as it is the arbiter of the governmental action, being independent. "The higher judiciary served not only as vindicator [defender] of Fundamental Rights, but as the single most persistent and significant agency of criticism of government operation of terms of constitutional norms."[163] On the cases pertaining to compensatory discrimination, the courts have been critical of government arrangements due to the intense political and social controversy involved. States drew most of the critical response on the issues of RPs from India's court system. In a total of 113 reported litigations about compensatory discrimination from 1950 to 1977, among the 57 litigations concerning preferential treatment conferred by the state governments, the courts ruled against the state governments in 24. But in 10 cases involving central preferences, they ruled against the Center in only 3.[164]

Since the Reservation Policies (RPs) benefits are mainly distributed through three channels: legislative branches, government offices and educational institutions, the Supreme Court deals almost exclusively with these three kinds of disputes. According to the statistics Marc Galanter collected, there were about 10 cases concerning the problems of reservation by state governments in South India for admission of OBCs in professional colleges (especially medical institutions); 5 cases over the promotion posts in the central services (especially Railways and the Central Secretariat) for SC/STs; 14 cases on the challenges to elections to legislative seats reserved for

---

[160] Supreme Court is the highest appellate court in all matters of criminal, civil and constitutional law Its authority extends to state as well as central law

[161] Below the High Courts are a hierarchy of subordinate courts such as the civil courts, family courts, criminal courts and various other district courts

[162] Glanter, Marc *Competing Equality Law and the Backward Classes in India* Berkkeley University of California Press, 1984 P 495

[163] Ibid P 482

[164] Ibid pp 482-7

SC/STs. These three strands of litigation account for 29 of the 38 cases that the Supreme Court has encountered the affirmative action policy.[165]

A judicial decision has interpretive effects on the process of policy forming and implementation of RPs. The government administrators and policy makers have to be responsive to the order of the court. They have either to modify/remove those specific features of the RP schemes which the court has found objectionable or carry out specific directions of the court. However, such relations between the courts and the state governments may become more complex according to the different state-level situations. Some states had continued to ignore the central governments' recommendations and Supreme Court's decision over the make-up of the Backward Classes (BCs). Tamil Nadu government is one of those states that had frequently to deal with the orders from the Supreme Court and that have become the instance of sustained resistance. The state maintained its system of communal quotas in distributing government posts. It has the highest percentage of reservations at 69%, which is much above the 50% ceiling fixed by the Supreme Court.

In contrast, there are other state governments that successively modified its BC order to conform to a succession of High Court judgments and then to the judgment of the Supreme Court. Karnataka is a case in point. As early as 1963, the relatively prosperous and politically dominant groups had been using the provisions for BCs for their own advantage. In order not to violate the commands of the courts, the state adopted the income/occupation tests of backwardness and a system of interview marks, which combine the communal considerations and secular and non-ascriptive criteria.

Since litigations transform a settled policy into an open issue, the results of litigations in the original place may influence the related institutions and people in other states.[166] For example, the Balaji litigation in Mysore (Karnataka) stimulated petitions in Andhra Pradesh and Kerala. The

---

[165] Glanter, Marc *Competing Equality Law and the Backward Classes in India* Berkkeley University of California Press, 1984 pp 506-7

[166] Litigation is the act or process of bringing or contesting a legal action in court

Supreme Court not only reinforced central government policy, but also served as an instrument for bringing the states into conformity with it. For instance, when the Center had urged the state governments to establish the state lists of OBCs, the Supreme Court adopted the centrally-favored economic criteria. Before 1965, Gujarat and Maharashtra had retained caste units without considering the scholarship arena. Punjab not only retained the caste test without the scholarship criteria, but also employed a list of communities where scholarship and income were criteria. Orissa had no schemes of its own for OBCs, Assam and West Bengal had none other than scholarships. Karnataka (Mysore) and Andhra Pradesh, with a high level of benefits to OBCs, adopted non-communal tests. In 1965, all eight states eventually complied with the centrally-favored economic criteria.[167]

Through the interpretive impacts on the policy-making and implementation process of Reservation Policies (RPs), the court orders also have effects on the interest groups of various kinds, and finally on various sections of the public. As a matter of fact, the interpretive influence of the courts may bring about the convergence or disintegration of interests at the same time. Marc Galanter has a specific explanation on this point.

"The striking down of a scheme may disarm groups that enjoyed a reservation. Since these groups sometimes have little to unify them other than the reservation itself, the loss of the reservation may dissolve them into a series of disparate elements with conflicting views on what the new scheme ought to be. On the other hand, the expectation of success in litigation may bring together groups to oppose the existing scheme. A new policy of reservation s may reflect (or generate)a new convergence of interests." [168]

For example, the Balaji litigation that shifted caste criterion to economic test tacitly changed the alignment of beneficiaries in Mysore (Karnataka). Before Balaji litigation, the thrust for

[167] But Andhra Pradesh reverted to caste units less than a year later as Mysore did more than a decade later. These data were cited fromGlanter, Marc. *Competing Equality Law and the Backward Classes in India* Berkkeley: University of California Press, 1984. pp.506-7

[168] Glanter, Marc *Competing Equality Law and the Backward Classes in India* Berkkeley: University of California Press, 1984. P528

identifying OBCs has gathered the poor non-*Brahmins* with a great multitude It was mainly *Brahmins* communities who opposed the policy through litigation. After the criteria have changed to economic tests, the new standard had included not only the politically dominant middle castes, but *Brahmins* also became the major beneficiaries of this policy. As a result, the middle castes began to align with the *Brahmins*, their most determined and resourceful opponents, and shift the burden (here of exclusion from medical colleges, etc.) to those least likely to mount a campaign against them. Eventually, the lower groups had politically to mobilize against the extensive benefits enjoyed by the wealthy OBC *Lingayats*.

To sum up, the effects of the court interpretation over the compensatory discrimination can be described in three aspects: even-distribution, flexibility and conformation. Firstly, the court system has prevented the unlimited expansion of OBC category and the unevenly diffusion of RP benefits by capping the total reservation percentage to 50 % and by setting the economic criteria. Secondly, the courts encouraged flexibility of compensatory discrimination by keeping open options that the beneficiaries do not have to be selected by some single pre-ordained criterion. "They have rejected both the 'modernist' view that communal units are impermissible and the 'historical' view that only communal units may be used to designate BCs, in favor of the "elastic" view that enables the government to utilize a variety of ways of selecting BCs."[169] Thirdly, all the above requirements suggest the role of the court system in India as an agent disseminating the central government's policy and overseeing its implementation at state level. Marc Galanter states that "These requirements have not only institutionalized periodic reassessment and encouraged collection of information which may facilitate better administration, but they have clearly contributed to making discourse on the subject of Backward Classes more precise and cogent."[170]

However, the interpretation of courts did not make the policy making and implementation of the RPs as explicitly as expected. Firstly, judges, who have the interpretive and deciding

[169] Ibid. P528
[170] Ibid. P534

advantage of dealing with concrete factual situations, can only work on the related cases from the normative learning about that society. Secondly, partly because of the incomprehensive and inconsistent understanding of the judges over the RP issues, there is still abiding confusion surrounding the main identification criteria of the backward classes: whether to use castes as the units that are deemed backward, or to use economic standing and educational status as measures of backwardness. Despite their general disapproval of caste criteria, the courts have given little guidance to discuss what alternative units can be used as criteria and what kind of tests can be used to select the real backward.

Thirdly, while promoting non-communal (economic and educational) tests of backwardness, the courts have not indicated clearly how these tests can be assessed and how these can be reconciled with communal unit tests. Fourthly, because of their concern with the abuses and excesses of RPs, the courts tend to treat all the "to be considered" caste groups uniformly. Yet, despite of their recognition that backwardness comes in kinds and degrees, the government limitations set by the courts could hamper the flexibility of government schemes for the backward at the state level. Fifthly, notwithstanding its independence, the judiciary is inevitably embroiled in battles between contending political and social forces. The disputes over RP benefit distribution do sometimes become a focus of group or communal struggle. As a result, the plural requirements by the courts have not lessened the interpretive ambiguity and incoherence of the RPs.

6.4.2 Various State Versions of the Reservation Policies

The courts act as a check instead of an expediter of the cases involving Reservation Policies (RPs). Although the courts have to oversee that the governments' behavior is consistent with constitutional boundaries, the main lines of policy formation and implementation –the use, extent, method, recipients, duration and administration –lie with the government. The Articles 15(4) and 16(4) suggest that the framers of the Constitution should rely primarily on the discretion of the politicians and administrators as they are major decision makers instead of the courts. These provisions give the executive and the legislature broad discretion in their application.

In practice, the implementation of the RPs is the arena where government officials could select backward classes and deliver benefits by their own standards. The Indian governments have not been very forthcoming with information. The problem is compounded by the lack of reliable information gathering apparatus and by the lack of impartial officials in charge of the implementation. Thus, the danger of distortion becomes greater if the rules have to be applied by a host of administrators making efforts to privatize the benefits.

Politicians enter the public sphere with the intention of controlling it and having their specific interests safeguarded through governmental action. As the privatizing of public resources is forbidden, the major mechanism for political manipulation therefore has to be patronage. It links the interests, rank, and activities of the elites to the appropriate levels of government. It is "an ability to retain the legal limits without losing exclusive control over the resource," which implies "a high level of political sophistication and skills of manipulating a variety of rules, regulations, and personalities."[171]

At the lowest level of the power hierarchy are the village leaders. They are educated and own considerable properties such as several acres of land and cattle. They either occupy positions within the government or maintain a patron-client relationship with someone occupying such a position. Village leaders may be the leaders of alliances, such as the leaders of Panchayat Raj (i.e. local self-governing body) or farm co-operatives. They are in the position to deliver or help deliver the RP schemes such as choosing teachers, distributing the old-age pensions and public housing funds etc.; and thus are able to monopolize or get access to the preferential goods and services formally destined by the state for general distribution.

[171] Lele, Jayant. *Elite Pluralism and Class Rule Political Development in Maharashtra, India* Toronto: University of Toronto Press, 1981. P117.

At a higher level of the power hierarchy such as that of district level and state level, the district magistrates and state ministers can access to the government resources in one way or another without breaking the line between the legal and illegal. Patronage usually takes the indirect form at the higher level of government agencies. For instance, a senior alliance leader at district or state level can create opportunities for his loyal supporters to directly get access to public resources. The bureaucracy can also play a role to block the supporters of rival alliances or promote supporters from friendly alliances. Jayant Lele concludes the patronage at the higher level of the governments as the following: "the hierarchical organization of bureaucratic units allows for greater use of indirect patronage at each higher level and gives higher-level alliance leaders greater access to negative sanctions through the use of formal and legal or bureaucratic and regulatory structures."[172]

6.4.3 Caste Identifications, Backward Caste Elites, and Reservation Policies

Judges have independent decision power over the interpretation of Reservation Policies (RPs) but have to rely strictly upon the Constitutional articles. In addition, the judges relate aloof to the factual situation of the Backward Classes (BCs) and thus are unable to fully realize the complexity of the identification process. The overwhelming majority of the Indian judges have been selected from prosperous and high status families. They are educated in elite institutions, have had distinguished professional careers and have very little political involvement. As a result, the interpretative role of judges has been the least disputable but most rigid.

In the post-1980s period, the Supreme Court devised an innovative way wherein a person or a civil society group could approach it seeking legal remedies in cases where public interest is at stake.[173] But the impact of judges' interpretation on the mass public is often indirect. The rules they design have to be implemented through the state administrators and bureaucrats. The administrators, at various levels of governments, are able to influence the distribution of RPs by

[172] Ibid. P117.

[173] The public can be involved either by filing a Writ Petition or by addressing a letter to Hon'ble the Chief Justice.

privatizing the benefits through patronage networks. Although they are empowered to access government resources, their impacts on the mass public have to be related with the backward caste elites who organize the mobilization of the real demand groups.

The backward caste elites not only have sufficient space to interpret the orders from courts and administrators, but have direct and strong links with the demand groups. The backward caste movement began in south India early in the last century and became a major political force across India by the first quarter of this century. The movements were initiated and led by the upper strata of the backward castes. Having improved economic conditions thanks to the change in agrarian structure and access to education, these backward caste elites, mainly landed peasantry, launched struggles for sanskritization in the social hierarchy and political power in the political hierarchy on caste lines.[174] They came together under the banner of backward castes, and mobilized the lower strata of the backward castes for enlarged support in the political sphere. These backward caste elites articulated political and economic demands for .the backward caste communities, mobilized caste members for a show of strength in the elections, and pressured the government to get greater influential political positions in state assemblies, cabinet and public institutions. Simultaneously, they pressed the government for reservations in government jobs and educational institutions.

Although they represent the common interests of the backward castes, these elite groups are primarily interested in serving their own political interests. They follow the same Brahminical ideology adhering to hierarchy and status, symbols and the idioms of the upper castes. Some studies show that the benefits of reservation are cornered by the more advanced sections of the backward communities.[175] Caste sentiments and solidarity are a means to political and economic power for them.

---

[174] Sanskritization refers to lower castes' emulating behavior of upper castes

[175] For example, see Shah, Ghanshyam. "Social backwardness and politics of reservation." *Economic and Political Weekly* 26, no. 11-12 (1991): 601-10.

The backward caste elites constitute the major links between patronage-based administrators and the demand groups. For the dual purposes of mobilizing electoral support as well as acquiring positions in the legislature and executive branches, may have established local political parties. On one hand, the primary function performed by the party organization is that of screening the applications of the leading candidates to various contests in the governmental sectors. Each political party seeks to place its own political leaders in the major policymaking offices of the government, thereby giving them the right to decide in the name of the entire political society.

On the other hand, the major political parties have to appeal to the lower caste groups to win elections. Through the party competition, these emerging lower-caste groups can be organized to compete with the established groups for political power and direct control of the governments. In most cases, the act of voting for the majority of the unprivileged sectors is usually the assertion of loyal relationships on caste lines. "Tradition becomes a manipulative strategy of rulership for the elite who control the political system to which they must deny access to others."[176] "Ritual voting" is especially predominant in the rural setting in India where kinship and caste are the primary contexts of a voting decision. For instance, the elite Marathas in Maharashtra can make effective use of the numerical strength of their caste community. The low Marathas faithfully deliver their votes to a candidate preferred by the dominant faction leaders. The elite can also expect patrimonially sanctioned compliance from the lower-caste members of their factions, and in turn, provide benefits to the lower castes as rewards in their loyalty.

The source of the loyal relationships between the supporters and the political parties come further from the propagandas and policy objectives that are designed by the party leaders. At a glance of Indian post-independent electoral politics, we can see how each party tried to carve out and consolidate a social constituency of its own. After the Mandal policy implementation in the 1990s, the focus of the major parties had to shift towards a large number of backward

---

[176] Lele, Jayant. *Elite Pluralism and Class Rule Political Development in Maharashtra, India* Toronto: University of Toronto Press, 1981.P.85.

communities. In order to win over these newly politicized caste groups, the political parties have to make their political ideology more compatible with that of the backward castes. For instance, the Congress party, whose leadership was drawn from the upper castes, provided protection and benefits to the targeted backward caste groups. The composition of the Congress leadership has changed sometimes to provide a greater voice to the backward castes. The lower-caste voters would for candidates from their own milieu, instead of supporting the traditional Congress notables. The BJP, another political party with high caste leadership, was forced to support Mandal to keep itself competitive.

As a result, the political parties, with their interpretive power directly working on the backward castes, have cultivated the caste-based divisions in the political system. In the 1990s in India, the political parties have made conscious efforts to carve out their respective constituencies among the different caste groups.[177] This approach used by the political parties to expand their political influence was seen as the ethnification of politics. Politicization of caste is an illustration of that.

6.5 The Mobilization Strategies of Political Parties: Congress Party, JD, BJP and CPM

In the following analysis of caste politicization, I use the "political party variable" - which party came to power or was in a majority in the assembly- to explain the politicization of OBC communities. The mobilization strategies of the political parties toward the lower castes can be manifested itself in its influence on the OBC representation in the assembly: whichever party has come to power in the post-Mandal period has maintained a high level of OBC MLAs. For instance, the electoral success of the 1993 alliance between the Samajwadi Party (an OBC-oriented party) and the BSP in Uttar Pradesh (UP), led by *Dalits*, accounts for the comparatively

[177] Here I quote Kanchan Chandra's definition of caste groups: it refers to the nominal members of an ascriptive cateogyr such as race, language, caste, tribe, or religion.

smaller proportion of upper-caste MLAs and a larger percentage of OBC MLAs in the UP assembly.

Looking back to the 1990s, I analyze the changes of representation of the various castes in government ruled by the Congress party, the Janata Dal, Bharatiya Janata Party (BJP) and CPM. Until the early 1990s, the Congress party had been in the dominant position in India's electoral politics. It was regarded as a "catch-all party" with its formula lying upon the capacity to encompass contending social groups, like the upper castes, the SC/STs, and the Muslims. This capacity of rallying the "coalition of extremes" has guaranteed the dominance of Congress Party in Indian politics for almost four decades. According to the all India opinion polls conducted by the CSDS, the Congress party was able to attract between 35.8% and 50.5% of the voters from any social group till the 1980s. As an opinion poll survey carried out after the 1989 elections shows that the Congress (I) won 39.5% of the valid votes, among which 41% of the *Brahmins*, 44.2% of the SCs/STs and 45.8% of the Muslims offered their support toward the Congress (I), which means a very small number of OBC voters voted for the Congress.[178]

The Congress lost its dominance, however, by the competition from its rival parties in the early 1990s and the loss of support from the lower end of the social spectrum. The 1990s witnessed an erosion of the Congress attraction amongst all sections. The Janata Dal party, the BJP and a large number of regional parties were the chief beneficiaries of this disintegration of the social coalition. It can be seen that the Other Backward Classes (OBCs) have reduced their support most dramatically from the Congress (I) after 1980s, dropping half the way from 42% in 1980 to 21.7% in 1996 Afterwards, the major political parties began to openly appeal to caste

[178] Verniers, Christophe Jaffrelot and Gilles "India's 2009 Elections The Resilience of Regionalism and Ethnicity " *South Asia Multidisciplinary Academic Journal, 3,* 2009 http //samaj revues org/index2787 html

identities central to their political programs. This phenomenon was defined by Chandra (2004) as the ethnification of Indian politics, which took place especially in the north India.[179]

The Janata Dal party, in order to bring together all the centrist parties opposed to the Rajiv Gandhi government (1984-1989), tried to build its own social constituency mainly for the OBC groups.[180] Focusing on the social justice-related issues and the implementation of Mandal Recommendations, V. P. Singh successfully consolidated the caste coalition that supported the Janata Dal in north India. The anti-Congress mobilization under V. P. Singh's leadership, though it did not hold out for long, significantly led to the emergence of the Mandal block. The OBCs as a major political force became consolidated, especially in north India.

The BJP was another major beneficiary from the erosion of Congress dominance in the late 1980s. Established in 1980, the BJP traditionally supported Indian nationalism and strongly advocates conservative social policies. Different from Janata Dal's focus on the backward castes, the BJP was able to attract many Hindus with their latest anti-Muslim rhetoric. The BJP in the 1990s aggressively entered the electoral arena with a clear-cut policy of Hindu majority mobilization.[181] It aimed to unify Hindus irrespective of their castes, and thus has been branded as a communal party by its political opponents. Initially, the BJP remained an urban-based party confined to north India with its greatest influence in business community. Gradually it attracted the support of the upper castes and has extended the influence of the party in the rural areas and among some OBCs.

Like the Congress party, the issue reservation brought to the fore the contradictions for the BJPs. It once stood with the anti-Mandal students' protests across India, and intensified the *Hindutva* mobilization as a counter to Mandal Commission implementations. However, it seemed

[179] Chandra, Kanchan "Post-Congress Politics in Uttar Pradesh The Ethnification of the Party System and its Consequences " In *Indian Politics and the 1998 Election, Regionalism, Hindutva and State Politics*, by Ramashray Roy and Paul Wallace New Delhi Sage Publications, 1999

[180] The Janata Dal was formed by merger of Jan Morcha, Janata Party, Lok Dal and Congress (S) It defeated the Congress Party in the 1989 election with the outside support from the Bharatiya Janata Party and the Communists

[181] Through its aggressive postures and organizational mechanism, the BJP was able to gain ground among the urban middle class irrespective of caste differences across India Later it was able to attract even the rural landowning gentry who became their backbone in north India

to start transforming into an advocate for reservation to gain electoral support among the OBCs. The BJP leaders expressed their bifocal visions in the pre-election press interview in 1999. "We work with a bifocal vision. We are neither breaking out of our commitment to those issues nor are we apologetic about our stand."[182] The Prime Minister, A.B.Vajpayee could not free himself from the caste factor, either. While addressing an election meeting in Rajasthan one day later, he stated if re-elected, his Government would seriously debate the issue of granting reservation to *Jats.* On one hand, he criticized his partymen for taking on the "communal" agenda and, on the other, he spoke in favor of a caste agenda to appease the powerful *Jat* community in Rajasthan.

The BJP's political strategy of attracting the OBCs is evident from the rather large proportion of OBC MLAs in 1991 and 1996, when it won the largest number of seats in parliament. The BJP, like other parties, had to adapt to change. Indeed, while the proportion of upper-caste MLAs in the BJP remained above 45 percent throughout 1990s, the share of OBCs stood at or above 20 percent during this period. After Mandal polarized Hindu society around an "upper versus lower caste" dichotomy, the BJP became aware of the divisive potential of the rise of OBCs. It chose to build electoral support by nominating OBC candidates. This turnaround indicates BJP leadership's own realization of its precarious predicament, especially the failure to usher in and consolidate the majority Hindu vote bank.[183]

The CPM, contrary to its class biases, also came to support the reservations for OBCs and SC/STs.[184] While supporting the reservation (totaling 27% and 22.5% at the Centre and varying in States according to the proportion of population of OBCs and SC/STs); the CPM held that Reservation Policies (RPs) is only a concession which does not tackle the roots of the problem necessary for their social and economic emancipation. This is why the CPM consistently demands

---

[182] Interviews with General Secretary of the BJP K.N.Govindacharya. Times Of India dated August 23.1999

[183] See Chinnaiah, Jangam. "BJP and Reservations Quota Politics or Electoral Convenience?" *Economic and Political Weekly*, July 2003: 3143-45.

[184] Like the SC/STs in West Bengal, it is a fact that the bulk of those who are categorized as OBCs in the state belong to the rural poor. They are sharecroppers, small tenants or poor peasants with small holdings. Further, in the rural areas the OBCs are in occupations which are still based on the traditional caste hierarchy such as dhobis, barbers, cattlerearers and artisans. Their lowly caste status prevents their entry into education and new occupations.

radical land reforms and building of the unity of agricultural laborers and poor peasants of all sections to provide the basis for a powerful agrarian movement to achieve the same. Ironically, in West Bengal and Kerala, the CPI (M) did little to achieve them in the two states they governed for a long period.

It can be argued that the CPM's attitude to OBC reservation stems from its class standpoint. The Communists analyze from a Marxist perspective that the anti-caste movement has to be linked with the movement for agrarian revolution in order to build the unity of the working people and advance the democratic movement. "The working class party, therefore, while supporting reservations, seeks to strengthen its links with the rural mass which will be a main force of the agrarian revolution. At the same time, it also considers the building of unity of the toiling people of all castes to be the crucial question."

In order to protect this unity among the working classes, the CPM refused to divide the entire rural poor in to caste divisions. "Large sections from these masses often stand alienated from the democratic and working class movement, and are swayed by sectional leadership which diverts their discontent and anger into narrow channels." [185] Thus the Marxist party wants an economic criterion within the reservation for the OBCs. This criterion, the CPM argues, need not necessarily be just an income ceiling, but can be a package in which income tax assessments, extent of landholding, professional status of parents, etc., can be taken into consideration.

6.6 A Comparative Study: Tamil Nadu v.s. West Bengal

To understand the lower-caste mobilization in response to different mobilizing strategies of interpreting Reservation Policies (RPs), the case studies of Tamil Nadu and West Bengal are explored in this section. Tamil Nadu and West Bengal do not seem like qualified candidates for comparison. The former state, which has tiny upper caste populations, almost has no middle

[185] It was addressed in its Political Resolution at the Thirteenth Congress of the CPM.

castes. Vast numbers of lower castes (including the OBCs and SC/STs), instituted state-level reservations long before Independence and have continued them into the present. In the latter state, where the upper and middle castes have a strong presence, the lower castes comprise less than 40 percent of the state population.[186] In addition to the social composition, the political party system showed a great difference too. Tamil Nadu has been dominated by two regional parties since the late 1960s, with Dravida Munnetra Kazagham (DMK) and All India Anna Dravida Munnetra Kazagham (AIADMK) alternating in power and Dravidian culture as the core of the two regional parties. Politics in West Bengal, on the other hand, has seen the dominance of an alliance of Communist parties since the late 1970s. The Left Front, after defeating the Congress Party in 1977, has been able to held power continuously until 2011. Its leadership was almost composed of upper castes, unlike the proletarian leadership in the south.

Despite their profound differences of social compositions, and the contrasts between the state-level political environments in which the political parties operate, the DMK/AIADMK and the Left Front have a number of interesting similarities. Both ended the dominance of Congress Party in the states after the 1970s. Both were continuously able to hold power by mobilizing grassroots support. Both have been led by the long-time leadership of one man (M. Karunanidhi for the DMK, Jyoti Basu for the Left Front). And both have been based on the cadre systems with wide networks of local cells, well-disciplined party command structures, and affiliated cultural and social organizations.[187]

Considering the similar party dominance in these states, the implementation of the RPs made effects in two diverging patterns. In Tamil Nadu, the preferential policies were introduced as early as 1920s with the aim of raising the economic and political status of the Dravidian castes. The programme in West Bengal was initiated in the 1980s and has been geared toward

---

[186] According to the NSS 62nd round (2005-06) records, Tamil Nadu has 4.48 percent of upper and middle castes, 22.6 percent of Scheduled Castes, 1.12 percent of Scheduled Tribes, and 72.34 percent of Other Backward Classes; while in West Bengal, there are 61.99 percent of upper and middle castes, 26.69 percent of Scheduled Castes, 5.79 percent of Scheduled Tribes, and 5.53 percent of Other Backward Classes.

[187] The CPM, however, lost to a large extent in 2011 state elections due to a loss of much OBC support.

overcoming the class divisions. Even though the sımilar set of RP rules were ıntroduced in these two states, the two states have seen the diverging factors of lower caste mobilization as a result of policy interpretation by the polıtical parties

6.6.1 West Bengal

The Left Front government in West Bengal has been continuously in power for 34 years since 1977. The Left Front was a coalition of a few left parties Communist Party of India (Maxist) or CPM forms the largest part of it.[188] As of 2004, the party claimed 57.9 percent of the electorate in West Bengal as its party members.[189] Atul Kohli credıts CPM for much of the improvement of poverty over a 20-year period after it came to power ın West Bengal. He argues that the leadership, ıdeology and organızation of CPM regime enable it to be repeatedly elected to office for over 30 years.[190] What was the CPM leadership composed of? How did they react to and interpret the caste reservatıons?

The upper castes have been largely dominating the politics of West Bengal since Independence As Atul Kohli states, "radical, conservative or reformist, modern Bengali politıcs has been dominated by an upper caste, well-off, educated minority."[191] Although Scheduled Castes, Scheduled Tribes as well as Muslims have massively shifted their loyalties from the Congress to the Left Front parties in the 1970s, the dominance of the Left since the 1970s has probably reinforced the hold of upper castes on the political leadership because the Bengali cadres of CPM are favorably recruited among the upper-caste elite group and these communists have typically ignored caste in their ideological framework and mobılizing process.

---

[188] The Left Front ıncludes Communıst Party of Indıa (Marxıst) (CPM), Communıst Party of Indıa Revolutıonary Socıalıst Party, All Indıa Forward Bloc, Revolutıonary Communıst Party of Indıa, Marxıst Forward Bloc, West Bengal Socıalıst Party now Samajwadı Party, Democratıc Socıalıst Party, and Bıplobı Bangla Congress Communıst Revolutıonary League of Indıa was a member of the West Bengal LF between 1995 and 2000

[189] Membershıp figures calculated from from http //www cpım org/pd/2005/0403/04032005_membershıp htm Electorate numbers taken from http //www ecı gov ın/SR_KeyHıghLıghts/LS_2004/Vol_I_LS_2004 pdf

[190] Kohlı, Atul *The State and Poverty ın Indıa The Polıtıcs of Reform* Cambrıdge Unıversıty Press, 1989 pp 96-97

[191] *From Elıte Actıvısm to Democratıc Consolıdatıon The Rıse of Reform Communısm ın West Bengal* Vol 2, ın *Domınance and State Power ın Modern Indıa Declıne of a Socıal Order*, by F Frankel and M S A Rao, 367–415 Delhı Oxford Unıversıty Press, 1990 P 367

The CPM was led until 2000 by Jyoti Basu, who came from a wealthy, upper-caste background. Jyoti Basu was close to the Bengali *Bhadralok* (the educated and cultured elite) due to his similar educational background.[192] He has served as the Chief Minister of West Bengal from 1977 to 2000, making him the longest-serving Chief Minister of any Indian state. Under his leadership, the Left Front government embarked on three tasks. 1) land reforms; 2) the program of "*Operation Barga*" divided the lands of landowners and assigned the ownership of plots to those sharecroppers (*Bargas)* who had been working on the land for more than three years; and 3) the *Panchayati Raj* system at local level was accordingly instituted. These local governments gave the poor peasants and all farmers a say in running the *Panchayati* institutions and on finance and development issues, according to the 73rd Amendment to the Constitution in 1992.

The upper-caste dominated leadership of CPM in West Bengal paid little attention to caste-based issues. The communists had to typically ignore caste in analyzing social relations and implementing relevant public policies for two major reasons. One, construction and consolidation of a broad-based political unity have been deemed very important for the democratic-developmental CPM. Two, class, instead of caste, is traditionally the privileged category in their ideological framework. Actually, CPM had succeeded to the extent that middle and small farmers (who often constitute the bulk of OBC in other Indian states) have been supporting the Left Front ever since it came to power and started implementing land reforms. Therefore, there seems to be no particular caste-based vote bank in West Bengal because no particular parties, including CPM, have presented such interest in mobilizing caste groups as in other states.

Regarding the implementation of RPs in West Bengal, CPM never took initiatives until the 1980s when the first Committee of Backward Classes was established. This made West Bengal one of the last among the Indian states to recognize the existence of Other Backward Classes (OBCs). Facing the Mandal Report, the former Chief Minister Jyoti Basu denied the existence of any OBCs in West Bengal and the people would be deprived under the new dispensation.

---

[192] Jyoti Basu was Educated in elite Calcutta schools and trained in law at the middle Temple in London.

Criticizing V. P. Singh for not having consulting either the Left Front or any other parties over the Mandal Report, Jyoti Basu states the Mandal Report has become outdated due to the changes had occurred during the intervening decade.[193]

Even when West Bengal had to follow the court order to establish a commission for OBC identification in the 1980s, the CPM interpreted the criteria and objectives of the Reservation Policies (RPs) that can be accepted by the communists. Jyoti Basu's government demanded the OBC identification should be based on economic instead of caste criteria. He stated that there were rich people among these backward castes and those rich should not grab the benefits of reservation. Jyoti Basu further emphasized that the only way to bring the Backward Castes on par with the rest of the population was by improving their lot through land reforms, irrigation, provisions of education and medical facilities and creation of more jobs. The CPM's general secretary, E.M.S, Namboodiripad announced CPM's "conditional support" to the reservation policy. He declared that reservations are acceptable but only if an economic criterion is included as well as provision made for some reservation for the poor of the other castes. [194]

The communist party modified the policy for their own interest. For example, the West Bengal government suggested the Center earmark 2% of those jobs which are to be brought under quotas for West Bengal, in accordance with only certain economic and not caste criteria. The meager 2% figure was suggested because CPM was afraid it would be the loss to West Bengal on account of not having any "OBCs". CPM also holds that the RP benefits should be distributed in favor of the most deprived. Given the increasing class inequalities, affirmative action - in terms of more scholarships, coaching centers and also reservation - should be considered for the students of poor families who do not come under the reserved category. For critics, CPM only created the opportunities for the poor upper-caste Hindus who are excluded from the RPs.

---

[193] The Mandal Report was submitted in the late 1970s but finally approved in the late 1980s.

[194] Prasad, Chanchreek. K. L and Saroj. *Mandal Commission Myth and Reality A Rational View point* Delhi: H.K Publishers, 1991.pp.62-67

To sum up, the CPM took cautious stance on the ideology inconsistence and political instability caused by RPs. It championed the legitimate struggle for caste-based reservations, not as an end in itself, but as a means to attract more electoral support from the OBC groups. In order to be consistent with the ideology of CPM, which "...emphasizes the preservation of democratic institutions on the one hand, and on the other hand emphasizes the use of state power for facilitating 'development with redistribution'", CPM introduced the RPs to consolidate electoral power by channeling reservation benefits to the middle and small farmers (who often constitute the bulk of OBC in West Bengal).[195]

Nevertheless, it is important to note that caste was seldom used by the CPM as a mobilizing tool in West Bengal. To be competitive in elections, there are more important sources of electoral support than caste. For instance, CPM took local loyalties as an important source of electoral support. The selected local candidates not only had to be politically "correct" but were also able to attract support based on "primordial loyalties", such as the Biharis and Jharkhandis in eastern districts and the Gurkhas in Darjeeling region. "None of this in West Bengal, however, adds up to the 'backward castes' movement of a Bihar type, or the concern with the 'dominant castes' in Karnataka."[196]

6.6.2 Tamil Nadu

Like its counterpart in West Bengal, the dominance of the Congress Party was replaced by the regional parties - the Dravida Munnetra kazagham (DMK) and All India Anna Dravida Munnetra Kazhagam (AIADMK) - in Tamil Nadu. The DMK was the main political party to grow out of the Dravidian revivalist movement initiated by the Justice Party in the 1920s. As a Dravidian party, the DMK consistently advocated "self-respect" among the Dravidians, against the traditional high caste Hinduism idea that the descendants "Aryans" (by which it meant not

[195] In fact, the middle and small farmers have been supporting the Left Front ever since it came to power and started implementing land reforms [195] The ideology of CPM is called by Atul Kohli as a developmental and democratic-socialist ideology Cited from Kohli, Atul *The State and Poverty in India The Politics of Reform* Cambridge University Press, 1989 pp 98-99

[196] Kohli, Atul *The State and Poverty in India The Politics of Reform* Cambridge University Press, 1989 P 104

only north Indians but Tamil *Brahmins*) are superior to Dravidians. After it first came to power in Tamil Nadu in 1967, the DMK claimed its favor for the Tamil language and culture and its rejection of caste-based Brahminical Hinduism. "The DMK draws resources and support from a proliferation of formal and non-formal civic associations, including book clubs, debating societies, and firm clubs, all of which encourage discussion and debate about Dravidian cultural and social issues."[197]

AIADMK was founded in 1972 by M.G.Ramachandran (popularly known as MGR) as a breakaway from the DMK led by M. Karunanidhi, owing to differences between the two. Despite the hostile relationship with DMK, AIADMK was also originated as a Dravidian and non-congress party, promoting the Dravidian identities and preferential policies for them. This powerful rhetorical appeal of combining regional and caste identities helped the DMK and AIADMK hold on the vast numbers of the poor and Dravidian voters and get through the party competition against the all-India major parties in Tamil Nadu: Congress Party and Communist Party of India (Maxist).

In the emphasis of Dravidian identities, the leadership of the regional parties has played an important role. Compared with the Left-wing cadres in West Bengal, who usually revolve around Marxist ideas, party issues or even memory games concerning past election results, the DMK and AIADMK activists' conversations typically range more widely into Tamil cultural issues, including indeed particularly, Tamil popular movies. M. Karunanidhi has been the leader of the DMK since the death of its founder C.N. Annadurai in 1969. He has contested in his political career spanning over 60 years and has served as chief minister five times (1969–71, 1971–76, 1989–91, 1996–2001 and 2006–2011). Karunanidhi entered politics by participating in anti-Hindi

[197] Banerjee, Mukulika. "Populist Leadership in West Bengal and Tamil Nadu: Mamata and Jayalalithaa Compared." In *Regional Reflections Comparing Politics Across India's States*, by Rob Jenkins. New Delhi. Oxford University Press, 2004

agitations in the 1930s.[198] In his long career of holding various positions in the party and government of Tamil Nadu, Karunanidhi consistently supported the caste-based preferential policies and promoted the welfare for the backward classes.

MGR, the founder of AIADMK, was seen as an icon for the Dravidian people and spread such message through films. MGR's success in politics can be based on his film popularity. Interestingly, his image in the film has been more of the leader/icon rather than the Dravidian people themselves. "MGR carefully crafted his screen persona to match the role he would eventually adopt as a politician: that of heroic fighter against injustice, savior of the poor and, above all, a gallant protector of women."[199] It can be argued that the theme of his films is consistent with DMK ideology, representing the demands of the Dravidians. It also represents the DMK's wish for the Dravidians to be "less about resistance from below than about noblesse oblige".[200] Under the influences of these leaders of Dravidian movement, policies of enhancing and promoting Dravidian identities became the priorities in Tamil Nadu.

Reserved quotas for the backward classes have been the signature issue of the Dravidian movement in Tamil Nadu and a way to empower the OBC masses. Tamil Nadu has had a long history of identifying the OBCs and providing preferential treatment for them. The preferential policy in Tamil Nadu first occurred in the form of the tuition subsidies (fees concessions) provided for the Muslims and Oriya speakers in 1872. Later it expanded to dozens of Hindu backward communities in the early 1900s.[201] By 1913 such educational concession was further extended to a larger pool of "backward classes" encompassing half the population.[202] This gradually expanded educational programme for the backward communities has led to the prompt

[198] Against the Hindi language, Karunanidhi circulated a hand written newspaper called Manavar Nesan to its members Later he founded a student organization called Tamil Nadu Tamil Manavar Manram which was the first student wing of the Dravidan Movement

[199] Swamy, Arun R "Parties, Political Identities and the Absence of Mass Political Violence in South India " In *Community Conflicts and the State in India*, by Amrita Basu & Atul Kohli Delhi Oxford University Press, 1998 P 134

[200] Ibid P 135

[201] Radhakrishnan, P "Reservations in Theory and Practice " *MIDS Bulletin* 20, no 4 (1990)

[202] F Irschick, Eugene "Tamil Revivalism in the 1930s " *Cre-A*, 1986 47-9

changes in identity in order to gain access to the concessions. A number of caste groups whose associations had been claiming Brahmin status redefined their status objectives in favor of "backwardness". The 1891 census reported a mysterious increase in the proportion of residents decaling Oriya as their mother tongue.[203]

The introduction of the preferential policies by various regional parties in Tamil Nadu has resulted in the split of Dravidian constituencies on a recurring basis. In 1927, the Justice Party introduced the caste-based quotas in the legislature and executive branches and educational institutions.[204] This comprehensive package of compensatory discrimination has inaugurated the battle over identifying the real "backward". The Justice Party's version of preferential policies incurred the attacks from within the non-Brahmin category for being monopolized by the elite non-Brahmin castes. In 1934, the Madras Provincial Backward Classes League was formed by the legislators belonging to lesser agricultural caste clusters, seeking to demonstrate the need for limiting preferential quotas to "Backward" as opposed to "Forward" non-Brahmin Hindus. As a result, a revised "Communal Government Order" was granted in 1947 to allot 2 out of 12 seats to "Backward non-Brhamin Hindus" and double the share of the Depressed Classes.

This Government Order had to face another revision as Supreme Court decreed that the practice of fixing quotas for all groups was unconstitutional. The reserved quotas were permissible only on the grounds of compensatory for the disadvantaged. The revised version of Government Order provided the reservation only for the "backward classes" and the constitutionally specified "SC/STs" who were given 25% and 16% respectively. All others, including the "Forward" non-Brahmin Hindu castes were henceforth assigned to the open competition category.[205] Following the declaration that only "backward" castes could be given preferential quotas, the vertical conflicts within the Dravidian constituencies reemerged,

[203] F Irschick, Eugene "Tamil Revivalism in the 1930s " *Cre-A*, 1986 47-9
[204] In 1927, Justice Party appointed to government positions by fixed quotas based on caste category, allotting 5 out of 12 seats for "non-Brahmin Hindus" collectively, 2 seats out of 12 for *Brahmins*, only 1 out of 12 seats for the Depressed Classes or "Untouchable" groups, 2 out of 12 for Muslims and Anglo-Indians(GOI 1989 164)
[205] "Government of India " 1980 165

revolving around the question: who should be included in the "backward" category? Whether should this category of "backward classes" be further compartmentalized by creating quotas for the "most backward" castes?

The political parties in Tamil Nadu have shown diverging views over these issues. The Congress party and AIADMK showed willingness to target reservations within the backward category, on both income and caste criteria. Thus the Kamaraj government introduced separate reservations for the "most backward" castes by dividing large clusters into "forward" and "backward" subcastes in 1971. However, the DMK has been reluctant to adopt the idea of further compartmentalization of the category. The DMK rejected the recommendation from the first Tamil Nadu Backward Classes Commission, which defines the Most Backward Classes (MBCs) and assigns them with separate reserved quotas.[206] The DMK also refused to constrain the existent quotas for those with an annual family income under Rs. 9000.[207] On the contrary, it accepted a proposal to expand the overall quotas.

Despite DMK's rejection of compartmentalizing the backward castes, the internal conflicts within the "backward class" category, however, became more intense. For instance, the PMK (Common People's Party) emerged in the political arena. It was supported principally by the members of the same OBC *Vanniyar* caste cluster whose earlier electoral vehicles had a short lived alliance with the DMK in the 1950s. This party's principal demand is for compartmentalizing "backward class" reservations and for granting *Vanniyars* separate quotas nationwide.

There has been a tendency of expanding the reservation quotas in Tamil Nadu, no matter what regional parties came into power. At Independence, the reservation for the Backward Classes was 25 per cent. In 1971, the DMK government hiked the reservation for the Backward

[206] From 1951 onwards, reservation for the Backward Classes in Tamil Nadu was 25 per cent but the first Tamil Nadu State Backward Classes Commission (Sattanathan Commission) recommended a separate educational and employment reservation of 16 per cent for the Most Backward Classes and 17 per cent for the Backward Classes.
[207] In the wake of DMK-led demonstrations, the income cut-off that was shortly implemented by MGR in 1979 was withdrawn.

Classes from 25 per cent to 31 per cent and for the Scheduled Castes and Scheduled Tribes from 16 per cent to 18 per cent. In 1980, MGR's AIADMK government increased the reservation for the Backward Classes from 31 per cent to 50 per cent. Until present, Tamil Nadu has the highest reservation quota of 69 percent, comprising 30 percent for BCs, 20 percent for MBCs and denotified communities (DCs), 18 percent for the SCs and 1 percent for the STs. This arrangement has been questioned by the Supreme Court on the basis of its judgment in the 1992 Indira Sawhney case (better known as the Mandal Commission case) where the judges ruled that the aggregate of reservations could not cross 50 percent. But few political parties and state governments in Tamil Nadu followed the court order at the expense of losing voting supports. The mobilization of the lower castes in Tamil Nadu, in the context of expanding and compartmentalizing quotas and benefits, grew in strength and in complexity.

6.6.3 Summary

There are several implications from the case studies of Tamil Nadu and West Bengal. Firstly, the different inheritance of the *Dalit* and OBC movements in these two states is somewhat expected. This was mainly analyzed from the strategies of the dominant parties in these two states. Both the DMK/AIADMK in Tamil Nadu and the CPM in West Bengal have been successful in broadening the social supports from the subaltern communities. But there remain striking differences in the means by which these parties have accomplished this shift. In Tamil Nadu, the two regional parties are both led by the lower-caste elites. It was the Dravidian identity that both parties pursued. In West Bengal, the upper-caste dominated CPM has seen the support of caste reservations as part of the wider picture of a "multi-class alliance".

Secondly, when the Supreme Court announced the economic criteria of identifying the RP beneficiaries, there are various responses at state level. Interestingly, the states with low levels of benefits for the OBCs tended to go along with the Center's shift to economic tests. In the states with higher levels of benefits for OBC, the effect was not to stimulate a changeover to an economic basis, but to stimulate the pruning and rationalization of the community-wise list. Thirdly, the state administrators, assumed by the party leaders and political elites, played important roles in interpreting and implementing the public policy. To conclude, the cases can help us understand how the party-level variables, combined with other state-level variables, explain the different strategies of mobilizing the same caste groups in these two states.

While our case studies come solely from West Bengal and Tamil Nadu due to their contrasting features of interpreting the Reservation Policies (RPs), the different reactions to the RPs can be observed in other Indian states. Even though the hegemonic elite, such as party leaders and administrators, are dispersed across regional and linguistic barriers, its collaborative strategies have insured nearly total control of the political society.

6.7 Conclusion

Although caste and politics influence each other, some scholars assert that "it is the latter which uses the former and even changes in the process".[208] The major political actors –political and administrative elites–have been competing for power in the democratic polity and always looking for new sources of support. Corresponding to the political rise of the caste group, they have found a new way of identification and commitment among voters. Through designing and interpreting the public policies, they can create groups and loyalties on new and varied bases. "The rulership strategies are the ways in which the elites and political elites respond to and manipulate the social structure."[209]

The effects of the manipulation can be realized through three levels. At the top are the responsive and progressive modernizing elites who are committed to the goal of empowerment and development. According to Jayant Lele, the political arena is the arena for elite bargaining.

---

[208] Kothari, Myron Weiner and Rajni. *India Voting Behaviour* Calcutta: Firma KL. Mukhopadhyaya. Krishna. Gopal, 1967. P.265

[209] Lele, Jayant. *Elite Pluralism and Class Rule Political Development in Maharashtra, India* Toronto: University of Toronto Press, 1981.P7

The elite, in turn, is not an ideologically unified minority but a heterogeneous group of accountable and responsive leaders concerned with maintaining some correspondence between individual wills and collective decisions.[210] At the bottom is the slowly but increasingly conscious, issue-oriented, and partisan electorate. The social groups chose between two or several sets of elites in the elections based on their perception and received benefits of the public policies. The "ferment from below" must accompany the "pressure from above". In this view of political mobilization the ferment from below is to be generated and carefully moderated by the modernizing elites.

However, the behavioral research on elections has thrown little light on this causal effect. In this chapter, I argue that mass mobilization can be explained through party identification - the loyalty of the mass public to a party. This is the middle level at which the elites can produce new party loyalties and alter the existent perceptions of the voters on certain public policies etc. The interpretive effect of the Reservation Policies on the political behavior of the lower castes, thus, can be a good perspective to understand this mechanism.

[210] Ibid. P3

Chapter 7

"Creamy Layer" Politics in Shape

Executive Summary: It is argued in this chapter that reservation, unintentionally but in their direct effect, have increased inequalities among the eligible OBC communities by reserving most of the benefits for the Creamy Layer: the affluent upper crust of the OBC society. This chapter analyzes the impacts of "Creamy Layer" phenomenon in India. Through the case study in Maharashtra and the procedure of issuing non-Creamy Layer caste certificate, it implies that reservations have secured casteism in the social and political arenas.

7.1 Introduction

For about three decades, the politics around reservation for Other Backward Classes (OBCs) has developed across India along two dimensions. At a primary level, it was characterized by the clashes between different political forces that stood in favor of or against the OBC quotas in education and employment. The pro-reservation groups perceive the reservation-based affirmative action as an instrument to uplift the subaltern sections of the society, while the opponents refused but had seen that the upper-caste hegemony was gradually replaced by the lower castes. This is what the previous two chapters discuss. At secondary level, the politics around OBC reservation has developed along the lines of excluding the "Creamy Layer" (CL) sections of the Backward Classes (BCs). This chapter will illustrate the CL phenomenon in India's politics.

In this chapter, it is argued that reservation, unintentionally but in their direct effect, have increased inequalities among the eligible OBC communities by reserving most of the benefits for the Creamy Layer: the affluent upper crust of the OBC society. To analyze the CL phenomenon in India's politics, this chapter is organized as follows. I begin in Section II by explaining the concept of Creamy Layer: who are they, where are they, how are they; and why are they special?

What are the principles of the CL endorsed by the judiciary system and how did the government implement the identification of this CL section of Backward Classes? In Section III, I examine the evidence on the impact of Creamy Layer Phenomenon in the political arena; and what were the state-level response and party-wide responses towards the rules of CL exclusion? In Section IV, I analyze two cases - the CL politics in Uttar Pradesh and the Caste Certificate Issuance, explicitly characterizing the political and administrative challenges for implementing the CL exclusion policy. Finally, in Section V, I summarize the implications of the CL phenomenon and predict the possible future of the CL exclusion policy.

7.2 Concept of Creamy Layer

The Creamy Layer (CL), as implied by the name, refers to the relatively wealthier and better educated members of OBCs. The term of CL was first introduced by the Sattanathan Commission, the first commission set up by the Tamil Nadu government for OBC identification in 1971.[211] It directed that the CL - the "upper crust" of the OBC communities - should be excluded from the reservations (quotas) of civil posts and services granted to the OBCs. A more recent definition of CL was provided by the Supreme Court in 1992. The court order has two major points: First, the benefit of reservation should not be given to OBC children whose parents were/are in the public positions.[212] Second, the OBC Children are not eligible for reservation benefits whose family earns a total gross annual income of Rs. 2.5 lakh because they belong to the creamy layer.[213] In other words, the ordinance regulates that these OBC children should be

---

[211] Sattanathan was Chairman of the first Tamil Nadu backward Classes Commission constituted in 1969 in the regime of DMK Government under M.Karunanidhi. One of its recommendations was an income limit to prevent the accumulation of reservation benefits by an "upper crust". However it was a short-live proposal and finally got withdrawn.

[212] These public positions include the constitutional functionaries such as President, judges of the Supreme Court and high courts, employees of central and state bureaucracies above a certain level, public sector employees, members of the armed forces and paramilitary personnel above the rank of colonel, lawyers, chartered accountants, doctors, financial and management consultants, engineers, film artistes, and authors.

[213] 1 lakh =10, 0000. Rs. 2.5 lakh was about US $5,500 in 1993 when the office memo was accepted.

excluded from being categorized as "socially & educationally backward", irrespective of their social/educational backwardness, if they came from an advantaged OBC family.

The "Creamy Layer" category was created as the result of the caste-based design of the Reservation Policies. In compensation for the historical deprivations of subaltern caste groups in India, a framework for reservations, made for ten years, have now endured for fifty years, and the beneficiaries of the reservations have been expanded from Scheduled Castes and Scheduled Tribes (SC/STs) toward the Other Backward Classes (OBCs). This government welfare benefit is unlikely to be abolished. The Mandal framework was seen as a scheme whereby "resources would be redistributed from the least advantaged members of the most advantaged groups to the most advantaged members of less advantaged groups." Marc Galanter has found the identification measures unfriendly with the backward section of the BCs, "measures for inclusion in elites should be complemented with more broadly based measures to enlarge opportunities. For all its failures in implementation, India's policy of compensatory discrimination has been remarkable in its scope and generosity." [214]

Not only in the central list, quite a few state OBC lists include some such communities that are not socially and educationally backward and are adequately represented in the public services under the state. However, their population size and political importance have enabled them to gain entry in the list and they continue to remain there. These instances include the entries that were made before 1992 as well as those approved by the State Commissions for Backward Classes (SCBC) after 1992. For instance, the case of *Vokaligas* in Karnataka belongs to the first category whereas the inclusion of *Jats* in Uttar Pradesh and Rajasthan belongs to the second category. The petition of *Jats* to be included in the central list of OBCs was rejected by the National Commission for the Backward Classes (NCBC). But their petition was still under the consideration of the SCBC of Uttar Pradesh. Even if the Supreme Court challenged the idea of

[214] Anything but a caste would be administratively difficult to handle Galanter, Marc "The Long Half-Life of Reservations " In *India's Living Constitution Ideas, Practices, Controversies*, by E Sridharan and R Sudarshan Zoya Hasan, 306-318 New Delhi Permanent Black, 2005 pp 306-318

inclusion of *Jats* in the state OBC list in Uttar Pradesh, the *Jats* are still enjoying the benefits of Articles 15(4) and 16(4) of Indian Constitution.[215]

With several developments in the last four or five decades of the post-colonial politics in India, many castes which were once termed as non-twice-born castes (such as *Shudra* castes) have ceased to be so for all practical purposes.[216] In the economic realm, these castes have received economic benefits and often replaced the erstwhile dominant *Zamindari* castes in much of rural India, as a result of the land reform policies and "Green Revolution". Subsequently, these better-off castes were also introduced to the empowered grassroots institutions of the *Panchayati Raj*, more particularly in view of their numbers. Thus they practically have already obtained an "upper caste" status and were categorized as peasant castes, and they were called "*neo-Kshatriyas*" in some places.[217] In the social sphere, they once preferred climbing upwardly in the hierarchical caste system through a process which M N Srinivas termed *sanskritisation.* But "with the advent of the democratic politics based on sheer number, these landed backward castes often resorted to increase their bargaining power through horizontal mobilization and fusion."[218]

It is impossible that the backwardness of all backward Classes is of the same magnitude. In the 1920s, the term "Backward Classes" was meant to include a wide range of social categories: "Depressed Classes", "Aboriginals", "Hill tribes", "Criminal Tribes" and "Wandering Tribes". Even though an attempt was taken to give a definite denotation to all the above terms in the 1930s, a clear cut definition of "Backward Classes" was nonexistent.[219] The Constituent Assembly did not define the term. "We have left it to be determined by each local government. A

---

[215] According to Article 15(4), nothing in this article prevent the State from making any special provision for the advancement of any socially and educationally backward classes of citizens or for the Scheduled Castes and the Scheduled Tribes. According to 16 (4), nothing in this article shall prevent the State from making any provision for the reservation of appointments or posts in favour of any backward class of citizens which, in the opinion of the State, is not adequately represented in the services under the State.

[216] The non-twice-born castes refer to the castes which originally cannot enjoy an upper status in the ritualistic hierarchy of castes.

[217] These people obtained an "upper caste" status by access to resources and sankritizing behavior. Kumar, Pradeep. "Reservations within Reservations: Real Dalit-Bahujans." *Economic and Political Weekly* 36, no. 37 (2001): 3505-3507.

[218] Ibid. P.3506

[219] Glanter, Marc. *Competing Equality: Law and the Backward Classes in India.* Berkkeley: University of California Press, 1984. pp.154-59

backward community is a community which is backward in the opinion of the government", Ambedkar explained.[220] Under articles 15(4) and 46, the state is required to make certain provisions to protect the interests of the weaker sections. A government can set up commission(s)/committee(s) to seek advice for the inclusion/exclusion of certain castes/ tribes/groups in the schedule. For this purpose certain criteria have been evolved to determine eligibility.[221]

7.2.1 Judiciary Judgments on Creamy Layer

The concept of "Creamy Layer "(CL) was first formally introduced by the Supreme Court in the Mandal judgment delivered in November 1992 to indicate an elite group among the Other Backward Classes. It was in the Indra Sawhney case in 1992 that eight judges of the Supreme Court, barring Justice Pandian, argued that the CL section of the Backward Classes should be excluded from reservations. According to the Court, some members of designated backward class are highly advanced in social, economic and educational terms. This "upper crust" of the Backward Classes (BCs) obtained most reservation benefits meant for that class, thus blocking benefits to reach the truly backward members. Justice K G Balakrishnan, the first SC to become the Chief Justice of India stated, "the special benefits cannot be further extended to them (those who have already attained economic well-being or educational advancement) and, if done so, it would be unreasonable, discriminatory or arbitrary resulting in reverse discrimination."[222] In order to weed out this forward part of the backward, the Supreme Court upheld implementation of separate reservation for other backward classes in central government jobs. It required the government to exclude the CL from enjoying reservation facilities to ensure that only the neediest among the OBCs to be benefited by reservation.

---

[220] Maharashtra, Government of "Dr Babasaheb Ambedkar Writings and Speeches, " Vol 13 1994

[221] Dahiwale, S M "Identifying 'Backwardness' in Maharashtra " *Economic and Political Weekly* 35, no 37 (2000) 3293-3297

[222] Venkatesan, J "Caste Can Be the Basis to Determine Backwardness, Rules Supreme Court " *The Hindu* April 11, 2008 http //www hindu com/2008/04/11/stories/2008041159961200 htm

Actually, the origins of the CL concept can be found even before the Indra Sawhney case. In the case of K. S. Jayasree V/S State of Kerala in 1976, the Supreme Court had approved a Kerala scheme to keep certain classes out from the reservation benefit by fixing economic ceiling.[223] Dealing with the N. M.. Thomas case, Justice Krishna Iyer, pointed out that "its [Reservation Policy] benefits, by and large, are snatched away by the top creamy layer of the 'Backward Caste' or class keeping away weak and leaving the fortunate layers to consume to the whole cake."[224]

It seemed to make sense in the Indian social context to make Caste the sole criterion in the identification process. For instance, the indicators of literacy rate and work participation rate (WPR) in Uttar Pradesh in the early 1910s showed a large difference across castes. According to the 1911 census, the average literacy rate was about 11 per cent for the high castes, only 1 per cent for the OBCs and 0.13 per cent for the SCs. In the same year in UP the average work participation rate (WPR) was 42 per cent for the high castes, 54 per cent for the OBCs and 57.5 per cent for the SCs.[225] The reasoning is simple: the poorer and illiterate families tended to send a larger proportion of their members to do manual work than the well-to-do and literate families.[226] Both the literacy rate and the work participation rate appeared to confirm that caste is a good indicator of deprivation. Moreover, almost all Indian consider Caste the most important element of their identity.

However, a scheme based largely on caste can be problematic. The above-mentioned averages actually conceal the enormous heterogeneity within the OBCs and the SCs. The literacy rates for the OBCs vary between 8 and 0.14 per cent, while the literacy rates for the SCs are within a much smaller range, between 0.11 and 0.48 per cent. The situation is more acute with respect to the economic condition. According to the statistics provided by Pradipta Chaudhury (2004), "the WPR for the OBCs varies between 39.82 and 66.61. Four of the OBCs, namely,

---

223 "K.S. Jayasree v State of Kerala ." 3 SCC 730, 1976.
224 N.M. Thomas, as a lower division clerk, was not promoted despite his passing the test.
225 " Census of India." Vols. XV, . 1911. Table XVI .and "Census of India." Vol. XVI. 1921. Table XXI.
226 Chaudhury, Pradipta. "The 'Creamy Layer': Political Economy of Reservations." 39, no. 20 (2004): 1989-1990.

Sonar, Jat, Gujar and Kisan, figure in the top eight places in the scale of economic status while five, namely, *Luniya, Barai, Bhar, Koeri* and *Kewat,* figure among the bottom seven places. The three poorest castes (*Bhar, Koeri* and *Kewat*) belong to the OBCs. Likewise, the economic status of the seven SCs varies a great deal; the WPR ranges between 44 (for *Khatik*) and 63.76 (for *Dusadh*)"[227] Therefore, it is virtually inappropriate to assume that the entire population of each caste category suffers from a uniformly high degree of deprivation.

In order to solve the problem of heterogeneity, it was suggested by some state commissions to arrange the backward castes by the degree of backwardness, to categorize them into sub-groups such as "more-backward" and "most-backward", and accordingly to redistribute sub-quotas within the total quota. But, the economic status of households varies a great deal within each caste. Each caste can contain landless laborers, cultivators as well as landlords. For instance, the most populous caste community who mainly live in the western Uttar Pradesh - the *Chamars*- was traditionally considered as land-less. The workers of this caste were about equally reported as laborers and cultivators - between 35 and 40 per cent in each. Some *Chamar* families cultivated landholdings of 10 acres or more in size while others of this caste were landless laborers.[228] The *Chamars* are considered at the top of these SC hierarchy.

The quantifiable economic criterion, thus, seems like a more rational or objective way to allocate reservations. Identifying the Creamy Layer (CL) based on economic principles can be traced back in South India in pre-independence period. The schemes of educational scholarships were first introduced in the South India, with the goal of financially supporting the students from the weaker sections of the society. For qualified candidates, the income limit/occupational status of their parents were fixed. Madras government was the first state to introduce supportive grants-in-aid schemes at educational institutions, providing special facilities and financial assistance to the students of the weaker sections of society in 1885. The income criterion was also adopted in

[227] Ibid. P.1990
[228] Ibid.

other states. For instance, income criterion was applied in allocating hostels of educational institutions in Andhra Pradesh, in local bodies in Maharashtra, in medical education in Bihar, in providing fee concessions in Rajasthan, Orissa and Delhi.[229] As Table 7.1 shows, the annual income limit of the students' family was fixed in some states to select the eligible receivers of scholarships and other facilities. (Table 7.1)

Table7.1: Evolution of the votes of Congress and its Allies (in %) by social group (1967-1998)

Castes & communities	Election year				
	1967	1971	1980	1996	1998
Upper castes	41.1	45.6	35.8	28.4	28.1
Dominant castes	NA	NA	NA	NA	NA
OBCs	38	39.4	42	21.7	22.5
Scheduled Castes	49.4	47.8	50.5	31.6	29.6
Scheduled Tribes	46.2	41.2	48.6	39.2	41.9

Source Surveys by the CSDS Data Unit (quoted in Mitra & Singh 1999 134)

The concept of an economic criterion was once again introduced after Independence. In Kerala, the Administrative Reforms Committee headed by E.M.S. Namboodiripad and the Nettoor Damodaran Commission suggested such a criterion for Backward Classes reservation in 1958 and 1971 respectively. The reservation in admissions to medical colleges in Kerala was also governed by an income criterion. Only those whose parents earn less than Rs, 20,000 per year are entitled to benefit from OBC reservation. In some other States, like Tamil Nadu and Karnataka, there are two or three categories of backward classes, with the more economically backward either getting more fee concessions and other facilities or getting a greater quantum of reservations.

Although the economic criterion of identifying "Creamy Layer" (CL) was created a long time ago, the CL concept has been "unconstitutional" because the Constitution prescribes no

[229] Government of India 1980 4-10, cited from Sukhadeo Thorat, Narender Kumar *In Search of Inclusive Policy Addressing Graded Inequality* New Delhi Rawat Publications, 2008

directive to exclusively discriminate among OBCs.[230] It is the Supreme Court that invented this concept and laid down principles of CL to justify OBC reservations during the Mandal implementation. The majority of the nine-judge Bench of the apex court authoritatively agreed that special privileges like job reservations were monopolized by the more affluent sections of Backward Classes; and the really backward sections among them kept on getting poorer and more backward. Except Justice Pandian, the other eight justices argued that reservation for the OBCs should be allowed subject to screening the CL among them. Among the eight judges, Justice Kania C. and Justice Venkatachaliah, Ahmadi and Jeevan Reddy, pointed out that CL should not receive benefit because of their capacity to compete with the forward classes.

Income or property holding criterion has been regarded as the major principle of identifying the affluent sections of the Backward Classes. It means those persons holding higher levels of agricultural land holdings or getting income beyond a limit have to be excluded from the Backward Classes. Justice Jeevan Reddy pointed out that income limits should be prescribed as being a criterion of social advancement. According to the Court, certain positions should be signified as socially advanced, such as becoming the members of Indian Administrative Service (IAS) or Indian Police Service (IPS) or any other All India Services. Justice Thommen and Kuldip Singh recommended a means-test measure. He emphasized that the means-test measures must be strictly and uniformly applied to exclude all those persons in the category reaching above the predetermined economic level. Justice Kuldip Singh argued that the eligible candidates are those who are totally unable to join the mainstream of upward mobility because of their utter helplessness arising from social and educational backwardness and aggravated by economic disability. However, some judges disagreed with notion of economic criteria as the basis of CL recognition. They observed that, "the very concept of a class denotes a number of persons having certain common traits which distinguish them from the others. In determining Backward Class

[230] It is always politically impossible to maneuver change of differentiating the CL from the rest of OBCs.

under Article 16(4), if the connecting link is the social backwardness, it should broadly be the same in a given class."[231]

The Court attempted to integrate the economic criterion with the notion of existent conditions to exclude the CL section of Backward Classes. The eligible candidates are always determined by the status of parents instead of the status of the individual, spouse or siblings. In the Mandal judgment in 1992, the Supreme Court ordered that OBC children, falling under the CL category include the children of constitutional functionaries, including the President, judges of the Supreme Court and High Courts, members of the Union Public Service Commission, Groups A and B or Class I or II officers of the All-India Central and State services and the children of public sector employees. Besides, the children of professionals are also excluded such as lawyers, chartered accountants, doctors, financial and management consultants, engineers, film artists, authors and playwrights. By the economic criterion, the OBC children belonging to any family that earns a total annual income of Rs. 4.5 lakh are also excluded from being categorized as the backward regardless of their social /educational backwardness.[232] To sum up, the Supreme Court regulates three principles on the CL exclusion. First; means test are imperative to remove the affluent sections of the BCs. Second, only the most deserving – the weakest section among the BCs should be given reservation benefits. Third, the identification of the OBCs under Article 16(4) can be made solely on the basis of economic criterion.

7.2.2 Identifying the Creamy Layer

Although the majority of the judges favored the application of Creamy Layer (CL), they were not sure about defining it - income, property, or status criteria. The Supreme Court therefore directed the Government of India to specify the basis of exclusion - on the basis of income, extent of land holding or other social criteria. As norms may differ from State to State or from region to

[231] "Mandal Case, Para 86, 121(3) (d), 450,451."
[232] The income ceiling for the Creamy Layer rose from 2.5 lakhs to 4.5 lakhs in October 2008.

region, the Central and State governments are obliged to create separate bodies to identify the CL within a time frame.

How did the central and state governments implement the identification of CL section of BCs? Under the direction of Supreme Court in the early 1990s, the central and state governments began to constitute commissions to deal with definitional issues, to make lists of OBCs, and to assess proposed additions to or subtractions from their lists. The central government instituted the National Commission for Backward Classes (NCBC). This permanent commission is responsible for creating a national list of OBCs based on the Mandal Commission's list and on the various state level lists. It indicates the concrete principles designed by the NCBC to exclude CL from reservations. (See Appendix 7.1)

Justice R.N. Prasad, the first head of the NCBC established in 1993, also headed a new Creamy Layer Committee to design criteria for the OBC reservations. As Prasad noted in an interview, the rules should allow for a situation in which a group is qualified to be an OBC community but individuals within that group can be excluded on the basis of advancement or prosperity.[233] Prasad's committee agreed upon a series of processes to examine applicants, their parents and, in the case of women, their husbands. The objective is to remove those who hold high-ranking government or military positions (or who have parents or husband in such a position), those who own a certain amount of irrigated land (cultivated land), and those with an annual income level over 100,000 rupees (about 2100 US dollars).[234]

For implementation, the NCBC has evolved a procedure to examine the petitions and complaints for inclusion in the OBC lists. A set of questionnaires were devised to call for the relevant information from the petitioners. The questionnaires are divided into two parts. Part I contains the general information about the caste. Part II includes the data on social, educational, economic status and representation in public services at central and state levels. Interestingly, the

---

[233] Prasad interview was done by Laura Dudley-Jenkins on18 September 1996

[234] Dudley-Jenkins, Laura. " Identity and identification in India: defining the disadvantaged." Psychology Press, 2003. P.149

NCBC designed the "fast-track" category to deal with the petitioners identified with traditional or hereditary occupations considered to be unclean or stigmatized.[235] The "fast-track" cases were taken on priority basis. It can be argued that the NCBC still put priority on the traditional caste criterion. At state level, the State Commissions/Committees of Backward Classes (SCBCs) were established for the similar purposes. In Indian states, the SCBCs usually follow the National Commission for BCs (NCBC). It is appropriate to indicate the methodology adopted by the NCBC has become the role model for the state-level implementation of CL identification. There are important cases bearing on Creamy Layer in different states. (See Appendix 7.2)

While prioritizing the reservation benefits for the more backward among the OBCs, it has been difficult to judge and measure who are the real Creamy Layer (CL) because no official Creamy Layer percentage census is available to demonstrate it. First of all, as mentioned above, there exists considerable heterogeneity within OBCs compared to the SCs and STs.[236] The differentiation is both inter-caste and within any given OBC caste in terms of the economic and educational indicators. The former differentiation refers to the fact that some castes within the OBC category are considerably more advanced as a caste than other OBC castes, and often not significantly behind the upper castes. Such differentiation also exists within any given OBC caste. But the Mandal Report did not account for the fact that backward castes are neither socially nor economically equal.

Secondly, the exclusion of CL became focus of the tensions between the legislature and the judicial system. It is argued that the utopian perception of the Supreme Court has undermined the will of the legislature. The legislature, on the other hands owns the sole prerogative of implementation since the judiciary has no constitutional mandate to implement policy decisions.

---

[235] These occupational categories cover traditional artisanal crafts such as fishing, hunting, bird snaring, agricultural labor on the lands of others, earth work, stone breaking, salt manufacturing, lime burning, toddy tapping, animal rearing, butchery, hair cutting, washing clothes, ferring by boat, scavenging, knife grinding, grain roasting, entertaining through song and dance, knife grinding, grain roasting, entertaining through song and dance, acrobatics/jugglery, snake charming, acting, begging or mendicancy. The above information was summarized from Dudley-Jenkins, Laura. " Identity and identification in India: defining the disadvantaged." Psychology Press, 2003.P.130

[236] The Creamy Layer concept is meant only for the OBCs, which is not applied to the unreserved category, Scheduled Castes and Scheduled Tribes.

For instance, in 2006 when the central government wanted to give reservation for the OBCs in Central Educational Institutions like IITs and IIMs, and medical institutions like AIMS without exclusion of CL section of the BCs, it was opposed and challenged in the Supreme Court.[237] The central government pleaded that the CL concept is applicable only in case of job reservation not in case of reservation in admission in educational institutions. But the Supreme Court opposed the view that the BCs at State and State-aided educational institutions are subject to the rule of CL exclusion from the OBCs.

The conflicts also existed between the court system and the state-level governments. The criteria for determining CL in Bihar and Uttar Pradesh set by the state governments were declared invalid for being against the norms indicated by the Supreme Court in the Mandal case.[238] The principles to identify CL in Bihar and Uttar Pradesh reveal that they had put some additional conditions, such as a salary of more than Rs.10, 000 (about 210 US dollars), the wife and husband are graduates and one of them owns a house in urban area. As for professionals, the annual income of Rs.10 lakh (about 2,1000 US dollars) was fixed as criterion.[239] It further provided that the wife or husband should be at least graduate and the family owns immovable property valued at least at Rs. 20 lakhs (about 4,2000 US dollars). Similarly, the criteria regarding traders, industrialists, agriculturists and others were also very high.[240] The Supreme Court required the state governments in Bihar and Uttar Pradesh to re-examine the principles of CL exclusion. It declared that the state governments should follow the Government of India and work on the similar criteria for identifying the CL.

---

[237] The central government decided the OBC quotas of 27% in the Central Educational Institution (Reservation in Admission) Act 2006 without CL exclusion. The Supreme Court opposed this Act in Ashoke Kumar Thakur v/s Union of India.

[238] The CL formula in Bihar and Uttar Pradesh were named "the Bihar Reservation of vacancies in Posts and Services (for Scheduled Castes, Scheduled Tribes and Other Backward Classes) (Amendment) Ordinance, 1995" and "State of U.P. the Uttar Pradesh Public Services Reservation of Scheduled Castes and Scheduled Tribes and Other Backward Classes Act, 1994"

[239] 1 lakh=100,000

[240] For instance, for industrialist it was required that they might have invested Rs.10 crores for at least 5 years and spouse was at least graduate, for agriculturalists, an income of Rs.10 lakhs in year from sources other than agriculture and graduation of spouse was essential, for any other person to mention the above categories, the income from all sources required for continuously 3 years was fixed at not less than Rs.10 lakhs, graduation of spouse and immovable property worth Rs.20 lakhs.

7.2.3 A Comparative Case Study: Uttar Pradesh and Tamil Nadu

Brahmins, Kshatriyas, Vaisyas and *Shudras* are four categories into which many *jatis* arrange themselves (i e. the actual kinship group is referred to as a caste). The economic differentiation among and within castes has also widened over the years The classification of OBCs by the Mandal Commission in 1980 was based on the economic conditions of households in the 1931 Census, which was the last comprehensive body of information on the economic conditions of different castes in India. The National Family Health Survey (NFHS) provides a new opportunity to study the relationship between caste and economic condition.[241] More specifically, the information in NFHS was collected on caste, by head of household and economic conditions of the household, such as type of house, source of lighting, availability of protected water, toilet facility, modern objects owned, viz, watch, radio, bicycle and literacy levels of the members of the household. Thus this data set presents a unique opportunity to study the differentials in socio-economic indicators by caste.[242]

From the data compiled in the NFHS, three categories - Scheduled Castes, Other Backward Classes, and Upper Castes (*Brahmins* and Intermediate Castes) –are defined. My study design is based on K. Srinivasan and S. Kumar (1999) to examine the differentials of literacy rates and economic conditions between different sub-castes in the major caste category and between major castes groups [243] The economic conditions of households in the categories of SCs, OBCs and Upper Castes were studied through six relevant indicators[244]

---

[241] NFHS was conducted with the primary objective of providing reliable and comparable estimates of fertility, infant mortality, contraceptive use, reproductive health, family size desires, etc, across the states of India But it also generated considerable data on caste and economic conditions

[242] Kumar, K Srinivasan and Sanjay "Economic and Caste Criteria in Definition of Backwardness " *Economic and Political Weekly* 32, no 42/43 (1999) 3052-3057

[243] Kumar, K Srinivasan and Sanjay "Economic and Caste Criteria in Definition of Backwardness " *Economic and Political Weekly* 32, no 42/43 (1999) 3052-3057 P 3054

[244] (1) Whether there is an adult literate person in the household code 0 if none, 1 otherwise, (2) Whether the house in which they are residing, is kutcha(crude, imperfect, or temporary residence) code 0 if yes, 1 other- wise, (3) Whether the house is electrified code 0 if not electrified, 1 otherwise, (4) Whether there is a toilet facility, owned or shared, for the household code 0 if no such facility, 1 otherwise, (5) Whether the household possesses irrigated land code 0 if no, 1 otherwise, and (6) Whether any household member possesses any of the following objects - a watch, a radio, or a bicycle code 0 if none, 1 otherwise A household economic score was computed on the basis of these six items in two steps by scoring as 0 and 1 against each item and summing them up Obviously, households with a score of zero are

For Uttar Pradesh 29 percent of all the households have no adult literate members, 52 per cent are living in kutcha houses, 66 per cent have no electricity, 76 per cent have no toilet facility, 44 per cent have no irrigated land, 27 percent have no modern items, such as a watch, bicycle or radio.[245] Generally, the SCs' economic lives have been far worse than the average. The OBCs' come from relatively better, but still stayed behind the forward castes. For example, among the *Pasi* (SCs), 95 per cent of the households have no toilet facility, compared to 87 per cent among *Kumhar* (OBCs) and 69 per cent among *Brahmins*; 90 per cent of *Pasi* households have no electricity compared to 76 per cent among *Kumhars* and 50 per cent among *Brahmins*; 88 per cent live in kutcha houses compared to 65 per cent among *Kumhar* castes and 36 per cent among *Brahmins*. In other words, the conditions of *Pasis* (SCs) who have been recipients of many privileges such as free education, housing loans, priority in employment, etc, did not seem to have improved by these privileges after Independence. The differentials between the lower castes (*Pasis* and *Kumhars*) and the *Brahmins* are quite wide. It can be seen that the conditions of OBC *Kumhar* castes households are relatively similar to *Pasis*. At some point, their economic conditions were even worse than *Pasis*. 42 per cent of *Kumhar* households were without any literate adult members (for *Pasis* it was 43 percent), 44 per cent without irrigated land (for *Pasis* it was 39 percent), and 30 percent had no modern objects (for *Pasis* it was 42 percent). This further implies that the special privileges for the SCs and OBCs did not appear to have had any impact on their lifestyles in the aggregate so far, even though they have had special benefits for more than two decades. (Table 2A)

However, an interesting finding from this survey is the existence of strong differentials among castes within the SC and OBC category. For example, the percentage of "most poor" in the rural areas is 39.5 among *Pasis,* 31.3 among *Chamars,* 28.8 among *Dhobis,* who all belong to SC category. Similarly, among OBCs, there is a variation in the proportion of "most poor" from

very poor and have practically no material possessions. For the purpose of this analysis, we considered the households with a score of 0 and 1 as "most poor", 2 and 3 as "poor" and 4, 5, 6 as "not poor". The findings are presented below.

[245] The survey work in UP was carried out between October 1992 and February 1993,

15 4 (*Kurmis*) to 30 9 (*Telis*) among the caste groups considered (*Kuhmars*, *Telis* and *Kurmis*) Thus, it appears that there are not only wide variations between the major caste groups but also between castes within the SCs and OBCs (Table 7 2 A)

Table7.2A: Social Economic Indicators of the Households of Specified Castes in Uttar Pradesh

(Percent)

Caste	Total Household	No Adult Literate Member	Living in Kutcha House	Without Electricity	No Toilet Facility	No Irrigated Land	No Watch Radio Bike, etc	% of "Most Poor"
All	10110	28 6	52 0	66 0	75 9	44 4	27 3	17 8
Brahmins	1255	8 0	36 2	49 6	69 3	38 2	15 9	5 2
Intermediate Castes								
Kayastha	189	16 9	45 5	44 4	46 0	64 0	15 3	14 4
Rajput	738	22 4	51 3	67 6	82 4	33 0	25 2	13 6
OBCs								
Kumhar	188	41 5	64 5	76 1	86 7	44 1	29 9	23 5
Teli	68	47 1	61 8	73 5	85 3	58 8	45 6	30 9
Kurmi	52	25 0	59 6	71 2	75 0	28 8	26 9	15 4
SCs								
Chamar	1316	40 0	68 8	83 4	95 1	48 8	41 9	31 3
Pasi	125	43 2	88 0	89 6	95 2	38 7	41 6	39 5
Dhobi	156	39 1	60 9	75	89 7	54 5	37 8	28 8

Source Data arranged from the tables in Kumar, K Srinivasan and Sanjay "Economic and Caste Criteria in Definition of Backwardness " *Economic and Political Weekly* 32, no 42/43 (1999)

In Tamil Nadu, 21 per cent of all households have no adult literate members, 37 per cent live in kutcha houses, 36 per cent have no electricity, 71 per cent have no toilet facility, 82 per cent of the households have no irrigated land, and 34 per cent have no modern objects (watch, bicycle or radio) [246] Tamil Nadu has a long history of social welfare and development programmes aiming at abolishing the caste differentials since 1920s However, the data from Table 2B reveals that there still exist sizeable economic differentials between castes For example, among *Muppans* (OBCs), 93 percent of the households have no toilet facility compared to 10 percent among *Brahmins,* 50 percent live in kutcha houses compared to 3 percent among *Brahmins*, 42 percent of the

[246] The survey work in TN was carried out between April and July of 1992

households have no modern objects (watch, bicycle or radio) compared to 2 percent among *Brahmins,* and 33 percent of the households have no adult literate member compared to 2 percent among *Brahmins*. The large differentials in economic conditions between the *Muppans* and the *Brahmins* suggests that more than seven decades of government efforts to bridge this gap have not yielded the desired results. The policy benefits aiming at the real backward classes seemed to be absorbed somewhere else. A similar finding can be found in Tamil Nadu in terms of the differentials among castes within OBC category. The percentage of "most poor" among OBCs varies from 4.9 (*Devangulus*) to 30.5 (*Muppans*). (Table 7.2B)

Table7.2B: Social Economic Indicators of the Households of Specified Castes in Tamil Nadu

(Percent)

Caste	Total Household	No Adult Literate Member	Living in Kutcha House	Without Electricity	No Toilet Facility	No Irrigated Land	No Watch Radio Bike, etc.	% of "Most Poor"
All	4287	20.8	36.8	36.2	70.6	82.2	34.3	20
Brahmins	68	1.5	2.9	2.9	10.3	86.7	1.5	0
Intermediate Caste								
Pillai	58	3.4	8.6	8.6	41.4	86.2	17.2	1.7
OBCs								
Devangulu	182	10.4	11.5	12.1	50.5	91.8	18.1	4.9
Vanniyan	340	23.2	55.3	36.5	85.6	65.6	39.4	20.6
Muppan	60	33.3	50.0	53.3	93.3	83.1	41.7	30.5
Padyachi	100	29	51.0	36.0	90.0	68.0	39.0	23.0
SCs								
Kallan	90	12.2	52.2	45.6	87.8	65.6	45.6	21.1
Parahia	607	36.2	64.1	56.0	84.5	91.3	56.6	40.7
Pala	131	32.1	55.7	65.6	89.3	84.7	55.0	43.5

Source· Data arranged from the tables in Kumar, K. Srinivasan and Sanjay. "Economic and Caste Criteria in Definition of Backwardness." *Economic and Political Weekly* 32, no. 42/43 (1999).

From the comparison of the Tamil Nadu and Uttar Pradesh, several observations can be drawn. First of all, the differentials between the lower and upper castes appear to be larger in Tamil Nadu than in Uttar Pradesh, which did not have similar long-standing programmes to reduce economic differentials among the caste groups. For example, in Tamil Nadu, 30.5 per cent of the *Muppans* (OBCs) are in the "most poor" category compared to 0 per cent among *Brahmins* and 1.7 per cent among *Pillais* both of which belong to forward caste category. In Uttar Pradesh,

30.9 per cent of the *Telis* (OBCs) belong to the "most poor" category compared to 5.2 per cent among *Brahmins* and 13.6 per cent among the Intermediate Caste *Rajputs* This may imply more of the benefits were distributed among the CL section of the Backward Classes in Tamil Nadu than in Uttar Pradesh. With a long history of implementation of Reservation Policies, Tamil Nadu has probably seen politics of "Creamy Layer" in the earlier time.

Moreover, in both Tamil Nadu and Uttar Pradesh there are very wide differentials among various castes within the SC and OBC category. As shown in the Table 4A and 4B, there are significant differentials among the different castes within SCs and OBCs. It can be implied that CL has become a widespread phenomenon across India. Thus, grouping of SCs or OBCs into one category for the purposes of providing special benefits does not appear to be a reasonable procedure when there are strong intra-caste variations in economic conditions within that category. In general, the comparison also highlights the point that economic criteria, along with caste considerations, should form the basis of any welfare programmes for the lower castes.[247]

This comparative study also demonstrates the complexity of the OBC problem: Within the category of OBCs, there is a significant inter-caste and intra-caste economic differentiation. The Indian government considers class in addition to caste, and considers individuals in addition to groups. Namely, the government can finely subdivide the categories for reserved seats and disqualify the most economically advanced families at the group levels. Only by this effort, the least-well-off sub-castes would be entitled to their own separate reservation category. For example, some states, such as Bihar and Tamil Nadu, have tried to create a "Most Backward Classes" category. But such distinctions add new definitional challenges. For example, the Supreme Court disagreed with the Uttar Pradesh government on the categorization of Backward, More Backward and Most Backward Classes.[248] The back-and-forth definitional differences

[247] However, anything else is judicially and administratively difficult to skim the CL off the reservation list

[248] *Appointment of 'most backward' in UP stayed* January 22, 2002

between the court system and the governments over the role of economic criteria could last for years to come.

7.3 Impacts of "Creamy Layer" Phenomenon

It is well noted now that the system of reservations has mainly helped those forward within lower castes and was practically incapable of substantially changing the situations of the backward among lower castes in aggregate. As Weiner notes, "material benefits to the lower castes have largely gone to their more advanced members, some castes (*Yadavs,* for example) have befitted substantially, others hardly at all. There are growing class divisions within each of the lower castes as the more successful individuals obtain positions in government while others receive few if any benefits."[249] For this reason, the Creamy Layer (CL) is not only a social phenomenon but also a political one.

Social mobility, partly a result of Reservation Policies has facilitated the shaping of better-off "Creamy layer" (CL) within the disadvantaged groups. Due to the characteristic of the unequal distribution of Reservation Policies, reservations have created an educated subset within the eligible groups, who were later employed in government service and have become a political force. It appears that reservations have served as a tool to elevate the social standing of the privileged sections of the lower castes. Rather than a picture of oppression at the bottom of the ritual hierarchy, these are the influential strata of the lower castes who not only own land or other properties, but are well represented in the political power structure. Under their leadership, the OBC movements were organized in the democratic India. The more advantaged have assumed roles of political leadership of these castes.

The democratization process in the decades following Independence has politically empowered the numerous and relatively wealthy backward castes. While the 1950s continued to

[249] Weiner, Myron. "The Struggle for Equality: Caste in Indian Politics." In *The Success of India's Democracy*, by Atul Kohli. New Jersey: Cambridge University Press, 2001.P.223

be dominated by the upper caste Hindus, the 1960s saw the peasantization of politics as some most powerful chief ministers came from the OBC peasant caste members. In the subsequent decades of the 1970s and the 1980s, an increasing number of backward castes participated in politics across India. Political power began to shift to them as more high officials came from these castes. This happened first in the southern states where Dev Raj Urs and Bangarappa were installed through the political supports among the backwards. Later in some northern states such as Bihar and Uttar Pradesh, the Yadavization of the politics were rising as peasant caste members Laloo Yadav, Mulayam Singh Yadav and Ram Naresh Yadav became the heads of governments. *Yadavs* have been among the most successful of the OBCs. For example, Mulayam Singh Yadav wields significant influence among *Yadavs* in Uttar Pradesh, where the *Yadavs* are estimated to account for nearly 10 per cent of the State's population. In the 1990s, the *Dalits* and OBCs both have gradually established their own political forces in the north, successfully setting up their own political parties and capturing the important government posts. The OBC MPs tended to form an important force in the Hindi belt states, from 14.0 percent of the total MPs in 1980 to 22.2 percent in 1999. (Table 7.3) In the state of Bihar, the percentage of the OBC MPs has jumped from 5.5 in 1952 to 37.5 per cent in 2004. In another northern state Uttar Pradesh, the share of OBC MLAs has been increasing from 16.91% in the 1980 toward 27.52% in 2002.

Table 7.3: Status of OBC Representation (MPs) in the Hindi Belt States (1980-1999)

Categories	OBCs MPs in Hindi Belt 1980-1999 (%)						
	1980	1984	1989	1991	1996	198	1999
Upper Castes	41.0	47.0	38.2	37.1	35.3	35.0	31.0
Intermediate Castes	5.3	5.31	8	5.4	7.53	9.0	6.4
Scheduled Castes	18.0	17.3	17.8	18.1	18.14	18.2	18.0
Scheduled Tribes	7.6	7.5	7.6	8.14	7.52	7.6	7.3
OBCs	14.0	11.1	21.0	22.6	25.0	23.6	22.2

Source: Adapted from Jaffrelot (2003) The Rise of the Lower Castes in North Indian Politics.

In the southern states and Maharashtra, reservations for non-Brahman castes were essentially aimed at procuring a large share of the government jobs. The long-term operation of the Reservation Policies has made their representation in bureaucracy quite in tune with their percentage in the population in most states. As Table 7.4 shows, in Tamil Nadu more than 60 percent of the positions of "Secretariats" and "Collectorates" were taken by the OBCs as early as 1970s. (Table 7.4) Partly due to the reservation benefits, these high-ranking non-Brahman castes had achieved higher economic and political status than the *Brahmins* in the early twentieth century. From the 1960s, the quotas were also given in public employment, and therefore a significant number of them had joined government jobs. These new elites belonging to the upper end of the lower castes resented the predominance of the *Brahmins* in the state politics. With the advent of the democratic politics with its emphasis on numbers, these upwardly mobile castes resorted to increasing their bargaining power through horizontal mobilization, fusion and Sanskritization. For example, the *Vokkaligas* and the *Lingayats* in Karnataka have successfully resisted their exclusion from the list of the backwards and have consequently succeeded in capturing political and economic power in the state.[250] The *Kunbis* in Maharashtra and the *Kapus* of Andhra Pradesh, however, have not been politically so active in this respect, and have lagged behind other OBC castes, despite their large number on account of their failure to "fuse" themselves as successfully as *Vokkaligas* and the *Lingayats* in Karnataka.

Table 7.4: OBCs in the Secretariat and in the "Collectorates" in Tamil Nadu, 1970 (%)

	Non-gazetted posts	Gazetted posts
Secretariat	39.8	20.8
"Collectorates"	47.5	24.8

Source Adapted from Sattanath, Report of the Backward Classes Commission, pp 140, cited from Jaffrelot, Christophe *India's Silent Revolution the Rise of the Lower Castes in North India* New York Columbia University Press, 2003 P239

[250] The Mandal Commission included Vokkaligas and the Lingayats in the backward category, however, the state-level Havanur Commission re-examined their economic and social status and re-categorized them into the non-backward in the OBC list

A similar pattern appeared in the north later. The numerically important backward castes, namely, *Ahir (Yadav), Kurmi, Lodha, Kahar and Gadariya* have lagged far behind the upper castes in the economic hierarchy during the first half of the 20th century. Those richer lower castes (*Barhai, Gujar, Jat, Kisan, Lohar, Mali and Sonar*) had small demographic weightage and were scattered. The upper castes in general and *Brahmins* in particular had thus dominated the state politics and administration till very recently. Only after 1977, the new OBC elites began to play as stakeholders in the political process. The politics of the last few decades were regarded as Yadavisation and Kurmiaisation of politics in Bihar and Uttar Pradesh, named after the two most pronounced OBC caste clusters. This horizontal integration of the *Shudra* castes has made many of them disproportionately powerful in the politics of their region. The *Yadavas,* the *Kurmis* and the *Koeris*, who constituted the *"triveni"*(trio) to fight the *Zamindari* system in Bihar in the 1920s, account for about 20 per cent of the population of the state but have cornered a disproportional number of political positions assigned to the backward castes, and were major beneficiaries of the Green Revolution, leaving little for the remaining 35 per cent backwards.[251] The recently inclusion of the well-off *Jats* in this category has made the imbalance even greater.

This is probably why most important political and administrative positions have been monopolized by the CL among the lower castes. The CL monopolization may last for quite some time. They not only have made intelligent use of their numbers to further consolidate themselves politically, but have preserved the privileges for their offsprings by keeping criteria as traditional caste categories. The reservations have created the "next-generation" CL among the sons and daughters of the public officers enumerated in the "Service Category" even after they retired. In order to preserve the privileged rights for their children, the new elites refused to accept the principle of CL exclusion. This is also true in the educational arena. Patwardhan and Palshikar (1992) contend that the beneficiaries of reserved seats are increasingly second-generation

[251] Kumar, Pradeep. "Reservations within Reservations: Real Dalit-Bahujans." *Economic and Political Weekly* 36, no. 37 (2001): 3505-3507. P.3506

students from the favored groups, whose families have benefited from positive discrimination to become middle to upper-middle class; while children from more backward sub-castes and tribes find it difficult to compete. This proposition receives clear empirical support in the experience of the elite IITs.[252] Rao (2001) corroborated the above observation "...the schemes of reservation (in higher education) tend to reproduce within the beneficiary class the same kind of clustering the reservation is meant to remedy...those among the beneficiaries who already enjoy the greatest advantages obtain disproportionately large shares of the benefits."[253].

7.3.1 Politics of "Creamy Layer": State-level Response to the Principles of CL exclusion

Even though an increasing number of OBC and *Dalit* leaders have captured the important government posts, most of the backward castes are nowhere near the Creamy Layer (CL) in terms of their economic and political clouts. The non-CL groups actually constitute the actual deprived of sections of the population today as they have failed to benefit from the affirmative action programmes. At this point, removing the Creamy Layer (CL) became an imperative adjustment of the reservation policy programmes. What are the major impacts of this action? Indeed, the legal principles of CL exclusion formulated by the Court and implemented by the governments have not shown expected results yet. Some consequences of Reservation Policies have become permanent even though the Reservation Policies were imposed as a temporary measure. The political balance between the castes, as a result of the unequally distributed reservation benefits, also ensured its perpetuation.

The implementation of quotas is both a political minefield and an administrative nightmare. The CL rules have resulted in political activism in terms of the classification issues. Because the CL rules constitute a policy shift from purely caste-based criteria toward individual economic

[252] Patwardhan, Vasant and S Palshikar "Reserved Seats and Medical Education A Study" *Journal of Education and Social Change* 5, no 4 (January - March 1992) This study was first brought out in Marathi and published in the Journal, Navabharat, Year 43, Issue 3, December 1989

[253] Rao, S S "Equality in Higher Education Impact of Affirmative Action Policies in India" Unpublished draft paper, Jawaharlal Nehru University, 2001 It was published in 2002 in *Global Collaborations the Role of Higher Education in Diverse Democracies*, by E F Beckham Washington, DC Association of American Colleges and Universities, 2002 P 511

criteria, the introduction of an economic criterion has met with strong resistance wherever the OBC reservations already existed. In general, only when a broad consensus is reached can it be ımplemented. All the states welcomed the 27% reservation quotas to socially and educationally backward communities (OBCs). But the concept of Creamy Layer and the new individual level restrictions have varied responses across Indian states. For example, the protest in the north was held by the anti-Mandal student protesters who did not want new OBC quotas in the educational institutions; while the anti-Creamy Layer activists in the southern states did not want new restrictions on OBC quotas.

As individual states have formed their own CL rules for state-level reservations, such state-level decisions provided examples of resistance against CL exclusion and manipulation of the CL categories.[254] In contrast to the violent demonstrations against the Mandal issues in the north, the new OBC reservations were more widely accepted from the outset in the southern states. While the CL regulations assuaged some of the concerns in the north about OBC reservations, some southern states did not even accept it. With a large population who already declared backward in the south, it has become politically more difficult to skim off the constituencies, particularly the most powerful members of those constituencies, through new CL exclusions. For instance, the CL principles have not been implemented in the southern state of Kerala because no agreement was reached. The politics of defining the creamy layer in Kerala has been particularly contentious. This is also true in other southern states. Till July 2011, the Tamil Nadu government still decided not to exclude "Creamy Layer" among Backward Classes from the ambit of 69 per cent reservation in the State.[255]

Take Kerala as an example. Kerala had a history of progressive politics for backward communities during the colonial era. As early as the mid-1930s, a Public Service Commission was appointed to allocate many posts in government service to a list of 14 communities on a

---

[254] Stats adopted the exclusıon of certaın CL castes, instead of excludıng the CL people wıthın a caste

[255] "Government not to exclude 'creamy layer' among backward classes from reservatıon " *The Hındu* July 13, 2011 http //www thehındu com/news/states/tamıl-nadu/artıcle2222119 ece

proportional basis. In the post-Independence period, three commissions were set up to assign OBC quotas in the technical and professional colleges and state government jobs. All of these steps were taken prior to the national Mandal Commission. In the 1990s, the Kerala government resisted the nationally mandated CL rules to trim the ranks of the backward. A few back-and-forth exchanges between the state government and the Supreme Court took place thereafter. The Kerala government passed a resolution in 1995 denying that there was any CL at all in the state, which was nullified by the Supreme Court.[256] In response, Kerala appointed Narendra Commission to come up with more lenient rules and shrink its CL. The Narendra Commission was explicitly charged by the Supreme Court to provide "maximum benefits permissible within the parameters of the December 13 Supreme Court verdict to backward communities".[257] The Commission also invited suggestions from most organizations of backward communities and minorities to help it in its task. Almost all organizations have taken the stand that there is no creamy layer among the backward communities in Kerala without presenting documentary support for the quantum of increase in the income ceiling.[258]

Kerala was not the only state to contest the new boundaries of backwardness. In the northern state of Uttar Pradesh, there was no periodical revision of CL formula. Nobody bothered to check and verify CL certificates. The political parties tended to ignore the implementation of CL exclusion because they did not want to lose their vote bank of OBCs, who were led by people from CL backgrounds. In another northern state, Bihar, the picture was somewhat different. Bihar adopted the Prasad Committee rules of excluding the CL. Despite a destructive anti-reservation movement when OBC reservations were being introduced for the first time in Bihar in 1978, a formula has been working since then. The 26 per cent reservation consists of 12 per cent of the most backward category listed, 8 per cent for other backward classes listed with an income ceiling of Rs 12,000 per annum, 3 per cent for women and 3 per cent for the poor of the forward

---

[256] "Supreme Court strikes down Kerala backward classes act." Rediff.com , December 13, 1999.
[257] "Government Appoints Panel on CL." *The Hindu.* January 13, 2000.
[258] Cited the Venugopal (2000) from Dudley-Jenkins, Laura. " Identity and identification in India: defining the disadvantaged." Psychology Press, 2003. P152.

castes. Bihar experience may bring about a workable solution toward the tense caste situation in India. It can be implied from the above cases that the anti-Mandal protesters and anti-CL protesters have very different attitudes toward reservations for OBCs; yet what unites them is their preference for older policies using caste as the criteria.

7.3.2 Politics of "Creamy Layer": Party-wide Response to the Principles of CL exclusion

Many mainstream political forces welcomed the additional 27% reservation to Other Backward Classes (OBCs). As discussed in last chapter, Not only did V. P. Singh's Janata Dal Party embrace the OBC reservations, but the Congress Party and BJP eventually included reservations for the OBCs in their manifestos. Various political parties have come up with their own nuanced interpretations of the judgment and its socio-political background. For instance, the BJP spokesperson, Prakash Javadekar, said that the BJP had always favored social justice measures and that the political force to benefit most from the implementation of the quota would be the BJP since it had the largest number of OBC members in Parliament.[259]

But, the Creamy Layer (CL) exclusion has varied responses from various levels of the political class. Most political parties, barring the Left parties, have been uncomfortable with the criteria and concept of CL. The Left parties have consistently advocated that the OBC reservations exclude the affluent sections and the truly deserving should get the benefits of reservation. Other parties and politicians have uniformly expressed their misgivings about the CL exclusion parameters raised by the Supreme Court. For example, the Rashtriya Janata Dal (RJD) leader and Railway Minister, Lalu Prasad, opposed the Supreme Court's suggestion in the Cabinet, arguing it could defeat the very purpose of OBC reservation. Janata Dal (United) leader Sharad Yadav also opposed CL exclusion. He held that reservation was meant to address social and educational backwardness, not economic backwardness. The Chief Minister of Uttar Pradesh

[259] Cited from Ramakrishnan, Venkitesh. "Political Consensus." *Frontline.* Vol. 25. no. 9. April-May 2008.

Mayawati explained that inflation had eaten into incomes and the economic limit of identifying the Creamy Layer became inappropriate.

Just like the OBC Reservation Policies, the CL proposal endorsed by the Supreme Court seemed turning into another instrument for political gamesmanship. For instance, the PMK in Tamil Nadu welcomed the extended quotas for OBCs in the educational institutions but opposed the CL concept endorsed by the Supreme Court. PMK founder S Ramadoss contended,“ there is no mention about the concept (of creamy layer) in the Constitution. All the leaders who work for social justice should work together to defeat the concept.”[260] As the first regional party in the ruling alliance at center, PMK's strong stance over the issue has already influenced the DMK, the bigger Tamil party in the United Progressive Alliance (UPA) government. The DMK leader and the Tamil Nadu Chief Minister M Karunanidhi required Prime Minister Manmohan Singh to take immediate measures for a “fair and just review” of the various parameters of what defines “Creamy Layer” including the income criteria.[261] As for the Congress party - the leading party of the UPA government - has also been under political pressures: on one hand, it tried to meet demands of its southern allies and RJD who opposed the idea of CL exclusion; on the other hand, it had to keep line with the requirements of Supreme Court.

The implementation of Creamy Layer exclusion scheme has been delayed in almost all states as well as the center. In the Rajya Sabha (the upper house of the Parliament of India) on March 16 2004, the then Prime Minister Atal Behari Vajpayee conceded that there has been delay in constituting the review committee since the last committee was constituted in 1993. After the Mandal verdict, only two revisions (in 2004, 2008) have been made, by which income limit has been increased up to 4.5 lakh for the exclusion of Creamy layer. The bottom line in most places is that caste is used as the sole criterion for benefits.

---

[260] Cited from "Creamy layer concept against Constitution PMK " *The Economic Times* April 15, 2008 http //economictimes indiatimes com/PoliticsNation/Creamy_layer_against_Constitution/articleshow/2951898 cms

[261] Ibid

7.4 Two Cases on Politics of Creamy Layer

It is commonly argued that reservations, at least in their direct effect, have increased inequalities among the eligible OBC communities by reserving most of the benefits for the affluent upper crust of the OBC society. The main focus, instead of reaching the real poor, was to mobilize the support of the OBC elites who are relatively wealthy and educated; if more importantly, these wealthier elements have taken control of caste councils and are able to mobilize the impoverished the OBC masses. Because the OBC upper crust has become the rising power brokers in the country, one has to face strong political and administrative hindrances to exclude them. The CL phenomenon in Maharashtra politics indicates how the CL element became the empowered politicians. In the case of Caste Certificate Issuance, the upper caste and CL officials manipulated the in-transparent procedures of issuing caste certificates, which led to more ineligible candidates included in the reservation programmes.

7.4.1 Politicians and Creamy Layer: Maharashtra

With a long history of low-caste movements, the Maharashtra government established three committees/commissions to identify the lower castes.[262] The category of OBCs was first introduced in the report of Depressed Classes and Aboriginal Tribes Committee constituted by the government of Bombay in July 1930. The committee worked to grant special help for their social and educational advancement, but did not fix any criteria for the inclusion of OBC communities. An OBC list of 125 castes was created then, but amended from time to time.[263] The second Committee under the Chairman B.D.Deshmukh was set up to report on Reservation of Backward Classes in the Service (1961-4). It created a list of 270 OBC communities along with

[262] The three commissions include 1) Depressed Classes and Aboriginal Tribes committee, Bombay Presidency (1930); 2) Committee to Report on Reservation of Backward Classes in the Service (1961-4), Chairman: Sh. B.D.Deshmukh; 3) The Other BackwardCclasses Committee and the Expert Commission on OBCs (1993-4)

[263] A list of 228 intermediate communities was declared by issuing GR dated April 23, 1942 for the purpose of recruitment to government service. The list includes peasant and artisan communities, Christians and Muslims. But this list was cancelled by the government of Bombay on November 1, 1950.

115 subgroups. The third state-level OBC Committee was constituted in 1993 to follow the weightage method of the Mandal Commission for recommending a community as backward/ forward.

In the updated list, most of the communities are the *"Shudras"* (i.e. OBCs) in the caste system. But some OBC communities were "deliberately" included in the reserved categories. For instance, the advanced *Sonar* (goldsmith) and *Gurav* (servants of the temple) had no history of either suffering from any social disability or the problem of access to resources/opportunities. But they were still granted OBC status. The peasant communities such as *Kunbi* and *Mali* had claimed the high-ritual *"Kshatriya"* status and even have become the ruling elite in their areas on account of their numerical majority. Because of their inclusion, the reserved seats in the educational institutions and public services under various government schemes have easily been distributed among them. The political appointments have also favored these people.

The policy loopholes to wrongly include the non-backward CL have left space for politicians to manipulate the situation for their own interests. In June of 1995, the Maharashtra government has prepared a list for Special Backward Classes (SBCs). Five communities - *Govari, Mana, Koshti, Koti* and *Mannerwar* – along with 36 sub- groups were categorized as SBCs. This special category was recommended by the Shiv Sena-Bharatiya Janata Party combine government. This recommendation served for a political purpose, since neither the state OBC commission was consulted nor a study undertaken. Interestingly, there has not been any writ petition in the Bombay High Court against the inclusion/exclusion of these communities in the state OBCs list.

.By wrong inclusion, the real backward groups are deprived of their rights. In the OBC-dominated villages, the long-term absence of drinking water and the abysmal literacy levels reflect the fact that the government was incapable and did not intend to supply drinking water to OBC villages, or to improve their literacy levels. It is thus necessary to initiate the process of descheduling of the well-off castes (*Kunbi* and *Mali*) and castes of higher rank (*Sonar* and *Gurav*) from the list of OBCs. Although the Other Backward Classes Commission was empowered by the Mandal Commission judgment (1992) to exclude the wrongly included communities, the state OBC commission is yet to act in this direction.[264]

7.4.2 The Non-Creamy Layer Caste Certificate

The benefits and concessions given by the state governments to the Other Backward Classes (OBCs) have gone further beyond the political and education opportunities. Some specific organizations were set up in charge of distributing economic benefits for the reserved OBC communities. Take Maharashtra as an example. The state government established in 1998 the Maharashtra State Other Backward Classes Finance and Development Corporation (MSOBCFDC), with the objective to develop economic activities for the benefit of OBCs and to assist the weaker section of the target group in skill development and self-employment activities. MSOBCFDC is a Government Undertaking Company under Social Justice, Welfare, and Cultural Affairs Department. It extended the government-aided-schemes to support the eligible OBC communities. The preferential government loans are provided for specific weaker sections of the OBC communities such as low-income groups, women and youths. (See Appendix 7.3)

Unfortunately, the richer reservation benefits have increased the difficulties to exclude the Creamy Layer (CL) from the Other Backward Classes (OBCs). The economic criteria can be as difficult, if not more so, to administer as caste criteria. The rules should be much more complex than a simply economic cut-off to include a wide variety of indicators relating to the employment, property and income of the applicant and the applicant's immediate family. Due to the lack of a systematic official investigation on the CL population, the process of identification has become opaque. D.L.Sheth, member of National Commission for Backward Classes, evaluated that "economic criteria are more difficult because there is a lot of informality, still, in this economy, in

[264] Dahıwale, S. M "Identıfyıng 'Backwardness' in Maharashtra." *Economıc and Polıtıcal Weekly* 35, no. 37 (2000) 3293-3297

[the] agricultural sector and people's income…it is common that people may be earning 20,000 rupees but show it as only 2000.So economic criteria are difficult to implement…occupational and caste categories are in fact neater."[265] The administrative challenges are not limited to the complexity of the rules. The unreliable economic data, as D.L.Sheth noted, has contributed to the growing corruption in the implementation process, which further obfuscated the economic criteria of selecting the CL group.

In the following, I will introduce the case of the non-Creamy Layer Caste Certificate to demonstrate the challenging implementation of CL exclusion. OBC certificates, which involve CL verification, are easily issued to the ineligible candidates. For the principles devised by the state level commissions for Other Backward Classes (OBCs), this new type of certificate is designed specifically for the non-Creamy Layer OBCs who have yearly income under certain amounts and whose parents do not hold the rank first official positions (Class I and II) in the state organizations. This certificate is produced to help the "non-creamy" OBCs applying for the reserved vacancies and posts/admission to central educational institutions under the Government of India. Just like the regular OBC certificates, the OBC "Non-Creamy Layer" certificates are issued by the competent authorities such as District Magistrate, Chief Presidency Magistrate, Revenue Officer not below the rank of Tahsildar, Sub-Divisional Officer of the area where the candidate and/or his family reside, and the similar-level officials of the above.[266]

To obtain the "non-creamy" OBC certificate, the applicants have to apply through his parents if alive or through any senior member of the family to the competent authorities mentioned above. The preprinted application form should be obtained from the relevant offices and should be submitted along with necessary documentary evidences. (See Appendix 7.4) Among the documents, the most important are the Income Certificate issued from the working

[265] D.L. Sheth's interview was done by Laura Dudley-Jenkins (1996) and cited in her book Dudley-Jenkins, Laura. " Identity and identification in India: defining the disadvantaged." Psychology Press, 2003. P.153

[266] Tahsildar is revenue administrative officer in India in-charge of obtaining taxation from a tehsil. A tehsil is also known as taluk (taluq, taluka), and mandal, is an administrative division of some countries of South Asia.

office, Domicile Certificate/Birth Certificate issued at the local government office in the living area.

Despite of the detailed administrative requirement, application of the Creamy Layer criteria all over the country can be very problematic. Firstly, the data of an applicant's extended family, which is relevant to their economic and social status, can be very difficult for the government to monitor. This is especially so in the mountain villages as many family members live separately in the villages that different *Panchayat* administrative staffs take charge. Also, the agricultural income can be hard to calculate in these areas because the agricultural laborers are mobile laborers from one village to another village where they can find temporary work to do.

Secondly, the corruption can grow easily from both sides of applicants and certificate issuing officers. It is doubtful that the upper-caste dominated bureaucracy followed the prescribed procedure thoroughly. Officers in the administration, mostly upper castes or CL officials, tended to hinder the granting of caste certificates to legitimate applicants by claiming a lack of information. There is little "transparency" to flush out the cream in the administrative process so that people can understand the inside stories, as Prasad noted in his interview.[267] The *Panchayat* administrative staffs became highly suspicious when I asked for the beneficiary list of the government-aid programs responding that, "these materials are confidential and are not supposed to be exposed to the public."[268]

On the other hand, the non-OBC or CL candidates tried to "influence" officials to get caste certificates through patronage networks. For instance, in the *Panchayat* (local council) institutions at village level, the bureaucrats usually have strong incentives to issue the relevant documents for their extended families and neighbors. Some documents, such as the parents' income certificates, are prepared for their children before they are born. One of the OBC families

[267] Prasad's interview was done by Laura Dudley-Jenkins (1996) and cited in her book Dudley-Jenkins, Laura. " Identity and identification in India: defining the disadvantaged." Psychology Press, 2003. P.153

[268] The author did the interviews with the local bureaucrats at the Jaldhaka region of West Bengal state, October,3 2008.

told me in the interview, "we did have these certificates provided well before our parents gave birth to us; and we know we need these certificates to get to colleges."[269]

Thirdly, because the "Non-Creamy Layer" certificates can only be issued based on certain certificates and documents which can easily be made fraud, there is a high possibility that the certificates are issued to the ineligible applicants. For example, reservations on economic grounds must be based on verified income certificates. But only a small segment of the population has reported their incomes to the Income Tax Department and their income certificates can hardly be reliably verified. As a matter of fact, the income-based reservations have generated a flourishing market in income certificates. The certificate issuing authorities, especially at local level, tended to attract a large-scale bribery from the undeserving rich at the expense of the deserving poor. Such document and certificate issuance also led to a vast increase in the scope of political patronage.

Whereas the non-OBC communities can obtain the "non-Creamy Layer" certificates easily through patronage network, the genuine OBC candidates found it very difficult to obtain certificates in time for their purposes. After the Mandal announcement, many of the recruiting agencies of the high educational institutions required the OBC certificates issued on their format and within a certain time limit. But the certificates issuing authorities do not issue them in that manner. Take the educational reservation as an example. According to the recruiting rules (2008-09) of some higher educational institutions, the first-year applicants of four year degree courses in engineering/technology have to meet the following requirements if they are eligible for the reserved quota:[270] Among them, 30 % seats of the total intake capacity are available as All India quota seats. The candidates who are interested in these seats should apply separately and directly

[269] The interview was done by the author with the local children at the Jaldhaka region of West Bengal state, September 29, 2008.
[270] These autonomous institutions include: College of Engineering, Pune; University Institute of Chemical Technology; Veermata Jijabai Technological Institute, Mumbai; Shri Guru Gobind Singhji Institute of Engineering and Technology, Nanded; Walchand College of Engineering, Sangli.

to the institutions with the Caste Validity Certificate and Non-Creamy Layer Certificate valid up to 31st Mar 2009.

7.5 Implications

As a result of unequally distributed reservations, a distinct cleavage formed within the target group in terms of privileged and under- privileged. Studies have revealed that those who benefited were the start of a chain of successes over successive generations - leading to the creation of a discernible Creamy Layer within the backward community.

Learning from the Creamy Layer (CL) phenomenon, we may conclude that impacts of Reservation Policies are sociologically and politically divisive. Although the Supreme Court recognized the complexity of the CL phenomenon in 1992, it may not have foreseen the degree of the divisive role played by the policies.[271] Firstly, reservations have secured casteism in the social and political arenas as the caste-based reservations created a structure of life-long privilege which is determined at the moment of birth instead of any index of achievement of economic status. In the process it has accomplished the divisions and variability of the Indian polity on the basis of caste and religion. Such political divisions have caused further economic differences. As Abhijit Banerjee and Rohini Somanathan state, among the historically disadvantaged social groups, those that mobilized themselves politically gained relative to the others. [272]

Secondly, reservations can further divide the sub-groups within each caste. Although some section of certain castes can climb the ladder of merit by using educational and employment opportunities, most of the people in the same caste had no access to the benefits. This is not simply the bifurcation between forward and backward castes, but fragmentation created within

[271] The Supreme Court suggested that to be an eligible beneficiary of Reservation Policies, it was not enough to be in a lower caste if one's father was government minister. It was also not enough to simply be poor if one was in a high caste.

[272] Abhijit Banerjee, Rohini Somanathan. "The Political Economy of Public Goods: Some Evidence from India." *Journal of Development Economics* 82 (2007): 287–314.

some specific castes. It can be argued that the identification of "CL" is in fact based upon horizontal division in each section of Backward Class into Creamy Layer or Non - Creamy Layer.

Thirdly, reservations also prevented the poor lower castes from uniting on class lines. The identity politics founded on reservations emerged in the 1990s across India, which pushed the economic issues facing the poor away from centre stage. Also, as the privileged sections of the lower castes absorbed in the ruling classes through reservations, these new elites tended to form "...electoral alliances or governing coalitions with parties that they had earlier branded as communal."[273]". As a result, the deprived masses were politically divided among different caste-based parties.

The Creamy Layer section of Backward Classes has made a huge impact in the political domain. Firstly, the Creamy Layer politics in the north and south has shown distinctive patterns. The OBCs have traditionally been dominating the politics of South India since the early 20th century. It inevitably helped a large number of Creamy Layer took hold in the political and administrative arenas. The Creamy Layer in the north, however, has shown its strength rapidly from the low-caste movements since the early 1980s. Not only have they gradually changed the composition of Parliament, they have been in power in most of the northern states in the Hindi belt. The clout of the community became enhanced from the manner and swiftness in which the 93rd (Constitution) Amendment (Higher Education Reservation) was passed. Interestingly, CL phenomenon in the north has not incurred as strong resistance as their counterparts in the south.

However, no matter whether it was anti-Mandal protests in the north or anti-CL activities in the south, the political activists preferred the status quo to the changes. As Jaffrelot (2001) argues, the challenges of adding new criteria to the existing categories may be solved only when different interests came to a consensus due to the growing recognition of the political power of the Backward Classes. At the same time, the undergoing economic liberalization may gradually

[273] Chaudhury, Pradipta. "The 'Creamy Layer': Political Economy of Reservations." 39, no. 20 (2004): 1989-1990.P.1990

attract young people's focus away from the public sector jobs. "'People have by and large reconciled,' says Rohit Sharma, then an anti-Mandal agitationist and now a marketing executive."[274]

Secondly, the political activities of the Creamy Layer also existed at the local level. The administrative design of issuing Caste Certificate empowered the local officials to manipulate the targeting population that benefited from the reservations. Critics of Reservation Policies for OBCs consistently claimed that the newly created OBC quotas have increased the inequalities within these groups and reduced opportunities for general-entry candidates from other groups who may be worse off than the beneficiaries. Therefore, it is important to separate the CL from the general category of the backwards, such as the mobile landed castes who have traditionally been cornering the lion's share from the general quota of the backwards in most states. For instance, the *Yadavs,* who constitute about 19 per cent of Uttar Pradesh population, have received 34 per cent reservation benefits according to the Social Justice Committee which was set up by the Uttar Pradesh Chief Minister Rajnath Singh.[275]

In order to reduce the political and administrative challenges in the process of identifying the CL, the differentiation of Other Backward Classes (OBCs) and Most Backward Classes (MBCs) is one of the workable measures. Some states have made attempts to set aside a proportionate quota for each of the important sub-castes in the OBC groups. For instance, the Bihar Commission has worked out the Karpoori Thakur formula which suggested the separate quotas for the intermediate (8 per cent), the MBCs (12 per cent), the women (3 per cent) and the poor among the upper castes (3 per cent). The Social Justice Committee in Uttar Pradesh has also attempted a similar exercise with regard to the MBCs and *Dalits*. The northern state governments seemed acting more actively than their southern counterparts, probably because CL phenomenon is relatively new in most northern states.

[274] "Mandal Battle fields Barren Now." *Indian Express* September 23 , 1993.

[275] Kumar, Pradeep. "Reservations within Reservations: Real Dalit-Bahujans." *Economic and Political Weekly* 36, no. 37 (2001): 3505-3507. P. 3507

However, will removing the Creamy Layer (CL) among OBCs ensure the reaching of benefits to non-CL of the OBCs? The reality is that the representation of Backward Classes is still miserably low. The representation of OBCs with 52% population and 27% reservation of seats had only 4.69% representation to class I till 1980 and 12.55% in all services. If CL is taken away, will the non -Creamy Layer be able to compete and fill 27% vacancies? The answer is probably negative. A job in government and a university admission requires an eligibility condition such as a bachelor's degree, a higher secondary certificate or at the very least, matriculation. Yet less than 2 percent of the general population graduate from colleges, only 3 per cent complete higher secondary school or its equivalent, and only 7 per cent matriculate.[276] Among the educationally backward castes the figures could be even lower: It can be implied that OBC government officials and college students may all come from this tiny minority. Even when the principles have been designed to exclude the CL, it is still difficult for the reservation benefits to "trickle down" to the majority of OBCs in a relatively short run. But the only way to improve the status of the lower castes requires two developments: 1) educational opportunities that can be offered to everyone; 2) a rapid and steady economy that affects most of the country. In fact, both are happening, which has resulted in a wide stretch of castes benefitting in education and careers.

[276] Guha, Ashok "Reservations in Myth and Reality" *Economic and Political Weekly* 25, no 50 (December 1990) 2716-2718

Chapter 8

Concluding Remarks

For some time now, political scientists and sociologists have been aware that some state policies promote political action from the mass public and elites while others impede it. It has also become known that policies have the ability to affect the identities, goals and behavior of individuals/groups over extensive periods of time (Mettler 2002).[277] But to date, we know little about the mechanisms through which pre-existing policies shape the identities, capabilities, goals and behavior of mass publics over time, as well as about the processes through which these effects become reflected in subsequent political processes. The analysis of such mechanism and processes has hardly been found in democratic countries, and even less so in the developing countries that had undergone radical and/or wide-ranging political transformations.

8.1 Task of the Study

The focus of this study is on the policy effects in India that has recently undergone wide-ranging political transformations for the mass public as well as political elites. More specifically, I explore the processes through which caste-oriented state policies affected the lower castes' activism. The reason why I concentrate on the policy for lower caste groups is two-fold. First, the state is known to have specific, relatively well delineated ideology and sets of policies focusing on social groups (in this dissertation the caste groups are focused). It is of methodological

[277] Mettler, Suzanne "Bringing the State Back In to Civic Engagement Policy Feedback Effects of the G I Bill for World War II Veterans " *American Political Science Review* 96, no 2 (June 2002) 351-365

significance for the Indian case because policy approach can serve as a clear criterion for distinguishing among various welfare regimes at subnational level.

Second, focusing on mass public and political elites helps understand the policy effects – resource effect as well as interpretive effect –on the social and political formation of these social groups. Theda Skocpol (1992) defines "policy feedback" as the ways in which "policies, once enacted, restructure subsequent political processes".[278] When policy benefits are distributed unequally, the less favored social groups, based on common purposes and social solidarities, will interact with elites or authorities in a sustained way for benefits. Such norms comprise a set of understandings that reflect how the lower castes pursued political power.

8.2 Main Arguments

My study has the character of a monograph, specifying the mechanism of Reservation Policies (RPs). This research is based on fieldwork and placed within the context of similar researches by other scholars with respect to RPs. An important question is regards the extent that results can be generalized for other parts of India? It is true that these dynamics can not be found in all parts of the country. Still, what is happening in these states seems to have certain general validity.

8.2.1 Caste and Politics

Although western scholars emphasize that the individual identities will gradually replace the role of caste in politics, this trend can hardly be seen in India. As Rudolphs argue, Indians do not see themselves as individuals but as members of social groups. Instead, the caste identity has been strengthened and caste-based politics have been enhanced. Caste gives an individual sense of belonging in a system in which he is otherwise getting alienated and atomized. It provides him

[278] Skocpol, Theda. *Protecting Soldiers and Mothers.* Cambridge, Mass. and London: Harvard University Press, 1992.

with an "institution" through which most people in the same group can be protected from outside threats including that from the state. Caste is used "as an instrument for social change. Caste is not disappearing, nor is 'casteism' – the political use of caste – for what is emerging in India is a social and political system which institutionalizes and transforms but does not abolish caste."[279] Therefore, the time when Indian governments began to identify the Other Backward Classes (OBCs) as a social category, the OBCs became crystallized not only as a legal-constitutional category but also a political category.

Caste politics is not a recent phenomenon in India. In the traditional and medieval eras, the caste groups have fought with each other to gain preeminence. Use of caste for political purpose has begun long before the introduction of adult franchise. Organizations based on caste for social, economic and political purposes came into existence even before Constitution came into force. The illiterate people who didn't understand politics were mobilized by the self-interested politicians who organize them by appealing to their caste sentiments and to gain benefits of a political system.

The modern version of caste politics in India has changed its format compared to the traditional competition and strife. Firstly, the modern state has become the mediator among different caste groups for power distribution. It is the modern state that has created new avenues for the economic and political uplifts of the lower caste groups. Secondly, though political contest has been mainly between the upper castes and the lower castes, the real picture probably has become more changeable between conflicts and agreements, competition and cooperation among various caste groups. *Jats* are against Gujars, together they are against urban castes; Kolis are against Patidars; the Vars oppress Pallars and the Devendrakula Vellalas; the Vanniyars Torment Adi Dravidas, even as many of them may be against, or for, Brahmans in their local settings.[280] The relationship between caste and politics in Indian has been intensively studied for decades.

[279] Weiner, Myron. "The Struggle for Equality: Caste in Indian Politics." In *The Success of India's Democracy*, by Atul Kohli. New Jersey: Cambridge University Press, 2001.
[280] Radhakrishnan, P. "'The Politics of Perdition." *The Hindu*. September 21, 2001.

The sociologists have analyzed various aspects of the relationship between caste and politics [281] Anil Bhatt observes that political interests became lower among higher caste groups while the lower castes showed a higher political awareness. [282] Lower castes by organizing themselves in pursuit of collective interest were able to achieve higher social, economic and political success. Rudolph and Rudolph emphasize the crucial role played by the caste associations in politics that has changed their position in hierarchical pattern of Hindu society.[283] In Andre Beteille's study of Tanjore district in Tamil Nadu, caste identity is also highlighted as to boost the political and economic status of the non-*Brahmins*.[284] From these views, one can conclude that caste has become one of the most formidable elements of group formation and solidarity in Indian Politics.

8.2.2 Group Identities Shaped by State

As one form of positive discrimination, Reservation Policies (RPs) in India aim to favor the disadvantaged ethnic groups by giving them reservations in employment, education as well as the political assemblies. I observe that state has been shaping new social categories through its legislative process and administrative practices. Once states use public policies to send the messages about the role of lower castes, a common identity and frames for engaging formal political institutions may be instituted. In the case of lower caste issues, RPs in the 1950s still serve as a dominant reference point against which the subaltern people in India formed their attitudes and actions in elections. This observation is especially delineated in Chapter 4. Chapter 4 focuses on the formation of group identities for the lower castes, especially the Other Backward Classes (OBCs), with central emphasis on the constructive role of RPs. Studying the legislative and administrative procedures of RPs, I argue that the political orientation of the subaltern people

[281] The well known sociologists including Andre Beteille, Rajni Kothari, and Anil Bhatt have highlighted the strengthened casteism in politics

[282] Bhatt, Anil "Politics and Social Mobility in India " *Contributions to Indian Sociology* 5, no 1 (January 1971) 99-114

[283] Rudolph , Lloyd I "The Political Role of India's Caste Associations " *Pacific Affairs* 33, no 1 (1960)

[284] Béteille, André *The Idea of Natural Inequality and other Essays* New York Oxford University Press, 1987

has become more constructed on caste basis as to deviate further from the traditional authority and elite politics in the states where reservations were provided in generous and definite forms.

According to Andre Beteille, the loyalties of castes are exploited in voting.[285] New alliances and caste-based demand groups cutting across castes are also formed. I find that caste enters the political process by making appeals to new caste loyalties of the defined reservation recipients. In Chapter 5, I emphasize caste alignment and caste polarization directly affected by RPs. The newly empowered caste groups have strengthened their influences by either associating with or resisting against the already powerful caste groups. As a result, the new caste identities regulated by RPs transformed the political scene in India.

8.2.3 Strengthened Casteism in Politics

In this dissertation I draw a general conclusion that expansion of reservations has not brought a commensurate increase of economic and political status among the lower castes. On the contrary, India's caste-related policies have intensified the political conflicts along caste lines in India. With its rigid caste-based identification and reservation benefits, the state has constructed and maintained casteism in the political landscape. Weiner (2001) views caste "as an instrument for social change......the political use of caste – for what is emerging in India is a social and political system which institutionalizes and transforms but does not abolish caste."[286] Traditionally, castes differentiate themselves from other castes in a hierarchical order.[287] This has changed in the sense that caste groups have been economically and politically empowered by modern state and its public policies. Indian modern state did revive caste after British rulers. Reservation Policies (RPs) since the early 1950s not only distributed the political and economic

[285] Béteille, André. *The Backward Classes in Contemporary India* New Delhi: Oxford University Press, 1992.

[286] Weiner, Myron. "The Struggle for Equality: Caste in Indian Politics." In *The Success of India's Democracy*, by Atul Kohli. New Jersey: Cambridge University Press, 2001.P.196

[287] According to Gupta, Dipankar (2000), the castes can be differentiated on multiple fronts: on how to get married; how to conduct funeral ceremonies; how to cook and eat; and on the basis of gods that they each caste considers to be special to its members. Gupta, Dipankar. *Interrogating Caste Understanding Hierarchy and Difference in Indian society* New Delhi: Penguin, 2000.

sources in favor of the lower castes, but also created a new group identity –Other Backward Classes (OBCs).

The empowered new caste identities have had increasing chances in the political scenario by its numerous heads to vote in the electoral competition. These numerous castes consequently started making numerous demands, whether for reservations, or for being categorized in OBCs etc. As results, the caste-related policies polarized the national politics; caste politics breed caste parties. Not a single party can avowedly break away from the dominate influence of Caste. Even National Congress or BJP have to consider a caste factor while allocating tickets to the candidates and allocating portfolios to the Ministers.[288] Caste tends to determine electoral nominations, voting behavior and government positions nowadays.

Casteism has penetrated in Indian politics so deeply as to shape state politics across India. Andre Beteille has pointed that the political process has a dual effect on the caste system. To the extent that caste and sub-caste loyalties are consistently exploited, and to the extent that it led to new alliance cutting across caste, it has changed the traditional structure.[289] The various caste groups, such as the Brahmin and non -Brahmin in Tamil Nadu; the Khamma and Reddy in Andhra Pradesh; the Vokkaliga and Lingayats in Kamataka, the Maratha and Mahar in Maharashtra, the Patidar and the Rajput in Gujrat, the Jat, Rajput, Meena, Brahmin and Vaisya in Rajasthan, and Nair, the Christian and Ezhava in Kerala were found politically powerful and determinative factors in the politics at the state level.

However, public policy can't be effective by itself. Political parties, court judges and state administers have enormous roles to play in the social awakening of India's democratic pattern. They endeavor to educate the people as per the ethics and organize public opinion to regularize the progressive changes. In Chapter 6, I emphasize the role of court judges, state

[288] But caste is not the only factor that parties give thoughts about; other factors such as experience of good governance are also considered to select the candidates.
[289] Béteille, André. *The Backward Classes in Contemporary India.* New Delhi: Oxford University Press, 1992.

administers as well as party leaders in interpreting RPs. The patronage and pecuniary sources available to the political leaders enable them to create a coalition of factions on caste basis in a complex network of personal obligational ties. Each of these leaders had a group of followers tied to him in accordance with the same set of caste principles. The political party leaders, especially during the elections, mobilize support along caste lines and articulate caste interests in an organized manner. As a matter of fact, grass-root political arenas have always remained and continue to remain dominated by these political elites, who compete with each other to form caste coalitions of supporters in order to maximize control over local resources and stayed as successful players in India's political scene.

8.3 Significance of the Study

As Skocpol states, in order to understand the complexities of democratic political processes, we need know how "policies transform and expand the identities, political goals, and capabilities of various social groups that subsequently struggle or ally in politics"[290]. As mentioned in the first place, some policies ultimately promote political action from the mass public while others impede it. This question of why this dichotomy is of particular importance in new democracies whose political regimes are yet to be fully consolidated. It is important to find answers to the questions about how citizens' experience with certain policies enhances or delimits their future political action and political attitudes. Inspired by existing descriptive studies of the lower caste groups in India, and by literature on policy effect within the historical-institutionalist division of the political science literature, this dissertation concentrates on processes and cases that have been understudied.

[290] Skocpol, Theda. *Protecting Soldiers and Mothers.* Cambridge, Mass. and London: Harvard University Press, 1992. P.58

8.3.1 Comparative Welfare Regimes

Globalization is seen as "the core of the problem" undermining the old social contract between the welfare states and social actors. However, it is not seen as something that might be affected by state policies. Whether or not India will achieve a new social contract is left in question; but it will be neither like the welfare states of "competitive corporatism" in the Scandinavian countries where the principles of universalism of social rights prevail and government plays a major role, nor like the "liberal" welfare states of the US, where social welfare plans are characterized by decentralization and private sector plays an important role.[291]

Two decades of economic liberalization in India has shown its strength and continuance in economic growth. India has achieved a GDP increase of around 8-9 percent annually since it embarked on economic reforms since the 1990s. As one asks the question that how many people have been positively involved in the wave of globalization, the other side of the same question is that how many has been adversely affected? By now higher growth rates and therefore higher per capita income, are not sufficient to improve the living conditions of all India's poor. Rapid economic growth only fueled demands for greater redistribution, especially since this growth is seen as unequalizing. "Trickle down" approach believed in many scholars in the early 1970s has lost its popularity since the 1980s. According to Atul Kohli, the solution to the problem of India's poverty will thus not emerge from higher rates of economic growth along, if they emerge at all, they are likely to involve conscious state intervention aimed at reconciling growth with distribution.[292]

The theoretical idea of this dissertation follows the school of historical institutionalism, which in the recent decade has become a mainstream position in comparative welfare state research. However, it has been recognized that the notion of "path-dependency" is often under

[291] In the development of US social programs, private sector shares a large role in providing health and medical care and employment related pensions etc.

[292] Kohli, Atul. *The State and Poverty in India The Politics of Reform* Cambridge University Press, 1989.

specified, i.e. it is not clearly spelled out how the feedback process actually works.[293] The comparative welfare regime theorists study how policy legacies shape new social reforms. In Esping-Andersen famous 1990 book, he distinguished between liberal, conservative, and social democratic welfare state regimes. As noted in Chapter 1, each of the three welfare regime types embraces a characteristic set of policy tools, beneficiaries, ideologies, and links between social protections and production. Even when welfare states are confronted with common exogenous pressures (such as globalization), they still develop the distinctive trajectories of welfare redistribution. Existing policies mold the construction of constituencies for new welfare state programs and create "policy ratchet" or "lock-in" effects that define solutions to new problems. Learning from previous and current welfare programs may provide certain prospects for future program expansion/retrenchment. For example, the U.S. public pension systems, such as the pay-as-you-go intergenerational contracts, have locked in particular paths of development.

Besides the resource provided by the states in terms of social protections and economic spending, different welfare regimes also have ideological legacies or interpretive effects: partly related to long-term patterns of party control and administrative management Citizens over time come to expect and accept certain things from welfare states inevitable (especially under long-term, left party domination). For instance, citizens in universal welfare states, such as Scandinavian countries, feel that they are treated equally, and that generate higher levels of trust in government than do liberal regimes.[294] Thus, one finds caste-based political contentions vary at state level in India in accordance with these regime distinctions which mirror the values, patterns of discourse, and institutional supports of each state's own context.

[293] Pierson, Paul. "Path Dependence, Increasing Returns, and the Study of Politics." *American Political Science Review* 94, no 2 (2000)· 251-267.

[294] Rothstein, Bo. *Just Institutions Matter* New York: Cambridge University Press, 1998.

8.3.2 Effect of Policy: Equality or Inequality

Till recently, Reservation Policies (RPs) still remained highly controversial and terms such as "Other Backward Classes" still invoke debates among many scholars and politicians. However, it is commonly agreed that the reservation policy legacies have led to the political involvement of lower castes who expect to build a more "equal" society. According to the Constitution of India, "the state shall not deny to any person, equality before the law or the equal protection of the laws within the territory of India."[295] As a pluralistic society, Indian policy makers swear not to discriminate on any ground, and hence RPs were adopted for alleviating inequalities in the political and economic scenarios.

The problem arises in targeting them and meeting the ends for which reservation is created. Also, the fact is that India is democratic and all groups-including poor compete for benefits of the state. RPs on basis of caste started when the Simon Commission came to India with the rule of separate electorates and reservations for the depressed. But a concrete legislation was passed only after Independence when Dr. B.R. Ambedkar fought for the rights of the Scheduled Castes, Scheduled Tribes and Other Backward Classes. During the Constitutional assembly debates, he supported the cause of backward castes and believed that RPs are the only way to eradicate these disparities. However, the provisional policies have been expanded for years as the government did not feel that the required amount of equality has been achieved in the social, economic or political life of people. Moreover, once a benefit given, it becomes almost impossible to withdraw it in a democratic country such as India.

Is the present reservation system a true reflection of an equal society that founders of Indian Constitution envisaged? The truth is that the reservations have eliminated certain disparities but cultivated others. Inequality has still been prevalent and existent in new forms. The noteworthy phenomenon is that of "Creamy Layer". Though pursuing the equal social status as the upper castes, there came the deepening economic and political gaps within the lower castes.

---

[295] It is Article 14 of India's Constitution which is construed as one of the fundamental rights.

RPs thus produced the particular stratum of the society which is termed as "Creamy Layer", who are relatively wealthier and better educated members of the Other Backward Classes (OBCs). In Chapter 7, I attempt to explain the politics of "Creamy Layer": how the exclusion of "Creamy Layer" became politically difficult in India, and why the CL are the major beneficiaries of quota policies.

Majoritarianism is a common development that persists in a democratic society. As the government is chosen by the majority and every decision that is taken depends upon the majority vote, the law tends to favor this majority.[296] However, in India, the Constitution makers wanted to avoid this situation of hierarchy and majority rule. A true democracy is established when all people have possible avenues to make the decisions. On one hand, there is a struggle for *equality*; but on the other hand, group and caste identities are sharpened and boundaries between groups reinforced. As paradoxical as it may seem, this contradiction is already present in the Indian Constitution, which on one hand calls for equality of opportunity and status for all citizens irrespective of caste, sex, religion etc. and on the other hand has a full package of reservations prepared for Scheduled Castes, Scheduled Tribes, and OBCs etc.

8.4 Limitations

This study on Reservation Policies (RPs), aiming to understand India's caste politics, follows the policy approach which starts by analyzing causal effect between policy and participation.

8.4.1 Limitation on the Policy Approach

The chapters in this dissertation emphasize that policy matters for participation. Shown in the previous chapters, the lower caste groups have responded to the unequally distributed

[296] As this feature of majoritarianism has come under criticism, democracies have consequently included constraints in what the parliamentary majority can do, in order to protect the fundamental rights of citizens.

programs with surging participation. Politicians see these surges in reaction to policy events and interpret them in general as demand for program changes or cuts. Congress members and representatives who hear more from their constituents are more protective of their programs. In some dramatic cases, lawmakers even switch their votes on caste-related policy in the face of protests by their constituents. Chapter 5 looks at the participation of the caste-based demand groups who received/did not receive government benefits: they associated or conflicted with other interest groups for which government programs have contributed to upward or downward participation-policy spirals. The comparative case study of West Bengal and Tamil Nadu in Chapter 6 illustrates that the program recipients participate at high levels in both states, but with different political attitudes and ideology based on the different interpretation of Reservation Policies.

However, as many scholars have studied, it is no less important that participants received even lower level welfare benefits largely because of their modest participant capacities. As a matter of fact, this participation-policy-participation cycle has suggested a lock-in effect that the unequal distribution of welfare benefits can not be corrected as planned by the state. In Chapter 7, the politics of "Creamy Layer" illustrates that the RPs have favored the "Creamy Layer" at expense of the qualified non-Cream Layers, which is repeatedly ignored because the empowered "Creamy Layer" used the system to dominate the reservation benefits.

To break the lock-in effect of the policy-politics cycle, the "learning effects" of policy approach on state actors or social groups is most important. In this dissertation, the political engagement of lower castes is a process started with their understanding of the relevant policies. Through the political learning of reservations, they have a better idea of how responsive the governments are and become more capable to deal with the government. The lock-in effects, therefore, would break due to their changing knowledge and behavior.

8.4.2 Limitation on the Employed Data

The search for data about the dynamics of policy implementation in India has encountered several limitations. Firstly, it is impossible to restrict myself to merely compiling data concerning the lower-caste households, by and large landless, in the two villages of my initial fieldwork. The complicated configuration of the reservation programs could not be understood if my study remained confined only to the two villages. It was not sufficient to try to compensate that shortcoming merely by tracing the process of policy implementation. Secondly, my academic work schedule in the U. S. does not allow for long spells of absence. This meant that field work had to be spread out in a way that would ensure the coverage over different locations in a rather short time. Such research with fragmented materials learning from the officials/intellectuals/low castes over a short period has its disadvantages, as the data collected does not reflect time consistency. Thus my fieldwork has to be complemented with information gathered by other scholars.

Taking my initial fieldwork villages as point of department, therefore, I compile large sets of data in discussing caste and politics. I use mass survey data to evaluate participation and attitudes of Other Backward Classes (OBCs) and other lower castes (Scheduled Castes and Scheduled Tribes). These data come from a variety of cross-sectional and time-series sources. For example, the election materials for this study come mainly from the National Election Study (NES) and Centre for the Study of Developing Societies (CSDS). The time series data is crucial for determining of participation rates of OBCs and other caste groups since the early 1950s. Although the data of lower-caste participation does not begin before implementation of reservation programs, it does extend back to 1952 (the first national election) in terms of SC/ST participation in the NES data.

In addition, I use some of the recent cross-sectional surveys conducted by CSDS to perform multivariate analyses of the influences behind lower-caste participation. The election surveys conducted by CSDS are comprehensive in terms of caste-based participatory activity currently available for cross-state research. It contains detailed questions about political engagement and caste mobilization unavailable in other datasets. It also contains OBC-specific participation items that are crucial to this study.

This study also employs official data from multi-level sources. In respect of spending programs for these caste groups, this study includes all-aspect fiscal spending data from the state-level Financial Reports, such as State Finance of State Government. It describes a good picture of welfare spending on the Scheduled Castes, Scheduled Tribes as well as Other Backward Classes. In addition to all the official datasets, I include other research data on the similar issues. In Chapter 6 I combine the village-based surveys in Uttar Pradesh and Tamil Nadu with my own data to assess the differentiations of the economic status among the lower castes and between lower castes and upper castes.

The identification of households or individuals that have been wrongly included or excluded from the OBC groups has shown varieties in various official sources. To analyze OBC phenomenon, I employ the official data that reflects the realty in the most appropriate term. For example, this study refers to several official sources in terms of OBC population. The recommendation by the B.P. Mandal Commission on reservation has estimated the OBC population at 52 percent of the total population, but it is separated into thousands of endogenous castes. Another estimate was drawn from the data compiled by the National Sample Survey Organization, which functions under the Ministry of Statistics and Programme Implementation. The National Sample Survey places their number at 36 percent of the population. The National Family Health Statistics (NFHS) conducted a survey in 1998 which estimated the non-Muslim OBCs constitutes 29.8 percent of the whole Indian population, which is a little higher than the reservations that the government extended for especially the OBCs from June 2007. However, Yogendra Yadav argues that the various data is in the official domain do not present the true picture of India's OBC population. [297] For my study, I employ the data of NFHS which is more reliable than others. On one hand it avoids the methodological problem of NSSO which asks the respondents most of whom do not even know their own caste category; on the other hand it avoids the simple calculation of OBCs as the residual population of the upper castes and *Dalits*.

Further, the reservation rules have been interpreted based on the special situations in different states. All this increased the difficulties for the policy research. To reduce the incomparable data collected from different states, the major explanation over the Reservation Policies has been cited mainly from the central government, central commissions of Backward Castes as well as nation-level surveys.

8.5 Summary

India witnessed the "second democratic upsurge"—a broad and intensive political participation among the disadvantaged social groups since the late 1980s. This dissertation focuses on the politics of lower castes especially the Other Backward Classes (OBCs), with the central emphasis on the constructive role of Reservation Policies (RPs) for them. I examine the mechanism how the lower castes are empowered through resource effect and interpretive effect of reservations as to transform the electoral politics and party preference in India.

Analyzing the process of designing and implementing RPs, I first conjecture that state is shaping or strengthening the new social categories, such as the OBCs. Through the historical understanding of legislative debates and the case study of Caste Certificate issuance, I attest that this new political identity of OBC groups is a construction originated in or strengthened by the positive discrimination policies.

[297] According to Yogendra *Yadav*, there is no final, conclusive empirical evidence of the size of the Other Backward Classes (OBCs) in India. He estimates the OBC population is between 40-44 percent based on the national election studies conducted over the past two decades.

Then, I contend that with its caste-based identification and reservation benefits, state has strengthened casteism in the political landscape. I especially analyze resource effect and interpretive effect of RPs, arguing that the insufficient and unequal allocation of reservation benefits and elites' manipulation of interpreting RPs have caused a politics of contention.

I further argue that rigidity of the state's continuous use of the same standards of caste recognition has unintentionally led to increasing inequality within the OBC groups, which is illustrated by the "Creamy Layer" phenomenon.

Surely, analysis of policy impacts is only half of the story. Understanding the complete policy-politics cycle can not ignore the feedback process that political participation of lower castes in turn influences policy making itself. (Diagram8.1) For instance, the non-Brahmin identities in Tamil Nadu are less a result of RPs but more of a factor leading to the first RPs coming into being. But when the RPs was implemented, it further strengthened the Dravidian identities and their assertiveness. Usually, the more policy recipients ably and confidently involve themselves in politics, the more likely they tend to participate actively, the more responsive the programs are towards the recipients' demands. For example, the court decision of excluding "Creamy Layer" from reservations was an active response toward the political request from the eligible lower castes who have not benefited from the reservation programs. In fact, "Creamy Layer" has not been excluded in actual implementation of RPs. However, this may change as the poorer OBC groups organize politically and gain more influence.

Diagram 8.1: Model of Policy Process

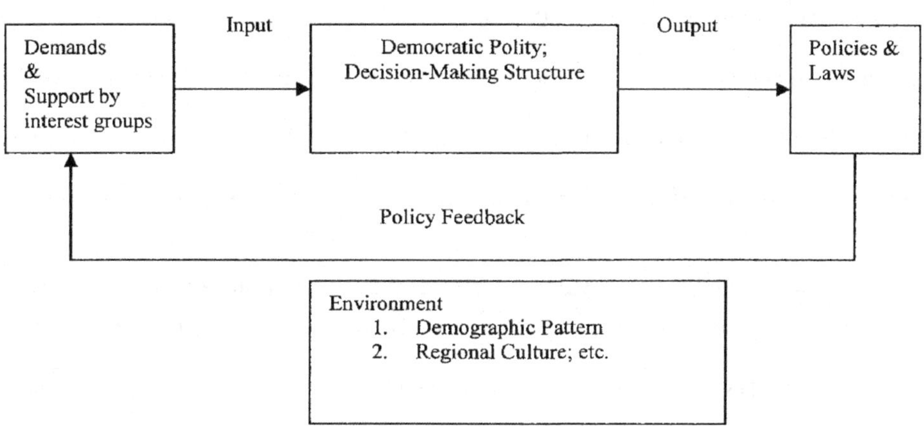

On the methodological front, this dissertation of India's Reservation Policies provides a good case for policy research. It attempts to prove three hypotheses in Chapter 2: 1) compared with Uttar Pradesh, the relatively generous and universal programs in Tamil Nadu have helped shape a broader political coalition among the cohesive SC/ST/OBC beneficiaries. 2) These beneficiaries politically participated in politics in a more orderly form than their counterparts in Uttar Pradesh partly because the reservation benefits in Tamil Nadu are provided longer and distributed more evenly. 3) The different strategies of mobilizing the same caste groups in West Bengal and Tamil Nadu has shaped the class-based electorate in the former and the caste-based participants in the latter.

Finally, further research needs to be done on the relationship between welfare regimes and political participation. The comparative study of Tamil Nadu, Uttar Pradesh and West Bengal provides different types of welfare regimes and political participation in India based on designs, interpretation and implementation of Reservation Policies (RPs). Tamil Nadu, dominated by the Dravidian elites, presents a pro-lower caste welfare system, where generous and universal reservation programs are provided. In this Dravidian state, the lower castes have been highly and orderly mobilized in the post-Independence period. By comparison, Uttar Pradesh, where RPs were designed later and distributed less evenly than Tamil Nadu, has seen the upsurge of participation of lower castes in the 1980s, but in a relatively disorganized manner. The upper-caste dominated communists in West Bengal, who were reluctant to use caste as a mobilizing tool, promoted class-based political participation. In contrast, the lower caste leaders in Tamil Nadu have successfully led Dravidian (i.e. non-*Brahmins*) movements. (Table 8.1)

Table 8.1: Reservation Policies (RPs) and Political Participation in India, the Case of OBCs

	Tamil Nadu	West Bengal	Uttar Pradesh
Welfare Regime Type	Dravidian-Democratic	Democratic-Developmental	*Kisan*-Socialist
Targeted Beneficiaries of RPs	Non-*Brahmins* (including all castes lower than *Brahmins* in the hierarchical Hindu system)	Middle and small farmers, can be clubbed with the middle castes	The middle castes between the *Brahmins* and *Dalits*
RP interpreters	Dravidian leaders	Upper-caste Communists	Socialists
Political Participation	Highly and orderly mobilized by the lower castes	Poor caste-based mobilization	Upsurge of participation of lower castes, but in a relatively disorganized manner
Political Attitudes/Ideology	Pro-Dravidian	Class-based redistribution of development	Pro-poor

Note: * One-party dominance was officially ended when Mamata Banerjee's Trinamool Congress, a non-communist party, won 2011 state election in West Bengal.

Appendix

Appendix 4.1: Timeline of Tamil Nadu Reservations since the Independence

Timeline	Reservation for SCs & STs		Reservation for OBCs		Total Reservation	Notes
1951	16%		25%		41%	Introduced as state act
1971	16%		16% (Backward Classes; BCs)	17% (Most Backward Classes, MBCs)	49%	Separated reservation policies for MBCs recommended by Sattanathan Commission; "Creamy Layer" and "Most Backward Classes" also introduced
	18%		31%		49%	Introduced by DMK government
1980	18%		50%		68%	"Creamy Layer Exclusion" implemented and withdrawn by ADMK; extension of OBC Reservation Policies introduced by ADMK government
1989	18% for SCs	1% extra for STs	30% for OBCs	20% for MBCs	69%	Separated Reservation Policies for ST and MBC introduced by DMK government
1994						69% Reservation was included in 9th Schedule

Appendix 4.2: Criteria or indicators to identify Backward Classes with effect from September 1st, 1999.

Indicators	Weightage to be allocated
Socially Backward	50%
Educationally Backward	40%
Economically Backward	10%

Source from the website of Tamil Nadu Department of Backward Classes and Most Backward Classes and Minorities Welfare

Appendix 4.3: How to categorize the Creamy Layer, OBCs and MBCs

	Categories
X<50%	Creamy Layer
50%X<65%	OBCs
X>65%	MBCs

Source from the website of Tamil Nadu Department of Backward Classes and Most Backward Classes and Minorities Welfare

Appendix 4.4: Percentage of Reservation to OBCs in the State Services

State	% of Reservation as suggested by the respective commissions	Presently Applicable
Maharashtra	34	32
Tamil Nadu	33	50
West Bengal	-	-
All-India	50	27

Source: Shish Ram Sharma, "Protective Discrimination: Other Backward Claasses in India", Raj Publication Delhi 2002

Appendix 4.5: Criteria for identifying the OBCs

Kalelkar Criteria

A. Social: Low social position in the traditional caste hierarchy of Hindu society.
B. Educational: Lack of general educational advancement among the major section of a caste or community.
C. Representational: Inadequate or no representation in government services.
D. Economic: Inadequate representation in the field of trade, commerce and industry.

Mandal Criteria

Indicators	Criteria
Social (12') (3points/Criteria)	(i) Castes/classes considered as socially backward by others.
	(ii) Castes/classes which mainly depend on manual labour for their livelihood.
	(iii) Castes/classes where at least 25 per cent females and 10 per cent males above the state average get married at an age below 17 years in rural areas and at least 10 per cent females and 5 per cent males do so in urban areas.
	(iv) Castes/classes where participation of females in work is at least 2 per cent above the state average.
Educational (6') (2points/Criteria)	(v) Castes/classes where the number of children in the age group of 5-15 years who never attended school is at least 25 per cent above the state average.
	(vi) Castes/classes where the rate of student drop-out in the age group of 5-15 years is at least 25 per cent above the state average.
	(vii) Castes/classes amongst whom the pro- portion of matriculates is at least 25 per cent below the state average.
Economic (4') (1points/Criteria)	(viii) Castes/classes where the average value of family assets is at least 25 per cent below the state average.
	(ix) Castes/classes where the number of families living in kuccha houses is at least 25 per cent above the state average.
	(x) Castes/classes where the source of drinking water is beyond half a kilometre for more than 50 per cent of the households.
	(xi) Castes/classes where the number of households having taken consumption loans is at least 25 per cent above the state average.

Appendix 4.6: State-wise Number of Caste/Communities Appear in the Mandal List, State list and Central list

S. No.	State	Mandal	State Commission	Central Commission
1	Andhra Pradesh	292	95	-
2	Assam	135	126	-
3	Bihar	168	138	-
4	Gujarat	105	127	79
5	Haryana	76	72	60
6	Himachar Pradesh	57	57	48
7	Jammu & Kashmir	63	20	20
8	Karnataka	333	200	170
9	Kerala	208	76	73
10	Madhya Pradesh	279	112	78
11	Maharashtra	272	355	209
12	Orissa	244	202	175
13	Punjab	83	68	61
14	Rajasthan	140	74	52
15	Tamil Nadu	288	252	172
16	Uttar Pradesh	116	79	53
17	West Bengal	177	60	14

Source: Shish Ram Sharma, "Protective Discrimination: Other Backward Classes in India", Raj Publication Delhi 2002

Appendix 5.1: State-wise Distribution of Number of Caste/Communities of Different Categories

S.No	State	Categories	No. of Caste communities covered
1	Andhra Pradesh	Group A (Aboriginal Tribes, Vimukta Jatis, Normadic and Semi-normadic trib(es))	40
		Group B (Vocational)	21
		Group C (*Harijan* Converts)	1
		Group D (Other Classes)	33
2	Assam	I (OBC)	119
		II (More OBC)	7
3	Bihar	I (Most Backward)	105
		II (Backward)	35
4	Haryana	Block A	67
		Block B	5
5	Karnataka	Category I	89
		Category II (a)	101
		Category II (b)	1
		Category III (a)	3
		Category III (b)	6
6	Maharashtra	BCs	307
		Special BCs	5
		Nomadic	13
		Semi-Nomadic	30

7	Matya Pradesh	Islamic Group	26
		Other BCs	86
8	Tamil Nadu	BCs	143
		MBCs	41
		Denotified Tribes	68
9	Uttar Pradesh	I Specific benefit in government jobs	15
		II Only for educational facilities	51

Source Shish Ram Sharma, "Protective Discrimination Other Backward Claasses in India", Raj Publication Delhi 2002

Appendix 7.1: Principles of Excluding Creamy Layer from Reservation

Description of category	To whom rule of exclusion will apply
I. Constitutional Posts	Sons and daughter(s) of – (a) President of India; (b) Vice-President of India; (c) Judges of the Supreme Court and of the High Courts; (d) Chairman and Members of UPSC and of the State Public Service Commission; Chief Election Commissioner; Comptroller and Auditor-General of India; (e) Persons holding constitutional positions of like nature.
II. Service Category A. Group 'A'/Class I Officers of the All India Central and State Services (Direct Recruits)	Son(s) and daughter(s) of – (a) parents, both of whom are Class I officers; (b) parents, either of whom is a Class I officer; c) parents, both of whom are Class I officers, but one of them dies or suffers permanent incapacitation; (d) parents, either of whom is a Class I officer and such parents dies or suffers permanent incapacitation and before such death or such incapacitation has had the benefit of employment in any International Organisation like UN, IMF, World bank, etc., for a period of not less than 5 years; (e) parents, both of whom are Class I officers die or suffer permanent incapacitation and before such death or such incapacitation of the both either of them has had the benefit of employment in any International Organisation like UN, IMF, World Bank, etc. for a period of not less than 5 years; Provided that the rule of exclusion shall not apply in the following cases :- (a) Sons and daughters of parents either of whom or both of whom are Class I officers and such parent(s) dies/die or suffer permanent incapacitation; (b) A lady belonging to OBC category has got married to a Class I officer, and may herself like to apply for job.
B. Group 'B'/Class II Officers of the Central and State Services (Direct Recruitment)	Son(s) and daughter(s) of – (a) parents, both of whom are Class II officers; (b) parents of whom only the husband is a Class II officer and he gets into Class I at the age of 40 or earlier; (c) parents, both of whom are Class II officers and one of them dies or suffers permanent incapacitation and either one of them has had the benefit of employment in any

	International Organisation UN, IMF, World Bank, etc., for a period of not less than 5 years before such death or permanent incapacitation; (d) parents of whom the husband is a Class I officer (direct recruitment or pre-forty promoted) and the wife is a Class II officer and the wife dies; or suffers permanent incapacitation; and (e) Parents, of whom the wife is a Class I officer (Direct Recruit or pre-forty promoted) and the husband is a Class II officer and the husband dies or suffers permanent incapacitation; Provided that the rule of exclusion shall not apply in the following cases:- Sons and daughters of – (a) Parents both of whom are Class II officers and one of them dies or suffers permanent incapacitation. (b) Parents, both of whom are Class II officers and both of them die or suffer permanent incapacitation, even though either of them has had the benefit of employment in any International Organisation like UN, IMF, World Bank, etc, for a period of not less than 5 years before their death or permanent incapacitation.
C. Employees in Public Sector Undertakings, etc.	The criteria enumerated in A and B above in this category will apply mutatis mutandis to officers holding equivalent or comparable posts in PSUs, Banks, Insurance Organisations, Universities, etc., and also to equivalent or comparable posts and positions under private employment, pending the evaluation of the posts on equivalent or comparable basis in these institutions, the criteria specified in Category VI below will apply to the officers in these Institutions.
III. Armed forces including Paramilitary Forces (Persons holding civil posts are not included).	Son(s) and daughter(s) of parents either or both of whom is or are in the rank of Colonel and above in the Army and to equivalent posts in the Navy and the Air Force and the Paramilitary Forces; Provided that – (i) If the wife of an armed forces officer is herself in the armed forces (i.e., the category under consideration) the rule of exclusion will apply only when she herself has reached the rank of Colonel; (ii) the service ranks below Colonel of husband and wife shall not be clubbed together; (iii) if the wife of an officer in the armed forces is in civil employment, this will not be taken into account for applying the rule of exclusion unless she falls in the service category under item No. II in which case the criteria and conditions enumerated therein will apply to her independently.
IV. Professional class and those engaged in Trade and Industry (i) Persons engaged in	Criteria specified against Category VI will apply

profession as a doctor, lawyer, chartered accountant, income tax consultant, financial or management consultant, dental surgeon, engineer, architect, computer specialist, film artists and other film professional, author, playwright, sports person, sports professional, media professional or any other vocations of like status.	
(ii) Persons engaged in trade, business and industry.	Criteria specified against Category VI will apply. EXPLANATION – (i) Where the husband is in some profession and the wife is in a Class II or lower grade employment, the income/wealth test will apply only on the basis of the husband's income. (ii) If the wife is in any profession and the husband is in employment in a Class II or lower rank post, then the income/wealth criterion will apply only on the basis of the wife's income and the husband's income will not be clubbed with it.
V. Property Owners A. Agricultural holding.	Son(s) and daughter(s) of persons belonging to a family (father, mother and minor children) which owns- (a) only irrigated land which is equal to or more than 85% of the statutory ceiling area, or (b) both irrigated and unirrigated land, as follows:- (i) The rule of exclusion will apply where the pre-condition exists that the irrigated area (having been brought to a single type under a common denominator) 40% or more of the statutory ceiling limit for irrigated land (this being calculated by excluding the unirrigated portion). If this pre-condition of not less than 40% exists, then only the area of unirrigated land will be taken into account. This will be done by converting, the unirrigated land on the basis of the conversion formula existing, into the irrigated type. The irrigated area so computed from unirrigated land shall be added to the actual area of irrigated land and if after such clubbing together the total area in terms of irrigated land is 85% or more of the statutory ceiling limit for irrigated land, then the rule of exclusion will apply and disentitlement will occur.) (ii) The rule of exclusion will not apply if the land holding of a family is exclusively unirrigated.
B. Plantations (i) Coffee, tea, rubber, etc. (ii) Mango, citrus, apple	Criteria of income/wealth specified in Category VI below will apply. Deemed as agricultural holding and hence criteria at A above under this category will apply. Criteria specified in Category VI below will apply.

plantations, etc.	
C. Vacant land and/or buildings in urban Agglomerations.	EXPLANATION:- Building may be used for residential, industrial or commercial purpose and the like two or more such purposes.
VI. Income/Wealth Test	Son(s) daughter(s) – (a) Persons having gross annual income of Rs. 1 lakh or above or possessing wealth above the exemption limit as prescribed in the Wealth Act for a period of three consecutive years. (b) Persons in Categories I, II, III and V-A who are not disentitled to the benefit of reservation but have income from other sources of wealth which will bring them within the income/wealth criteria mentioned in (a) above. EXPLANATION:- (i) Income from salaries or agricultural land shall not be clubbed; (ii) The income criteria in terms of rupee will be modified taking into account the change in its value every three years. If the situation, however, so demands, the interregnum may be less. EXPLANATION—Wherever the expression "permanent incapacitation" occur in this schedule, it shall mean incapacitation which results in putting an officer out of service.

Source: National Commission for Backward Classes

Appendix 7.2: Important Cases at State-Level Bearing on Creamy Layer

1) M.R. Balaji vs. State of Mysore (1963): Use of the criteria of economic status and occupation is permissible;
2) State of Andhra Pradesh vs. Balram (1972): Factual support obtained by a full and complete survey should be the basis of declaring a given caste as socially and economically backward. In this case, the Supreme Court also held that poverty, occupation, its nature and remuneration, place of habitation and similar other factors may be taken into account while determining the backwardness of the citizens.
3) Triloki Nath vs. State of J &K (1972): Mere poverty cannot be a test of backwardness. Cultivators of land, designated as backward on measure of the size of holdings, is impermissible. Economic consideration alone, opposed to other considerations (e.g. educational backwardness), is not sufficient to designate a community as backward.
4) State of Uttar Pradesh vs. Pradeep Tandon (1975): The Supreme Court rejected poverty and residence in rural area as the bases for reservation of seats in medical colleges.
5) State of Kerala vs. Thomas (1976): The Supreme Court held that social, educational and economic backwardness should be taken into account.
6)Jayashree vs State of Kerala (1976): The Supreme Court held that occupation, place of habitation and castes may all be relevant factors in determining social and educational backwardness. However, it accepted the rule of Kerala government, which prescribed that if annual income exceeds Rs. 6000 per annum, the favored class is not entitled for reservation quota.
7) Vasanth Kumar vs. State of Andhra Pradesh (1980): Different judges applied varying yardsticks in this case and these are indicated here:
a) As per Chandrachud, CJ: Two tests should be applied in determining social and educational backwardness: i) comparability to SCs/STs in the matter of backwardness; and ii) satisfaction

with the means test to be laid down by the state government in the context of prevailing economic conditions.

b) As per Desai and Sen, JJ: Economic criterion should alone be the test to determine backwardness.

c) As per Chinnappa Reddy, J: Class, poverty, way of life, standard of living and place in social hierarchy are the cumulative tests that should be applied an din so applying, it would be found that the caste largely represent the backwardness.

The forgoing brings out the fact that these are eligibility criteria for identifying the OBCs, but they do have clear bearing on the question of creamy layer.

8) Indra Sawhney and Others vs. Union of India (1992): The judgment given by nine judges can be grouped into majority, concurring and dissenting separate judgments.

Appendix 7.3: Economic Benefits for OBCs: Maharashtra

Term Loan:

Under this scheme, the project cost is up to Rs. 5 lacs out of which 85% loans is sectioned by the Central Corporation. 10% State Corporation and 5% beneficiaries. However, as per the guidelines of the Central Corporation 75% proposals are to be sanctioned having project cost up to Rs. 50,000/- and 25% proposal should be sanctioned having project cost from Rs.50,000/- to Rs. 5 lacs.

Margin Money Schemes:

Under this scheme 50% is Bank loan, 40% is Central Corporation Loan, 5% each is from State Corporation and beneficiary and project cost is Rs. up to 5 lacs. Rate of interest for the 40% Central Corporation loan between 6% and State Corporation loan carry the rate of interest @ 6% and Bank charges their Rate of interest as per their terms and conditions.

Micro finance:

Under this Scheme Non-Governmental Organizations which have established the Self Help Groups (SHG) are granted loans up to Rs 5 lacs for disbursement of SHGs. The NGO is expected to distribute this loan to the members of the OBC, the upper limit per beneficiary is Rs.20,000/-. The loan is granted to the NGO @ 5% and NGO is expected to grant the loan to SHG @ 9%. The loan is repayable within 36 months.

Mahila Samrudhi Yojana:

Under this scheme the loan is sanctioned to Self Help Group up to Rs. 5 lacs for disbursement to the 20 members of Self Help Group. The maximum limit to per member is Rs. 25,000/-. The loan is granted to the members of SHG @ 4% p.a.

Swarnima Scheme:

With a view of empowerment of the women, Central Corporation has introduced this scheme from the current financial year (2006-07). Under this scheme women having income up to the below poverty level are sanctioned loans up to Rs. 50,000/- for small activity, which carry the interest @ 4% only. The women beneficiaries are not required to contribute 5% and repayment period 2 year more than the normal scheme.

Education Loan:

The scheme was introduced in 2006. Under the scheme education loan is sanctioned to beneficiaries of the Corporation who have secured admission in the professional courses e.g. Health Sciences, Engineering, Computer, Management etc in the institutions which have been approved by the Central Councils. The Minimum Loan p.a. is Rs. 75,000 and Maximum Amount of Loan is Rs. 3 lacs which carry interest @ 4%. The loan is repayable after 6 months of the completion of the course in 5 years' period.

Swayam Saksham Scheme:
In order to inculcate the spirit of self-confidence among youths through self-employment and utilize their wisdom and expense gained through professional training and education the Corporation may consider providing financial assistance at concessional rate of interest to these professionally trained youths belonging to Backward Classes. Under this scheme loan up to Rs., 5.00 lakhs is sanctioned for starting the activities @ 5%. The beneficiaries between the age group of 18 to 35 are eligible under this scheme. Other conditions are similar to other schemes.

Appendix 7.4: Application for the Non-Creamy Layer Certificate

Questions	**Answers**
Who can apply	If the husband is in one profession and the wife is in a Class II or Lower Graded Employment, the income is considered. The applicant's parents should not be Class I / II Officers. If the applicant (husband) is in one profession and the wife is in a Class II or Lower Graded Employment, State (income is considered) Income limit for State & Central Government purpose: State Government purpose the income limit is Rs. 3 lakhs Central Government Institutions the limit is Rs. 1 lakh.
Whom to apply	Tahsildar*
Where To Apply	Taluk Office*
Documents required	All relevant records to prove the required details for the issue of Non Creamy Layer Certificate
Approval Authority	- District Magistrate/Additional District Magistrate/Collector/Deputy Commissioner/ Additional Deputy Commissioner/Deputy Collector/ 1st Class stipendiary Magistrate/ Sub Divisional Magistrate/ Taluk Magistrate/Executive Magistrate/Extra Assistant Commissioner (not below the rank of 1st Class Stipendiary Magistrate) - Chief Presidency Mgistrate/Additional Chief Presidency Magistrate/ Presidency Magistrate - Revenue Officer not below the rank of Tahsildar and - Sub Divisional Officer of the area where the candidate and/or his family normally resides
Fees	A count fee stamp worth Rs. 5/- is to be affixed

* Tahsildar is revenue administrative officer in India in-charge of obtaining taxation from a tehsil. A tehsil is also known as taluk (taluq, taluka), and mandal, is an administrative division of some countries of South Asia.

Bibliography

Abhijit Banerjee, Rohini Somanathan. "The Political Economy of Public Goods: Some Evidence from India." *Journal of Development Economics* 82 (2007): 287–314.

Alam, Javeed. "Is Caste Appeal Casteism? Oppressed Castes in Politics." *Economic and Political Weekly* 34, no. 13 (March 1999): 757-61.

Appointment of 'most backward' in UP stayed. January 22, 2002.

Are Gujjars any less backward than Jats in Rajasthan? December 25, 2010. http://articles.timesofindia.indiatimes.com/2010-12-25/india/28218277_1_jat-community-jat-reservation-obcs.

Banerjee, Mukulika. "Populist Leadership in West Bengal and Tamil Nadu: Mamata and Jayalalithaa Compared." In *Regional Reflections: Comparing Politics Across India's States*, by Rob Jenkins. New Delhi: Oxford University Press, 2004.

Banerjee, Shoumojit. "Bihar hunger deaths: lower level bureaucracy apathetic." *The Hindu.* The Hindu, Auguest 23, 2009.

Bardhan, P.K. "Poverty and Trickle-down in Rural India—A Quantitative Analysis." In *Agricultural Change and Rural Poverty.*, by J.W. Mellor and G.M. Desai, 76-94. New Delhi: Oxford University Press, 1986.

Bayly, Susan. *Castem, Society and Politics in India from the Eighteen Century to the Modern Age.* Cambridge: Cambridge University Press, 1999.

Bayly, Susan. "State Policy and "Reservations": the Politicization of Caste-Based Social Welfare Schemes." Chap. 7 in *Caste, Society and Politics in India from the Eighteenth Century to the Modern Age*, by Susan Bayly. Cambridge: Cambridge University Press, 1999.

Béteille, André. *The Backward Classes in Contemporary India.* New Delhi: Oxford University Press, 1992.

—. *The Idea of Natural Inequality and other Essays.* New York: Oxford University Press, 1987.

Bhatt, Anil. "Politics and Social Mobility in India." *Contributions to Indian Sociology* 5, no. 1 (January 1971): 99-114.

Campbell, Andrea Louise. *How Policies Make Citizens: Senior Citizen Activism and the American Welfare State.* Princeton University Press, 2003.

—. *How Policies Make Citizens:Senior Political Activism and the American Welfare State.* Princeton University Press, 2005.

—. "The Third Rail of American Politics: Senior Citizen Activism and the American Welfare State." *Ph.D. dissertation.* University of California, Berkeley, 2000.

"Census of India." Vols. XV, . 1911. Table XVI .

"Census of India." Vol. XVI. 1921. Table XXI.

Chandra, Kanchan. "Post-Congress Politics in Uttar Pradesh: The Ethnification of the Party System and its Consequences." In *Indian Politics and the 1998 Election, Regionalism, Hindutva and State Politics*, by Ramashray Roy and Paul Wallace. New Delhi: Sage Publications, 1999.

—. *Why Ethnic Parties Succeed.* New York: Cambridge University Press, 2004.

Chaudhury, Pradipta. "The 'Creamy Layer': Political Economy of Reservations." 39, no. 20 (2004): 1989-1990.

Chinnaiah, Jangam. "BJP and Reservations Quota Politics or Electoral Convenience?" *Economic and Political Weekly*, July 2003: 3143-45.

Church, Roderick. "Chapter 9: Conclusion: The Pattern of State Politics in Indira Gandhi's India." In *State Politics in Contemporary India: Crisis or Continuity?*, by John R. Boulder and London: Westview Press, 1984.

"Constituent Assembly Debates." Vol. 1. New Delhi: Lok Sabha Secretariat, 1989. 59.

"Constituent Assembly Debates." *supra* (Book1) 3, no. 10 (April 1947): 702.

"Constitution of India." Lucknow: Eastern Book Company, 1981.

"Creamy layer concept against Constitution: PMK." *The Economic Times.* April 15, 2008. http://economictimes.indiatimes.com/PoliticsNation/Creamy_layer_against_Constitution/articleshow/2951898.cms.

Dahiwale, S. M. "Identifying 'Backwardness' in Maharashtra." *Economic and Political Weekly* 35, no. 37 (2000): 3293-3297.

Dandavati, Padmaraj. "The Saga of Quotas in Karnataka." *Deccan Herald.* September 13, 2005. http://www.deccanherald.com/deccanherald/sep132005/state1910142005912.asp .

Drèze J. and Sen, A.K. *Hunger and Public Action.* Oxford University Press, 1989.

Dudley-Jenkins, Laura. " Identity and identification in India: defining the disadvantaged." Psychology Press, 2003.

Esping-Andersen, Gosta. *The Three Worlds of Welfare Capitalism.* Cambridge: Princeton University Press, 1990.

F. Irschick, Eugene. "Tamil Revivalism in the 1930s." *Cre-A*, 1986: 47-9.

Galanter, Marc. "The Long Half-Life of Reservations." In *India's Living Constitution: Ideas, Practices, Controversies*, by E. Sridharan and R. Sudarshan Zoya Hasan, 306-318. New Delhi: Permanent Black, 2005.

Gilens, Martin. *Why Americans Hate Welfare: Race, Media, and the Politics of Antipoverty Policy.* University of Chicago Press, 1999.

Glanter, Marc. *Competing Equality: Law and the Backward Classes in India.* Berkkeley: University of California Press, 1984.

"Government Appoints Panel on CL." *The Hindu.* January 13, 2000.

"Government not to exclude 'creamy layer' among backward classes from reservation. ." *The Hindu.* July 13, 2011. http://www.thehindu.com/news/states/tamil-nadu/article2222119.ece.

"Government of India." 1980. 165.

Guha, Ashok. "Reservations in Myth and Reality." *Economic and Political Weekly* 25, no. 50 (December 1990): 2716-2718.

Gupta, Dipankar. *Caste in Question: Identity or Hierarchy?* New Delhi: Sage Publications, 2004.

—. *Interrogating Caste: Understanding Hierarchy and Difference in Indian society.* New Delhi: Penguin, 2000.

Hasan, Zoya. *Quest for Power: Oppositional Movements and Post-Congress Politics in Uttar Pradesh.* New Delhi: Oxford University Press, 1998.

Hasan, Zoya. "Representation and Redistribution: The New Lower Caste Politics of North India ." In *Parties and Party Politics in India*, by Zoya Hasan. New Delhi: Oxford University Press, 2002.

Ingram, Anne Schneider and Helen. *The impact of policy for Democracy.* University of Kansas Press, 1997.

Jadhav., Vishal. " Elite Politics and Maharashtra's Employment Guarantee Scheme." *Economic and Political Weekly*, December 2006: 5157-5162.

Jaffrelot, Christophe. *India's Silent Revolution: the Rise of the Lower Castes in North India.* New York: Columbia University Press, 2003.

Jaffrelot, Christophe. "The Rise of the Other Backward Classes in the Hindi Belt." *The Journal of Asian Studies* 59, no. 1 (February 2000): 86-108.

Jha, Giridhar. "Upper Caste Voters Gain Prominence as Frantic Parties Woo Them with Sops." *India Today.* October 24, 2010. http://indiatoday.intoday.in/story/upper-caste-voters-gain-prominence-as-frantic-parties-woo-them-with-sops/1/117559.html.

—. "Upper Caste Voters Gain Prominence as Frantic Parties Woo Them with Sops." *India Today.* October 24, 2010. http://indiatoday.intoday.in/story/upper-caste-voters-gain-prominence-as-frantic-parties-woo-them-with-sops/1/117559.html.

Joshi, Barbara R. *Democracy in Search of Equailty: Untouchable Politics and Indian Social Change.* New Jersey: Humanities Press Inc., 1982.

K. Srinivasan, Sanjay Kumar. "Economic and Caste Criteria in Definition of Backwardness." *Economic and Political Weekly,* 1999: 3052-3057.

"K.S. Jayasree v State of Kerala ." 3 SCC 730, 1976.

Kohli, Atul. *The State and Development in the Third World.* Princeton University Press, 1986.

—. *The State and Poverty in India: The Politics of Reform.* Cambridge University Press, 1989.

Kothari, Myron Weiner and Rajni. *India Voting Behaviour.* Calcutta: Firma KL. Mukhopadhyaya. Krishna. Gopal, 1967.

Kumar, K. Srinivasan and Sanjay. "Economic and Caste Criteria in Definition of Backwardness." *Economic and Political Weekly* 32, no. 42/43 (1999): 3052-3057.

Kumar, Pradeep. "Reservations within Reservations: Real Dalit-Bahujans." *Economic and Political Weekly* 36, no. 37 (2001): 3505-3507.

Kumar, Suhas Palshikar and Sanjay. "How India Voted – Verdict 2004." The Hindu, May 20 (Thursday), 2004.

Lele, Jayant. *Elite Pluralism and Class Rule: Political Development in Maharashtra, India.* Toronto: University of Toronto Press, 1981.

Lowi, Theodore J. "Four Systems of Policy, Politics, and Choice." *Public Administration Review* 32, no. 4 (1972): 298-310.

"Orientalist Empiricism: Transformations of Colonial Knowledge." In *Orientalism and the Postcolonial Predicament: Perspectives on South Asia,* by D.C. A. Breckenridge and P. van der Veer Ludden, 250-278. Philadelphia: University of Pennsylvania, 1993.

Maharashtra, Government of. "Dr Babasaheb Ambedkar: Writings and Speeches,." Vol. 13. 1994.

"Mandal Battle fields Barren Now." *Indian Express.* September 23 , 1993.

"Mandal Case, Para 86, 121(3) (d), 450,451."

"Mandal Memories Revived." *The Hindustan Times.* April 9, 2006.

Mayawati writes to PM, demands quota for upper caste poor. *The Statesman.* September 19 , 2011.
http://thestatesman.net/index.php?option=com_content&view=article&id=383795&catid=36.

Mettler, Suzanne. "Bringing the State Back In to Civic Engagement: Policy Feedback Effects of the G.I. Bill for World War II Veterans." *American Political Science Review* 96, no. 2 (June 2002): 351-365.

Mooij, J. E. "Food Policy and Politics. The Public Distribution System in Karnataka and Kerala, South India." 1996.

P.Radhakrishnan. "Backward Classes in Tamil Nadu, 1872 -1988." *Economic and Political Weekly* 25, no. 10 (1990): 509-517.

Pai, Sudha. "Electoral Identity Politics in Uttar Pradesh: Hung Assembly Again." *Economic and Political Weekly* 37, no. 14 (2002): 1334-41.

"Parliamentary Debates." Vols. 12-13 (Part II). col. 9006.

Patwardhan, Vasant and S. Palshikar. "Reserved Seats and Medical Education: A Study." *Journal of Education and Social Change* 5, no. 4 (January - March 1992).

Pierson, Paul. "Path Dependence, Increasing Returns, and the Study of Politics." *American Political Science Review* 94, no. 2 (2000): 251-267.

Pierson, Paul. "When Effect Becomes Cause, Policy Feedback and Political Change." *World Politics*, 1993: 595-628.

Prasad, Chanchreek. K. L and Saroj. *Mandal Commission. Myth and Reality: A Rational View point.* Delhi: H.K.Publishers, 1991.

Radhakrishnan, P. "'The Politics of Perdition." *The Hindu.* September 21, 2001.

Radhakrishnan, P. "Reservations in Theory and Practice." *MIDS Bulletin* 20, no. 4 (1990).

Ramakrishnan, Venkitesh. "Political Consensus." *Frontline.* Vol. 25. no. 9. April-May 2008.

Rao, B. Shiva. "Report of the Sub-Committee on Fundamental Rights to the Advisory Committee." In *The Framing of India's Constitution – Select Documents*, by B. Shiva Rao. Bombay: NM Tripathi, 1967.

From Elite Activism to Democratic Consolidation: The Rise of Reform Communism in West Bengal. Vol. 2, in *Dominance and State Power in Modern India: Decline of a Social Order*, by F. Frankel and M. S. A. Rao, 367–415. Delhi: Oxford University Press, 1990.

Rao, M.S.A. "Social Movements among the Backward Classes and the Clocks: Homology in the Source of Identity." In *Social Movements in India*, by M.S.A. Rao. Delhi: Manohar, 1984.

Rao, S.S. "Equality in Higher Education: Impact of Affirmative Action Policies in India." In *Global Collaborations: the Role of Higher Education in Diverse Democracies*, by E.F. Beckham. Washington, DC: Association of American Colleges and Universities, 2002.

Report of the Backward Classes Commission. Government of India Press, New Delhi: Government of India, 1980.

Rothstein, Bo. *Just Institutions Matter.* New York: Cambridge University Press, 1998.

Rudolph, Lloyd I. Rudolph and Susanne Hoeber. *In Pursuit of Lakshmi: The Political Economy of the Indian State.* Chicago: University of Chicago Press, 1987.

Rudolph., Lloyd I. "The Political Role of India's Caste Associations." *Pacific Affairs* 33, no. 1 (1960).

Schneider, Helen Ingram and Anne. "The Social Construction of Target populations: Implication for politics and policy." *The American Political Science Review* 87, no. 2 (1993): 334-347.

Shah, Ghanshyam. "Social backwardness and politics of reservation." *Economic and Political Weekly* 26, no. 11-12 (1991): 601-10.

Skocpol, Theda. *Protecting Soldiers and Mothers.* Cambridge, Mass. and London: Harvard University Press, 1992.

Srivastava, Piyush. *2012 UP Polls: Mayawati Government to Woo Displeased Brahmins, Lucknow.* November 8, 2011. http://indiatoday.intoday.in/story/mayawati-government-brahmin-community/1/159084.html.

Stuart Corgridge, Glyn Williams, Manoj Srivastava and Reve Veron. *Seeing the State: Governance and Governmentality in India.* UK: Cambridge University Press, 2005.

Sujatha, V.S. " Chapter 4 OBCs: Composition, Decomposition, Characteristics and Empowerment Tasks." In *The OBCs and the Ruling Classes in India*, by Hs Verma. Rawat Publications, 2005.

Sukhadeo Thorat, Narender Kumar. *In Search of Inclusive Policy: Addressing Graded Inequality.* New Delhi: Rawat Publications, 2008.

"Supreme Court strikes down Kerala backward classes act." Rediff.com , December 13, 1999.

Swamy, Arun R. "Parties, Political Identities and the Absence of Mass Political Violence in South India." In *Community Conflicts and the State in India*, by Amrita Basu & Atul Kohli. Delhi: Oxford University Press, 1998.

Varshney, Ashutosh. "Mass Politics or Elite Politics? India's Economic Reforms in Comparative Perspective." In *India in the Era of Economic Reforms*, by Ashutosh Varshney, Nirupam Bajpai Jeffrey D. Sachs. New York: Oxford University Press, 1999.

Venkatesan, J. "Caste Can Be the Basis to Determine Backwardness, Rules Supreme Court." *The Hindu.* April 11, 2008. http://www.hindu.com/2008/04/11/stories/2008041159961200.htm .

Verniers, Christophe Jaffrelot and Gilles. "India's 2009 Elections: The Resilience of Regionalism and Ethnicity." *South Asia Multidisciplinary Academic Journal, 3*, 2009: http://samaj.revues.org/index2787.html .

Weiner, Myron. "The Struggle for Equality: Caste in Indian Politics." In *The Success of India's Democracy*, by Atul Kohli. New Jersey: Cambridge University Press, 2001.

Yadav, Yogendra. " Understanding the Second Democratic Upsurge." In *Transforming India: Social and Political Dynamics of Democracy*, by Francine Frankel, 120-45. Delhi: Oxford University Press, 2000.

Yadav, Yogendra. "Reconfiguration in Indian politics: State Assembly Election 1993-95." *Economic and Political Weekly* 31, no. 2 and 3 (January 1996): 95-104.

Zerinini-Brotel, Christophe Jaffrelot and Jasmine. ""Post-"Mandal"" Politics in Uttar Pradesh and Madhya Pradesh." In *Regional Reflections: Comparing Politics Across India's States.*, by Rob Jenkins. New Delhi: Oxford University Press, 2004.

Zwart, Frank de. "The Logic of Affirmative Action: Caste, Class and Quotas in India." *Acta Sociologica* 43, no. 3 (2000): 235-249.

SAI MA

Curriculum Vitae

CONTACT INFORMATION

South Asia Studies
The Paul H. Nitze School of Advanced International Studies
Johns Hopkins University
1619 Massachusetts Avenue NW
Washington, D.C. 20036
U.S.A.

Email: sma@jhu.edu
Phone : 202.689.7643

EDUCATION

PhD South Asia Studies, Johns Hopkins University, November 2011
Dissertation: "Impact of Reservation Policies: India's Quota Politics during the Post-Independence Period, 1950-2011."
Committee: Pravin Krishna (Chair), Walter Andersen, Sunil Khilnani, Cinnamon Dornsife, Pranab Bardhan (University of California, Berkeley).

MA International Politics, Beijing University, July 2003

BA Indian Language and Culture, Beijing University, July 2000

BA Economics (Double Major), Beijing University, July 2000

ADDITIONAL EDUCATION

The Consortium on Qualitative Research Methods designed to improve qualitative and multi-method research in political science, Institute for Qualitative and Multi-Method Research (IQMR), Arizona State University, January 2008

RESEARCH INTERESTS

Comparative Political Economy, Welfare State Development, Public Policy, Indo-China Relationship

PUBLICATIONS

Peer-Reviewed Articles

Sai Ma. 2008. "Sustainability of India's Welfare System in the Context of Globalization: A Comparative Study of Maharashtra and Tamil Nadu." *Southeast Review of Asian Studies*30:67–83

Project Articles

Justina Wong, Sai Ma. "Establishing the Individual Credit Registry System in China." Leadership Academy of Development, Promoting the Private Sector through Public Policy. (upcoming)

Newspaper Articles

Sai Ma. 2009. "India's Street and Political Scene Similar." *The Global Times.* Beijing, China. May.13. P.11

CONFERENCE PRESENTATIONS

2010. "Impacts of Reservation Policies: Quota Politics in India during the Post-Independence Period." The 67th Annual Meeting of Midwest Political Science Association, Chicago, April.

2010. "Replacing the State: A Case Study of Self-Help Groups and Localized Education in Jaldhaka, India." The 67th Annual Meeting of Midwest Political Science Association, Chicago, April.

2010. "Diversity and Sharing: A Local Version of Financial Crisis Management in India." 2010 Western Political Science Association Annual Meeting, San Francisco, April.

2009 "Displacing Farmers: a Comparative Study of the State Level Land Reform Policies in India." The 67th Annual Meeting of Midwest Political Science Association, Chicago, April.

2008. "Sustainability of India's Social Welfare System in the Context of Globalization." The 66th Annual Meeting of Midwest Political Science Association, Chicago, April.

2008. "A State-level Study of Declined Social Welfare Regimes in India during the Post-Reform Period." The 47th Annual Meeting of Southeast Conference of the Association for Asian Studies, South Carolina, January.

INVITED TALKS

2009. "Sino-Indian Trading Relationship: Past and Present." Guest lecturer at the Centre for Chinese and South East Asian Studies, Jawaharlal Nehru University, New Delhi, India.

RESEARCH EXPERIENCE

2008-09. Visiting Scholar, National Institute of Public Finance and Policy, New Delhi, India

2007. Research Assistant for Dr. Prema Kurien on the project of the role of Indian American Lobby Groups at the Capitol Hill. the Woodrow Wilson International Center, Washington D.C.

2006. Visiting Scholar, the Center of Policy Research, New Delhi, India

2004-05. Research Assistant for Dr. Stanley Kochanek on the project of the republished book: "India: Government and Politics in a Developing Nation." Washington D.C.

WORK EXPERIENCE

2010-11. Case-Writer on "Chinese Credit Bureau" for Leadership Academy of Development, Promoting the Private Sector through Public Policy, supervised by Dr. Roger Leeds and Dr.
Francis Fukuyama, Washington D.C., U.S.A.

2003-04. Editor & Program Planner (Full-Time), China Central Television (CCTV), Beijing, China

1999-2001. Editor (Part-Time), China Center for Economic Research, Beijing University, Beijing, China

PROFESSIONAL MEMBERSHIPS

The American Political Science Association
The Midwest Political Science Association

SELECTED FELLOWSHIPS AND AWARDS

2004-08. SAIS Four-year Ph.D. Fellowship, Johns Hopkins University
2005-07. SAIS Ph.D. Summer Travel and Research Grant, Johns Hopkins University
2001. Ford Scholarship for attendance of Indian workshops, Ford Foundation
2000. Honor Graduate, Beijing University
1997-2000. Three-year YouDa Fellowship, Beijing University

LANGUAGES

Chinese – native language.
English – speak fluently, read and write with high proficiency.
Hindi – speak fluently, read with proficiency, and write with basic competence.

CPSIA information can be obtained at www.ICGtesting.com
Printed in the USA
LVOW03s2149061114

412374LV00019B/1266/P